Library of
Davidson College

European détente

European détente

Case studies of the politics of East–West Relations

Edited by
Kenneth Dyson

St Martin's Press, New York

© Kenneth Dyson, 1986

All rights reserved. For information, write:
Scholarly & Reference Division,
St. Martin's Press, Inc., 175 Fifth Avenue, New York, NY 10010

First published in the United States of America in 1986

Printed in Great Britain

Library of Congress Cataloging-in-Publication Data
Dyson, Kenneth, H.F.
　European détente.

　Includes index.
　1. Europe — Foreign relations — 1945–　　— Addresses, essays, lectures.　2. Détente — Addresses, essays, lectures.　I. Title.
D1058.D97　　1986　　　327.4　　85-26271
ISBN 0-312-27061-5

Contents

	Preface	ix
	Introduction	1
1	European détente in historical perspective: ambiguities and paradoxes Kenneth Dyson	14
2	Détente and East–West relations: American, Soviet and European perspectives Andrew Carter	56
3	The Conference on Security and Cooperation in Europe: Europe before and after the Helsinki Final Act Kenneth Dyson	83
4	Berlin, the German question and the future of Europe: long-term perspectives Eberhard Schulz	113
5	*Deutschlandpolitik, Ostpolitik* and the Western Alliance: German perspectives on détente Michael Stürmer	134
6	Soviet–GDR relations and European détente Martin McCauley	155
7	The Soviet Union and European détente John Erickson	172
8	National independence and Atlanticism: the dialectic of French policies Philip Cerny and Jolyon Howorth	198
9	Britain, détente and the Conference on Security and Cooperation in Europe Philip Williams	221
10	Britain and European Political Cooperation in the CSCE Michael Clarke	237
11	Conclusions: a three-dimensional view of East–West relations Kenneth Dyson	254
	Index	273

'When spider webs unite, they can tie up a lion'
Ethiopian proverb

'There are only two forces that unite men — fear and interest . . . A man will fight harder for his interests than his rights'
Napoleon I, *Maxims*

List of contributors

Andrew Carter is an official of the British Foreign and Commonwealth Office, on secondment to the Royal Institute of International Affairs for 1984–5.

Dr Philip Cerny is Lecturer in Politics at the University of York.

Michael Clarke is Lecturer in Politics at the University of Newcastle.

Kenneth Dyson is Professor of European Studies at the University of Bradford and a founder member of the Association for the Study of German Politics.

Professor John Erickson is director of Defence Studies at the University of Edinburgh.

Jolyon Howorth is Professor of French Civilization at the University of Bath.

Dr Martin McCauley is Senior Lecturer in Soviet and East European Studies at the School of Slavonic and East European Studies at the University of London.

Dr Eberhard Schulz is Honorary Professor at the University of Bonn and deputy director of the research institute of the German Society for Foreign Policy in Bonn.

Dr Michael Stürmer is Professor of Modern History at the University of Erlangen.

Dr Philip Williams is Senior Lecturer in Politics at the University of Southampton and, in 1984–5, was on secondment to the Royal Institute of International Affairs.

Preface

The two quotes at the front of this volume sum up the ambiguity that lies at the heart of the politics of East–West relations. This ambiguity, and the irreducible complexity that it entails, is the central theme of the book. Against the background of crises in Eastern Europe (as in Czechoslovakia in 1968 and Poland in 1981–2), of troubles in the Atlantic Alliance (over cruise and Pershing deployments, burden sharing in European defence, sanctions against the Soviet bloc and the Strategic Defence Initiative), and of the chilling reminder that thousands of nuclear warheads are stationed in Europe, it will be readily apparent that the subject of this book is of monumental significance to the world at large as well as to Europeans. The achievements of détente in Europe are often not fully appreciated, particularly by those who measure it by the speed with which human rights and free movement become a reality for citizens of the Soviet bloc. Nevertheless, European politics has travelled a long way since the Berlin crises of 1948 and 1958–61 to the Quadripartite Agreement on Berlin of 1971 and the Helsinki Final Act of 1975. Perhaps more seriously, the character of the politics of détente in Europe is frequently misunderstood, and often by people who ought to know better.

This book is concerned with 'détente', a term borrowed from French diplomacy. Détente is to be distinguished from 'entente', meaning 'friendly understanding between states'. Its character, and the expectations to be properly associated with it, are more modest. Détente means 'easing the strained relations between states', 'relaxation of tensions'. The term seems to have been first employed in this sense in English by *The Times* in August 1908. Détente gained wider currency in the 1960s in the wake of President Charles de Gaulle's new initiative in East–West relations. The new Eastern policy of the Federal Republic of Germany was in fact to prove more important in its practical consequences for Europe. Correspondingly, the German term *Ostpolitik* was also to be taken up in the English-speaking world as a key element in the politics of European détente. In analysing European détente as policy it is necessary to focus on Germany. The book has, therefore, three chapters on Germany: Eberhard Schulz on Berlin, the Quadripartite Agreement, and Germany and the Helsinki process; Michael Stürmer on the inner-German relations policy and *Ostpolitik* of Bonn in the context of the Western alliance system; and Martin McCauley on the German Democratic Republic, seeking recognition and respect from European détente and caught between its role as Moscow's closest ally and its role in inner-German relations.

A prolonged period of trouble and confusion in the Atlantic Alliance about the proper conduct of East–West relations has centred chiefly on conflicts between successive American administrations and Western Europe. The role of regional détente has figured prominently in these conflicts, as Andrew Carter indicates in his chapter. The United States and Western Europe have had different interests in, and expectations of, European détente. In the 1980s there was a deeper commitment to détente and a stronger perception of Soviet frailty in Western Europe than in the American administration. Western Europe offered fewer opportunities than before to Soviet diplomacy, with closer European political integration and not least as 'revisionist' Eurocommunist parties in the West became of less relevance to (indeed threatened) Soviet strategy. Meanwhile the deep economic problems of Poland and Romania and the economic concerns of Hungary and the GDR were compounded by doubts about their political reliability. The Soviet Union was more readily accepted as a status quo power in Europe, less a deadly evil than a threatening and insecure opponent beset by intractable problems of economic inefficiency and stagnation at home, of political control in Eastern Europe, of ideological challenge from China and from Eurocommunism, and of decline as an ideological force after the 1960s. In such a difficult period, when internal conflicts within Western Europe and the United States serve simultaneously to cross-cut and reinforce this basic cleavage, it is especially important that academics should attempt to clarify détente as idea and as policy in Europe. The book places European détente in its historical context and seeks to draw conclusions from the experience of détente about the proper conduct of East–West relations. It draws out contrasting interests in, and expectations of, détente within Western Europe: for instance, the relationship between détente, on the one hand, and national independence and the politics of nuclear diplomacy, on the other, in France; and, in the German case, between détente and the German question. Not least, détente has seen the emergence of the GDR as a key European state.

The book derives from an Anglo-German conference organized at the University of Bradford in conjunction with the Association for the Study of German Politics. My particular thanks are due to Herr Waldo Maass, of the Goethe Institute, for his support to the conference and on many other occasions to the School of European Studies at the University of Bradford. As ever, special thanks are due to the secretaries of the School of European Studies, who had the dual labour of conference organization as well as typing, and to my wife Ann for her patient and loving support to an occasionally harrassed editor.

Kenneth Dyson
September 1985

Introduction

From its slow and complex emergence in the fifteenth and sixteenth centuries the modern European state has presented difficult problems of political morality.[1] Though these problems have grown, the state has remained the basic and most durable element in international life, perhaps the most significant political contribution of Europe to the world. Writing in the sixteenth century, the eminent French legal and political theorist, Jean Bodin, argued that the absolute and binding quality of its new sovereign power over all its subjects provided the indispensable means for security. The state promised order in a new age of social change and religious and dynastic wars. On the other hand, the European states system was from the outset characterized by warfare. Indeed the outlines of that system first became apparent in 1648 with the Treaty of Westphalia, which ended the awesome slaughter and devastation of the Thirty Years War in Germany. War and conquest played a large part in shaping modern Europe. The European states system was prey to conflicts based on territorial claims, on sharp disagreements about the proper political organization of the state, and on fears that the organization of the states system in shifting alliances would fail to provide a genuine and reliable balance of power. More ominously, industrialization, technological change, nationalism and the debate about democracy and 'the social question' introduced an unstable dynamism of change into the European states system after the eighteenth century. Contemporary European history has been the story of wars of ever-increasing destructiveness: from the Franco-Prussian War of 1870–1 to the First World War of 1914–18 and the Second World War of 1939–45. Part and parcel of this story have been the relegation of the European states system to an aspect of a new global balance presided over by the Soviet Union and the United States; and the recognition that, in the new age of nuclear and missile technology, war can no longer be an acceptable way in which to manage the relations amongst European states.

In the twentieth century Europe has lived through catastrophe and moral outrage and must now bear the burden of their political consequences. Occupying the world region in which the modern state was born and matured, Europeans had more reasons than most to learn, through bitter experience, about the aggressive vitality and overweaning ambition of 'great powers', their capacity for arrogance and hypocrisy, for arrogating special privileges to themselves and neglecting their wider international responsibilities.[2] These 'great power' characteristics could still surface in the post-war period, for instance, in Britain's attempt to hold on to her 'world role' and in French *grandeur*. The results were, on the one hand, French humiliations in Indo-China and Algeria in the 1950s, the shared humiliation of the Suez invasion of 1956 and the debilitating economic effects of successive sterling crises for Britain in the 1950s and 1960s; and, on the other hand, the enormous costs of developing and maintaining independent nuclear deterrents. Though many Europeans carried illusions into the post-war period, the learning process about the madness of universal involvement was nearly complete by the time the United States sought to come to terms with the agony of her war in Vietnam. Despite voices of caution, typically from American specialists on European affairs, the two superpowers found avoidance of imperious behaviour much more difficult.[3] Such behaviour sparked off in turn antagonism and suspicion from Europeans.

To very differing degrees, and with contrasting emphases, some European states began to feel their way towards playing a role as 'pivot powers', as states sustaining and facilitating relationships between the superpowers by pursuing a problem-solving and businesslike dialogue and generally seeking, within their own sphere of superpower influence, to constrain superpower behaviour. This process has evoked mistrust and often misunderstanding, most noticeably about inner-German relations.[4] The superpowers have come to expect and even value the role of the neutral and non-aligned states of Europe as middlemen: as we shall see, countries like Austria, Finland, Sweden, Switzerland and Yugoslavia formed a recognizable and constructive grouping within the Helsinki process. By contrast, the two German states are so important, economically and strategically, that their respective alliance systems cannot afford a subtle shift from their role in sustaining East–West dialogue to a status as neutral or non-aligned. Here we come to the paradox of the post-war situation of Germany in Europe. Born out of defeat, occupation and the cold war, neither German state has had the same opportunity as Britain and France to harbour illusions about its international role. Loyalty and predictability were readily adopted as their maxims of policy; they were expected anyway from the great powers that had presided over their creation. At the same time, the scale of the tragedy into which Bismarck's Germany had been led under Adolf Hitler collapsed the learning process about the monstrous consequences of the behaviour of imperious powers into a shorter period than elsewhere in Europe. A post-war generation of politicians, represented by Chancellor Adenauer (1949–63), was determined to replace narrow national interest by 'enlightened' national interest. Both German states remained the most loyal allies of their superpowers, aware of their historical responsibility. However, as their political systems matured, they became increasingly prepared to present their role in East–West relations as 'damage limitation', described by Honecker as 'a coalition of reason'. The strength of the peace movement in the Federal Republic of Germany indicated in a more pronounced way another European theme: anger at, and impatience with, imperious superpowers, and more generally with the 'states system' that had given birth to them.

Against this historical background it is scarcely surprising that tension exists between the liberal idealism that continues to inform American foreign policy and the more practical morality exhibited in Western Europe.[5] West Europeans often bemoan the arrogance, hypocrisy and ambition of the United States; Americans complain in turn about effete, world-weary and inward-looking Europeans. The contrast is not, of course, absolute. There are influential Americans who speak out for a European-type perspective on East–West relations; correspondingly, many Europeans are deeply wedded to an Atlanticist view that takes on board the notion of being involved in the struggle for a common cause. Nevertheless, Europeans have, on the whole, been uncomfortable with the moral zeal of successive American administrations, whether the focus was human rights under President Carter or 'making America strong again' under

President Reagan. They have been more ready to recognize the many-sided moral dilemmas and nuances in East–West relations, the way in which moral principles compete and often collide and the different shades and directions of moral sensitivity. The emphasis has been more clearly on dialogue and quiet diplomacy to promote mutual understanding, on forbearance and on taking careful account of political, economic and social constraints. Clear American ideological and strategic positions are counterbalanced by subtle European political positions.

The purpose of this book is not simply to argue the case for European détente by reference to these special historical and political circumstances and sensitivities of Europeans. Ideological struggle and strategic threat are as much part of East–West relations as the search for common security and cooperation. Hence détente does not offer a single concept in terms of which East–West relations can be either described or reformed. It is part of a more complex equation. This point will not reassure those who hope to gain from the book a single clear solution or set of solutions to the problems of East–West relations. Détente stresses the need for a common code of behaviour in East–West relations, for the revival of a constitutional tradition of diplomacy. Even after the Helsinki Final Act of 1975 there remains an enormous amount of diplomatic work to be done in order to ensure that moral constraints apply in the relations of European states. Yet diplomatic judgements must also take account of the practical political demands associated with ideological and strategic factors.

Equally significant is the absence of a unified theory of détente from which it would be possible to derive specific policy recommendations around which a consensus might develop. The book underlines the role of muddle, suspicion, polemics and divided counsels in the process of détente. It points in Chapter 1 to the intractable ambiguities and paradoxes in the idea of détente. The development of détente policies is, accordingly, a story of intelligible contradictions; and the practical implication is that there can be no final solution to the problems of détente, let alone of East–West relations in its wider sense.

These points are worth making, and practically important because East–West relations have been confused by moral zealots who have been wedded to a single, well-ordered account of East–West relations in terms of détente: in particular, the Soviet insistence on absolute security by means of 'military détente', and Western insistence on détente as a means of promoting respect for individual rights. In one Soviet view of the desirable political order in Europe the United States would be disengaged ('uncoupled') from Western Europe; in one Western view the Eastern bloc would be liberalized.[6] Behind this difference of moral vision about European détente lies a second dimension: the acquisition and consolidation of the power and interests of particular states. In the politics of détente these two dimensions — of moral zeal and guile — overlap and interweave in a most subtle manner. The West is attacked for using détente to bring about the 'internal erosion' of the socialist community; the East is accused of seeking military superiority behind the camouflage of rhetoric about a European common security pact. Deception and self-seeking are never far away from the process of détente.

At the same time, détente is about inculcating broader notions of responsibility in order to prevent the abuse of power that comes from a ruthless and crazily wilful pursuit of national interest. In other words, détente appeals to a common interest in preventing such abuse. Respect for moral considerations cannot just be left to the strength of critical voices of other states in the international system; though one should never forget just how important it is that these voices are raised. It is necessary to create more varied channels through which common interests can be refined and cooperation developed, thereby spinning a web of interdependency that constrains the behaviour of states. This latter phenomenon has been a most striking achievement of détente in inner-German relations, as we shall see. By spinning a web of relations, the pressure for cooperation is likely to remain strong when détente erodes. By these means détente aims to change the terms in which East–West relations are conducted. At the end of the day, however, its maintenance depends on the way in which states perceive their interests and exercise their power. Détente must deal with a world in which moral zealots can influence the exercise of power and even acquire office and in which the bargaining reputation of both sides is a variable but very doubtful commodity.

Five themes interweave in this book. Firstly, historical sensitivities are essential for a proper understanding and effective management of East–West relations. Policies are, after all, justified by reference to past events, and historical interpretation itself becomes a weapon in East–West relations. Soviet policies are wedded to memories of 'the great patriotic war' of 1941–5 and, as Professor Erikson indicates, have a long historical pedigree; French policy-makers think more readily of 1938, when Nazi dictatorship and aggression was unsuccessfully 'appeased' at Munich, and of 1940 when France paid for her political, economic and strategic weaknesses with rapid and ignominious defeat; whilst in the Federal Republic of Germany the reference points are the Nazi seizure of power in 1933, German responsibility for war in 1939 and the catastrophe of 1945. Correspondingly, the Soviet Union stresses 'vigilance' in defence of her 'sacred borders'; France pursues *grandeur*, expressed in the nuclear *force de frappe* and the associated idea of national independence; and the West Germans combine a 'militant democracy' at home with a concern that war shall never again break out on German soil (embodied in the final communiqué of the meeting between Schmidt and Honecker in December 1981).[7] Historical reference, argument and mythology are part of the texture of East–West relations, sometimes as a convenient tool for policy-makers, on other occasions seeming to imprison them and unduly constrain their freedom of maneouvre.

Secondly, the major role of the German question, of Berlin and of inner-German relations in East–West relations in Europe must be understood. A key theme of the détente process has been the emergence of the GDR as a European actor and a process of normalization in its relations with the Soviet Union that has been associated with conflicts, especially in 1983–4. Though inner-German relations remain limited in scope, they are pervasive in their effects on policy. They differentiate the Federal Republic from her West European partners, for whom inner-German relations are the odd dimension, unfamiliar in their own working environment and hence capable of being misunderstood. These misunderstandings were reflected most clearly in 1983–4 by the *New York Times* and *Le Monde*. More to the point were the scepticism and suspicion of West Germany's allies about the dangers of the Kohl government's renewed stress on the openness of the German question after 1982. By seeming to re-elevate the normative dimension over the pragmatic the Federal Republic risked creating anxiety about the territorial settlement in Europe. This shift of policy played into the hands of the Soviet Union which had an interest in questioning the motives of West Germany: the *revanchisme* campaign against West Germany not only evoked harsh memories of Germany but in particular served to secure relations with Poland. The concerns of the Western allies were occasionally about motives (particularly in Paris) but more about consequences, not least driving the Poles into the hands of the Soviet Union. By 1985 Bonn seemed to be losing its central role in Soviet diplomacy in favour of London and Paris.[8]

Thirdly, détente policies are condemned to complexity, and to unremitting hard labour, by the irreducibly two-sided and Janus-like character of détente. In one sense détente is a matter of civilizing the relations amongst states, of creating an international community in which each state recognizes the significance of others and displays a measure of solidarity in its conduct. In another sense détente is a process of politicking, of tough criticism and bargaining, of advancing interests and power. States and blocs seek to establish community on terms that will be acceptable to them. To speak about détente in one of these senses, whilst belittling or ignoring the other, is to risk talking about something that one does not know and to confuse oneself and others about the problems and prospects of détente. Reorientation of the interests of states and blocs to new norms of international conduct is an arduous and continual task. There is no prospect of a final solution of any problem and no promise of a linear development towards 'civilized' East–West relations.

Fourthly, détente is part of a complex equation of East–West relations that includes ideology and strategy. In Europe two contrasting value systems breathe down each other's necks: liberal democracy, with its respect for individual rights, circumscribed political power and pluralism; and Marxism-Leninism, with its promise of liberation of an oppressed proletariat and of a classless society. The West fears the totalitarian reality or potential of the Soviet Union and points to the treatment of dissidents and to the experience of the 'subject' peoples of Eastern Europe (notably the communist seizure of power in Prague in 1948, the suppression of popular revolt in the German Democratic Republic in 1953 and of reforms in Hungary in 1956 and Czechoslovakia in 1968, and the tragic history of Poland up to and beyond the declaration of martial law in 1981). The East stresses the unpredictability and aggressiveness of Western imperialism, disposed to wage class war as capitalism moves into crisis, and points to the attacks on the Soviet Union from Poland at the end of the First World War and from Nazi Germany. Ideological struggle is further compounded by strategic threat. The peninsular states of Western Europe face the enormous continental power of a Soviet Union astride the Euro-Asian land mass and extended after 1945 deep into central and southern Europe. In geopolitical terms they have reason to see the West European situation as precarious. The Soviet Union sees itself as encircled and isolated from Norway down through Turkey and the Indian Ocean to the Far East. For Western Europe the strategic lessons were nuclear dependence on the United States in the Atlantic Alliance and alliance solidarity; for the Soviet Union the lessons were a *cordon sanitaire* of East European satellite states with friendly, reliable governments and a 'decoupling' of Western Europe from the United States. From the combination of strategic threat with ideological struggle comes a deeply antagonistic conception of security, a reliance on instruments of propaganda and subversion and on deterrence and war-fighting strategies (which have come to incorporate nuclear weapons).

Détente seeks to broaden the terms of East–West debate beyond ideological and military categories to the political balance of interests. Such policies involve a search both for common security interests in limiting the arms' race and in improving East–West crisis management and for cooperation in economic, technological, environmental and cultural affairs. Winning a particular propaganda battle or being in balance or ahead in a particular statistic of missile deployments take secondary place to improvement of the overall political relationships on which East–West relations depend. The basic requirement is a conceptual discussion about what each side is trying to achieve as a preliminary to concrete negotiations about arms control, disarmament and cooperation. At the end of the day, however, détente has to live with the tendency of each side to take advantage of opportunities for propaganda or to steal an extra increment of security. More ominously, it has to contend with a military balance that, under the impact of rapid technological change, is becoming ever more complex and unstable. The central question is whether détente should give priority to arms control and disarmament measures or concentrate on other measures of cooperation. In the realm of security, political progress on confidence-building measures (CBMs) may hold out more prospects than rigorous formulae and juggling about with numbers and percentages, as military technology seems to be escaping the grasp of quantitative and qualitative limitations.

Fifthly, East–West relations have been a long learning process, apparent in the transition from wartime alliance to cold war (Chapter 1), from cold war to détente and from détente to confrontation (Chapter 2). This learning process has often involved relearning old lessons. We are now in a better position to appreciate the appropriate role for détente policies against the background of their historical interaction with ideological and strategic factors. A tendency to take a partial view of East–West relations, in terms of ideology, strategy or détente, has bedevilled the learning process and introduced difficult, even dangerous problems of readjustment and mutual understanding not just in East–West relations but in West–West relations and East–East relations. Equally important, the pursuit of effective détente policies requires certain techniques and political and administrative conditions. Governments must be good at recognizing and creating opportunities for negotiation, at carefully preparing discussions and at probing the intentions of other parties. They must be prepared to use and develop a variety of negotiating channels, especially 'back channels' through which reasons for particular actions can be offered. Careful preparation means attaining internal harmony in one's team and taking account of indirect effects within one's alliance. Particular attention needs to be given to persuasive techniques in establishing a common definition of the problem and in devising formulae as well as to safeguarding one's reputation as a bargaining partner. Above all, it is necessary to be sensitive to the peculiar atmospherics of East–West relations, which means being able to read and guess the other side. These techniques of détente suggest certain personal qualities in the politician and diplomat: patience that comes from long practice of negotiations and experience of the importance of prior conditions and timing for their success; breadth of outlook that develops from intensive study of the problems; depth of insight that results from long experience of one's opponents and allies; and resilience to domestic political lobbies that stems from recognition of the need to act as a public educator on exceedingly complex problems. They depend also on a political and administrative system that combines accountability with a cohesive policy network for the management of East–West relations and that encourages rather than discourages appropriate personal qualities of diplomatic professionalism. Comparison of America's Soviet policy-making with European, and especially German, policy-making shows how the nature of an increasingly searching public scrutiny and Congressional scrutiny has led to a spillover of domestic debate and lobbying into American external behaviour that has confused and frustrated allies as well as the Soviet Union.[9]

Ideological struggle and strategic threat mean that containment is a necessary feature of the management of East–West relations. The attempt to provide an account of East–West relations solely in terms of détente is fraught with danger, not least of complacency and of elevating faith in procedure over analysis of substance. Post-war Europe's character is defined by conflict between the two superpowers, and the alliances based around them, and between their respective political and social systems. The extent and problems of this conflict are not to be explained just by reference to power rivalries. One needs to understand its ideological and institutional character. In particular, the Soviet Union is ruled by an all-embracing ideological party which justifies its supremacy by an unbridgeable opposition of systems that can only be overcome by the disappearance of all other systems. In sharp and important contrast to the Third Reich, their disappearance is not seen as requiring war. The laws of historical development, as outlined by Karl Marx and Friedrich Engels, indicate the inexorable strengthening of 'real socialism' against its capitalist opponents. The Communist Party of the Soviet Union stands in the vanguard of history, refining a Soviet model that is globally relevant. Hence the power of 'the socialist community' can be extended without risk by simply waiting for the inevitable changes in power relationships. Clearly the Soviet concept of 'peaceful coexistence' erects major barriers to détente. It is, of course, possible to find ideas of unavoidable and permanent conflict of systems in the West. There, however, institutional factors of pluralism and electoral competition act as a corrective to such ideas. The rigid orthodoxy and absolutism of the Soviet Union is buttressed in institutional terms by the principle of 'democratic centralism', with its emphasis on party loyalty and discipline and the binding character of decisions taken by the highest party organs.

Détente adds a dimension of moderation to containment. It cautions against raucous abuse as counterproductive and seeks to delimit the scope of ideological competition. At the ideological level there seems, however, little room for maneouvre in détente. What is needed is an ability to communicate so that, at political and strategic levels, more opportunities are available for mutual recognition of each other's vital interests and restraint in these areas. Moderation is required, firstly, because of the political and strategic risks of universal involvement. Otherwise priorities will be established not by one's long-term vital interests but by a doctrine of linkage that encourages one to respond to events, to overcommit resources and to squander reputation. Complex tactics drive out strategy.[10] Secondly, détente is necessary as a political counterweight to an arms' race that is given institutional and economic momentum via the military-industrial complex in both blocs but that is destabilizing and costly in terms of social priorities. The risks involved in the 'second cold war' were far graver than in the first cold war.[11] Thirdly, the Soviet Union is an introverted, self-preoccupied and morbid power, obsessive about encirclement, isolation and threats to its security and repeatedly reminded of the limits of its power, not least of its economy and technology.[12] One's sympathy may be limited; these characteristics seem in part ideologically self-inflicted and the consequences of Soviet blunders and miscalculations. Nevertheless, the use of political channels to encourage a more open Soviet posture would enhance international security. Détente offers at least the long-term possibility that the Soviet Union might begin to reflect on the legitimate security concerns of others.

Having identified the major themes, and the significance of détente in East–West relations, it is necessary to turn to the context of détente in Europe before looking at its two major dimensions: inner-German relations and the Helsinki process.

Notes

1. Kenneth Dyson, *The State Tradition in Western Europe* (Oxford: Martin Robertson, 1981); Gianfranco Poggi, *The Development of the Modern State* (London: Hutchinson, 1978); Charles Tilly, ed., *The Formation of National States in Western Europe* (Princeton: Princeton University Press, 1975).
2. David Calleo, *The German Problem Reconsidered: Germany and the World Order, 1870 to the Present* (Cambridge: Cambridge University Press, 1979).
3. David Calleo, *The Imperious Economy* (Cambridge, Mass: Harvard University Press, 1982); George Kennan, *The Cloud of Danger: Some Current Problems of American Foreign Policy* (London: Hutchinson, 1977).
4. Eberhard Schulz and Peter Danylow, *Bewegung in der deutschen Frage? Die ausländischen Besorgnisse über die Entwicklung in den beiden deutschen Staaten*, 2nd edn (Bonn: Forschungsinstitut der Deutschen Gesellschaft für Auswärtige Politik, 1985).
5. On the background to American policy see Louis Hartz, *The Liberal Tradition in America* (New York: Harcourt, Brace and World, 1955). A European perspective is cogently presented in H. Butterfield and M. Wight, eds, *Diplomatic Investigations: Essays in the Theory of International Politics* (London: Allen and Unwin, 1966) and in Michael Howard, *Causes of War and Other Essays* (London: Allen and Unwin, 1984). More generally, see K.W. Thompson, *Morality and Foreign Policy* (Baton Rouge: Louisiana State University Press, 1980) and S. Hoffmann, *Duties Beyond Borders* (Syracuse: Syracuse University Press, 1981).
6. H.J. Ellison, ed., *Soviet Policy Toward Western Europe* (Seattle: University of Washington Press, 1984), and S.M. Terry, ed., *Soviet Policy in Eastern Europe* (New Haven: Yale University Press, 1984). See also Edwina Moreton and Gerald Segal, eds, *Soviet Strategy towards Western Europe* (London: Allen and Unwin, 1984).
7. On the Soviet Union see F. Northedge and A. Wells, *Britain and Soviet Communism: The Impact of a Revolution* (London: Macmillan, 1982) and Jonathan Steel, *World Power: Soviet Foreign Policy under Brezhnev and Andropov* (London: Michael Joseph, 1983); on France see Philip Cerny, *The Politics of Grandeur* (Ithaca, NY: Cornell University Press, 1974) and F. Roy Willis, *The French Paradox* (Stanford, California: Hoover Institution Press, 1982); and on the Federal Republic see E. Krippendorff and V. Rittberger, eds, *The Foreign Policy of West Germany* (Beverly Hills: Sage, 1980) and Wolfman Hanrieder, ed., *West German Foreign Policy: 1949–1979* (Boulder, Colorado: Westview, 1980).
8. Fred Oldenburg, 'Sowjetische Deutschland-Politik: von Breschnjew zu Gorbatschow', *Osteuropa*, 1985, pp. 303–19.
9. Joseph Nye, ed., *The Making of America's Soviet Policy* (New Haven: Yale University Press, 1984); C. Bertram, ed., *America's Security in the 1980s* (London: Macmillan, 1982).

10. George Kennan, *The Cloud of Danger: Some Current Problems of American Foreign Policy* (London: Hutchinson, 1977).
11. Fred Halliday, *The Making of the Second Cold War* (London: Verso and NLB, 1983).
12. *Prospects of Soviet Power in the 1980s, Part 1* (London: International Institute for Strategic Studies, 1979).

1 European détente in historical perspective: ambiguities and paradoxes

Kenneth Dyson

The achievements, problems and prospects of détente in Europe need to be considered in the historical, ideological and strategic context of these policies. It is necessary to begin by outlining the factors that shaped the post-war European order; the way in which the division of Europe was accompanied by the emergence of the cold war; and how new policies of détente from the 1960s were rooted in, and constrained by, historical, ideological and strategic factors. The theme of this chapter is that an understanding of détente policies, of their inherent ambiguities and paradoxes, requires a proper appreciation of the origins and development of post-war Europe. Ideas about East–West relations, and proposals for their improvement, are all too easily divorced from this framework. Indeed there is considerable ignorance and vagueness about the history and issues of East–West relations in Europe, not least about the German question. More recently, the Helsinki process has failed to penetrate the general political consciousness.

As the origins of post-war Europe receded in time, and post-war generations achieved positions of influence, the problem of historical judgement in East–West relations grew. In the 1980s eminent professional observers of European affairs were tempted to see signals of historic mutation in Europe. Zbigniew Brzezinski, National Security Adviser under President Carter (1977–81), pointed to developments in inner-German relations as an intimation of a 'post-Yalta' Europe that was emerging by slow stealth: perhaps ultimately a neutralized, confederal Germany based on the two German states within a neutral Europe.[1] Pierre Lellouche, a luminary of the French strategic affairs establishment, identified the sources of the historic mutation in the growing aversion to the nuclear option in the West and signs of neo-isolationism, global unilateralism and shift of interest to Central and South America and to the Western Pacific on the part of the United States.[2] Doubts about the American nuclear umbrella for Europe could only be dispelled by France's commitment (nuclear and non-nuclear) to the forward defence of West Germany. Like Brzezinski he saw in Franco-German collaboration the core of a new West European defence identity that opened up new possibilities for the conduct of East–West relations in Europe. In so far as greater political flexibility does exist in Europe such scenarios need to be informed by careful political judgement that combines a fine sense of history, ideology and strategy. What do we need to know and remember?

The European catastrophe

The post-war European order emerged out of a German and European catastrophe whose dimensions are difficult to absorb but must be appreciated if one is to begin to understand the contemporary problems and prospects of that order. In historical terms this linkage of German and European catastrophe is not new. Germany's geopolitical situation in the centre of Europe has meant that she has always been a European problem, an object of ambition and fear, a source of conflict and war. Who controls the Germans has been a recurrent European theme, pre-dating the great surge of nationalism in nineteenth- and twentieth-century Europe.[3] Germany has experienced the vulnerability of political fragmentation over centuries, limited national unification in the nineteenth century courtesy of Prussian arms and a subsequent problem of reconciling national ambitions with the constraints of geopolitical realities in the centre of Europe. The impact of the great European forces of the Reformation, industrialization and nationalism was always disproportionately great in Germany. Germany's saga as a European problem stretches from the devastations of the Thirty Years War in the seventeenth century to the Napoleonic invasions, from unification in 1871 in the wake of the Franco-Prussian War, via the reckless foreign policy of the Wilhelminian Reich and the ravages of the Third Reich, to a divided Germany in a divided Europe after

1945. The German problem in Europe was the concern of the Treaty of Westphalia in 1648, of the Congress of Vienna in 1815, of the Versailles Peace Treaty of 1919 and of the victorious Allies before and after the capitulation of the German *Wehrmacht* in 1945. The European catastrophe of the twentieth century seemed to have the hallmarks of a second Thirty Years War; the horrors of the First World War (1914-18) being followed by the 'twenty-year crisis' culminating in the Second World War (1939-45). Such historical parallels are, of course, fraught with difficulties. In this case they must take account of one major difference. After 1945 there was no peace treaty. The Allies had demanded unconditional surrender since the meeting of Prime Minister Churchill and President Roosevelt at Casablanca in January 1943, and the Third Reich fought on to total defeat. Subsequently, the victors — Britain, France, the Soviet Union and the United States — proved unable to agree about the future shape of a successor regime in Germany. The result was the division of Germany, and of Berlin, as well as of the rest of Europe. The German problem that had brought together the wartime allies drove them apart; the transitory promise of a condominium of the great powers in 1944-5 gave way to the European states system of 1948-9, to bloc politics and containment.[4]

Post-war Europe, divided into East and West, was born out of the harsh realities of power politics, notably as they affected the new Soviet-Polish frontier and the revised eastern border of Germany based on the Oder-Neisse line. When analysing this power politics, and its varying ingredients of idealism and cynicism, one should never lose sight of the backcloth provided by the immensity of the human catastrophe before and after 1945. One should not forget that the scale of this tragedy was far greater in Eastern than in Western Europe. There was a deep sense of outrage, though the vast geographical dimensions of the war meant that the objects of outrage varied from country to country. The durable memories were different. The appalling atrocities of the German SS against the Jews — millions were consumed by the holocaust — made Auschwitz, Belsen and Buchenwald symbols of shock to the self-confidence and esteem of European civilisation. Germany's campaign in the East involved the most horrendous suffering for Poles and Russians. Poland represented a Calvary of personal suffering. With 6 million dead Poland lost about one-fifth of its population. Though much aided by material provisions from Britain and the United States, the Soviet Red Army never faced less than 65 per cent of the German *Wehrmacht* divisions. The Soviet Union had some 20 million dead; the single city of Leningrad counted more dead than Britain and the United States combined during the whole war. Byelorussia, the Soviet republic longest occupied by the Germans, lost about one-quarter of its inhabitants. The size of these losses is to be explained by the awesome scale of the warfare in the East, combined with Russian scorched-earth policy and pillage by the retreating Germans. Fear of the advancing Soviet forces was endemic in Eastern Europe, symbolized at the time by the massacre of some 10,000 Polish officers at Katyn in summer 1940 and then by the atrocities against civilians in the East Prussian village of Nemmersdorf in October 1944. The combination of refugees fleeing from the Russians with forced expulsions meant the war was followed by what Churchill described as a 'tragedy of inconceivable dimensions'.[5] Article 13 of the Potsdam Protocol, signed by the victorious allies in 1945, provided that the eastern Germans — in East Prussia, Pomerania and Silesia and in Bohemia — would have to be transferred to what was left of the German Reich at the end of the war. This displacement of some 16 million Germans was to be conducted in an 'orderly and humane manner'. In practice over 2 million Germans did not survive this process as a consequence of murder, starvation, disease and exhaustion. In the horrific fire-bombing of Dresden in February 1945, larger in human impact than the atomic bombings of Hiroshima and Nagasaki combined, many of the estimated 135,000 killed were refugees from Silesia.

If outrage was sharpened by these appalling events, moral and human sensibilities were dulled. Brutality and cynicism were rife in 1945. The Second World War ended in utter confusion. So fast moving were the events, and so complex their interplay with ideas, interests and personalities, that reconstruction of the period, let alone explanation, is exceedingly difficult. Unlike in 1815 and 1918, there was no grand denouement, followed by a relatively clear-cut peace-making process. Peace-making started before the defeat of Hitler, notably at Tehran and Yalta, and in the end was never completed. Countries like France and Poland were liberated over many months. Victory celebrations were transitory, engulfed by horror about the war and its grim legacy of human suffering, economic misery and political bitterness. Chaos was complemented by fear: fear of the millions of Russian troops, not just of an alien ideology and system but of revenge in an indiscriminatory manner; and fear of the awesome destructive power of the new age of atomic warfare unveiled in Hiroshima and Nagasaki by the United States in August 1945 just after the Potsdam Conference. The Western allies were confronted by the military superiority of the Soviet Union as a European power at the end of the war and by the dramatic implications of Soviet liberation and occupation of Eastern Europe. In turn the Soviet Union noted that the United States had had a relatively 'good war'; with 406,000 killed, the continental United States had not been ravaged, materially or morally, by the war. American military superiority was clearly revealed by the manner of the ending of the war with Japan, just as its economic strength was to be reflected in the confidence and generosity of the Marshall Plan of 1947 for the reconstruction of Europe.

The war was a source of bitter memories and grief, as well as of pride to the Soviet Union. Internally, it provided a dramatic legitimation of the Soviet system, a proof of its strength and a source of cohesion that had previously been lacking in Soviet society. Externally, the legacy was ambivalent. On the one hand, the Soviet Union found itself in an entrenched position in Eastern Europe; the Red Army was able to dictate the terms of a political settlement in Poland, Czechoslovakia, Hungary, Romania and Bulgaria and to influence, as part of a four-power occupation, the terms of any settlement in Germany and in Austria.[6] The Soviet Union was thrust into the world arena as a major world power. On the other hand, American economic and military superiority was to become an obsessive concern of the Soviet elite and to feed a yearning for recognition and respect as a world power of first rank. Its own Marxist-Leninist ideology indicated that the Soviet Union was the model for the world society of the future. Yet the Soviet Union's aspirations seemed to be denied in the present and near future. The experience of the Second World War and American post-war superiority counselled vigilance as the leitmotif of Soviet policy and supported a central role for the Red Army in the power structures of the Soviet state.

Despite President Roosevelt's vision of 'One World', presided over by a condominium of the four great powers, the fantasy world of 1919 was not repeated. After the experience of the Versailles settlement, the twenty-years crisis and a brutal, exhausting war, the victors were not on the whole disposed to hold high expectations about the post-war European order. Allied disagreements about Poland in 1944–5 indicated that there would be a troubled peace. A combination of paranoia, grounded in harsh experience, with ideological ambition and rapid military successes between 1943 and 1945 made the Soviet Union a dangerous giant. The inter-war period, and especially the phase of appeasement of Nazi Germany, symbolized by the Munich Agreement of 1938, was interpreted as a lesson about the importance of realism in international affairs. Foreign policy needed to be founded on a concern for concrete interests and power.[7] This realism found expression both in the crucial importance that came to be attached to economic reconstruction for political stability and vitality of Europe and in the evolution of strategic doctrine around the 'tough' concept of deterrence. The new realism was, nevertheless, a learning process, made difficult by the confusion and complexity of the period. In the first place, in 1945 there was often a lack of clarity about American and British interests in Europe: policy was surrounded by fog and confusion.[8] James Byrnes, the US Secretary of State, and Ernest Bevin, the British Foreign Secretary, were not as well briefed and consistent in purpose as their Soviet opposite number Vyacheslav Molotov. Problems of succession, with the new Truman administration in Washington and the new Attlee government in London represented at the Potsdam Conference, were compounded by the relative ignorance about Eastern Europe of powers whose prime engagements were outside Europe. As early as the summer of 1945 the American diplomat George Kennan provided a realistic assessment of the need for containment of the Soviet Union.[9] In practice, however, Western interests were clarified in the period 1945–7 against the background of frustrating immobilism in the Allied Control Council in Berlin and the abject failures of the Council of Foreign Ministers at their sessions in April 1947 in Moscow and November–December 1947 in London. The Prague coup of 1948 and the Berlin Blockade of 1948–9 completed the often painful learning process in the West. By then the Western powers had already agreed to establish a separate government in western Germany and to assure its economic success by pouring Marshall Plan aid into it.

Secondly, views on realism were deeply influenced by different perceptions of Anglo-American interests. For President Roosevelt at the Yalta Conference realism meant enlisting Stalin's support for the war against Japan. The Far East was a pressing factor in American judgements.[10] Realism for General Eisenhower as Supreme Commander of the Allied Expeditionary Force in Europe meant destroying the German *Wehrmacht* with the least possible loss of Allied soldiers. Churchill's plan for a Balkan front in order to achieve a political hold on central Europe was dismissed by Eisenhower as adventurism. The United States and Britain confined their main military campaign to Western Europe, 'the second front'.[11]

Thirdly, in 1944–5 realism involved a recognition of Russian suffering and of the crucial military contribution of the Soviet Union to the defeat of the Third Reich. During his visit to Moscow in October 1944, Churchill accepted Stalin's wish for the decisive voice in the future of Bulgaria, Hungary and Romania, Hitler's allies.[12] He was relieved that Stalin's claims did not extend to Greece and Italy. Churchill saw a justice in this outcome: those who had borne the brunt of the barbaric fighting and the casualties should have the largest say in future borders and political arrangements. This case seemed especially clear in the cases of Bulgaria, Hungary and Romania, whose forces had participated in the German attack on the Soviet Union and whose capitals were occupied by the Red Army at the time when their political future was in question. Britain took a different, tougher stand on Poland, based on her pre-war treaty with Poland, the fact that Britain went to war over the German invasion of Poland, and Poland's own terrible sufferings under German rule. Churchill was prepared to accept a return to the Soviet Union of territory lost as a result of her defeat by Poland in 1921: the eastern third of Poland and the former Tsarist Baltic provinces of Estonia, Latvia, Lithuania, which had enjoyed twenty years of independent statehood during the inter-war period. He agreed that Poland should be compensated in the west by German territory in East Prussia and

Silesia. The Potsdam Conference eventually accepted as a *fait accompli*, however, a new Polish frontier as far west as the Oder–Neisse line, albeit as provisional pending a final peace settlement. If Stalin's heavy-handed behaviour about Polish border questions was a source of grave disquiet, the question of the political composition of Poland's post-war government erupted into a major quarrel. The result was determined by the fact that Poland had been liberated by the Red Army. Realism no longer meant just recognizing Soviet suffering and the realities of Soviet occupation in Eastern Europe. It meant being equal to Stalin's brand of power politics and imposing a limit on his growing ambitions.

The learning process for Europeans went much deeper than the level of the reciprocal expectations of the Allied elites. It involved a recognition that European power and reputation were the losers, with for instance Britain transformed suddenly into a net overseas debtor. The scale of Europe's self-inflicted wounds, the material destruction of its cities (like Leningrad, Stalingrad, Warsaw and Berlin), the physical condition of its inhabitants, and the shock to the self-confidence of its civilization from mass atrocities — all seemed to point to a fundamental crisis of the traditional European order. Ferocity, duplicity and barbarism seemed to stalk a continent that had earlier been esteemed as the centre of world civilization. European policy-makers turned their attention to 'damage limitation' as the criterion of policy. Proud, historic European states were humbled, compromised or weakened; the ugly face of Europe's tapestry of nationalism revealed in sharp focus. In the end the restraint of European savagery required the massive intervention of two outside powers — the Soviet Union and the United States — each bringing very different experiences and attitudes to the post-war problems of reconstructing Europe. By 1948 post-war Europe was divided between East and West, each within the sphere of influence of a superpower and relegated to a part of the latter's emerging concern with the wider global balance. The European powers were displaced from their role at the centre of international history; Germany itself, at the centre of the European power game since its unification in 1871, was divided between East and West.

As the structures of a divided Europe, a divided Germany and bloc politics took on a firm form, and as the labours of reconstruction bore fruit in unprecedented economic growth, the question of a *modus vivendi* for post-war Europe became of increasing political interest to European politicians. Détente, the relaxation of tensions, was most fervently embraced by European politicians who sought to rehabilitate Europe in the sense of 'normalizing' relations there. Chancellor Willy Brandt saw this rehabilitation essentially in moral terms: as re-emphasizing the shared cultural heritage, interests and sympathies and common responsibilities for peace of Europeans.[13] President Charles de Gaulle was, by contrast, more conerned with rehabilitation of Europe in terms of power: détente was a vehicle for national independence in Europe, a means of overcoming the inertia associated with the structures of bloc politics.[14] For most European politicians détente was the product of a more gradual, less systematic learning process. Whatever the motives for European détente, American and Soviet politicians were reminded of the need once again to take account of the complexities and passions of European politics. The post-war division of Europe had helped to contain the phenomenon of nationalism, whilst reduction in the number of great powers had centralized and simplified the workings of the international system. Yet with the 1970s and 1980s bloc politics was increasingly threatened by corrosive forces: by dissidence and nationalism in the East (notably Poland); by the conflict of Atlanticist and European perspectives within NATO (with attempts to revive the Western European Union in 1984); by mounting trade and monetary policy rivalries accompanying protracted recession in the West; and by uncertainty about the proper combination of military strategy and diplomacy.[15] The costs of bloc politics in Europe to the two superpowers were to prove very considerable indeed.

The interpretation of the European catastrophe was itself the cause and expression of much bitterness.[16] For the Soviet Union the Third Reich, and its attack on the Soviet Union in 1941, was the ultimate expression of the aggressive, exploitative imperialism that is unleased by the capitalist economic system. The Nazi invasion was carried out by 'the shock troops of imperialism'. The Munich Agreement of 1938 was interpreted as an Anglo-French attempt to turn Hitler against the Soviet Union, the Nazi–Soviet Pact of August

1939 as a cunning attempt to frustrate this 'criminal' policy. In the West Soviet communism began to be seen as a phenomenon similar to German National Socialism.[17] Both were totalitarian ideologies of mass mobilization behind an illiberal ideology that gave a leading group or figure the right to intervene comprehensively in society and that relied heavily on instruments of political terror. Both were inherently aggressive ideologies that had to be deterred effectively in the interest of world peace. The Soviet lesson was vigilance, the Western lesson was avoidance of appeasement. The wartime allies could agree about little other than the strategic necessity to fight a common enemy, Nazi Germany. They could not even agree about the nature of that political phenomenon, let alone about what they were fighting for. The harsh common experience of fighting against fascism generated nothing more than an ephemeral sense of shared interest, expressed in the so-called 'spirit of the Elbe' when American and Soviet soldiers first met at Torgau. On both sides, in reaction to each other, exclusive and mean-spirited interpretations of history arose that failed to capture the panorama of war and peace in all its component parts and that did little to honour the dead of Europe on both sides. Ideology and power politics, fuelled by outrage and fear, generated in the immediate post-war period approaches to European politics that were short on moral sensitivities.

As moral sensitivities developed, they were likely to do so in an asymmetrical way. The greater openness of Western liberal democratic ideology, combined with the more rapid reconstruction and dynamism of Western economies, encouraged a more comprehensive and ambitious conception of détente there. Détente's moral appeal to liberal democrats in Western Europe is readily comprehensible. Détente enabled them not only to ensure that war would never break out again on European soil but also to rediscover a civilizing mission in international affairs. It represented an aspect of Europe's coming of age in the post-war world, its rehabilitation. Such a process is rarely smooth, and détente was no exception. Frustration with the rigidities and inhumanities of bloc politics and desire for atonement were not sufficient guides to European conduct. Factors of ideology, power and interest had still to be brought into the equation of responsible international conduct. As we shall see, the different ideological contexts in East and West introduced from the outset a conceptual problem into détente policies. The language of détente carried various meanings. Second, as Halford Mackinder noted, democracies have a tendency to refuse to think strategically unless and until compelled to do so for purposes of defence.[18] Whilst there may be very special reasons to pursue détente policies in Europe, analysis of ideological and strategic factors require a wider world view.

The post-war settlement

One of the first casualties of the escalating brutality of the Second World War was the moderate peace programme outlined in the Atlantic Charter by Churchill and Roosevelt in August 1941. At the conclusion of the Atlantic Conference they agreed to renounce 'aggrandizement, territorial or other' and to oppose 'territorial changes that do not accord with the freely expressed wishes of the people concerned'. In January 1942 these liberal principles for a post-war settlement were embodied in a joint declaration of the United Nations, signed by all governments at war with Germany, including the Soviet Union.[19] Such moderation did not survive the unspeakable inhumanities of the war. Little interest in, let alone respect for, the Atlantic Charter was apparent in the key Allied meetings that shaped (or rather recognized *de facto*) what the Western powers saw as a provisional post-war settlement: the Tehran Conference (28 November–1 December 1943), Churchill's visit to Moscow in October 1944, the Yalta Conference (4–11 February 1945) and the Potsdam Conference (July 1945).

The complex sequence of meetings, combined with the difficulties of the agenda, and the absence of a final peace treaty, gave exceptional scope for divergent interpretations of what had been agreed. Thus American interpretations of the Yalta Conference have tended, from Secretary of State Dean Rusk to Secretary of State George Shultz, to emphasize the joint declaration on liberated Europe and to castigate the Soviet Union for breaking its provision that all previously oppressed peoples should choose in free elections their own form of government. By contrast, de Gaulle, Helmut

Schmidt and François Mitterrand regarded Yalta as an endorsement of 'spheres of influence' and hence of the division of Europe.[20] A further complicating factor was that the military and political context altered from meeting to meeting in ways that strengthened the hand of Stalin. At the time of the Yalta Conference the Western Allies had been held up by Hitler's Ardennes offensive, whereas the Red Army had reached the river Oder and had the German eastern territories and Poland effectively in its hands. The three great capitals of central Europe — Vienna, Prague and Berlin — were almost within the Soviet grasp. Roosevelt was mortally ill (he died in April 1945), and Churchill was not in the best of health. In the light of later developments the elements of competition and suspicion in the Anglo-American alliance during this period were often underestimated.[21] Roosevelt regarded Churchill as an old-fashioned imperialist in contrast to the new world represented by the United States and the Soviet Union. Accordingly, Stalin approached the Yalta and Potsdam Conferences in the confident assumption that they would serve to consolidate his military and political successes.

Churchill has often been blamed for encouraging Stalin in this assumption by accepting the idea of legitimate spheres of influence at his famous meeting with Stalin in Moscow in October 1944: a 90 per cent Soviet predominance in Romania, a 90 per cent British share in Greece, a 75 per cent Soviet share in Bulgaria, and a half share each in Hungary and Yugoslavia. In suggesting such figures Churchill was perhaps being optimistic. On the other hand, he displayed a strategic sense.[22] By this time the Red Army was already in military control of Bulgaria and Romania and parts of Yugoslavia and Hungary. Yet there were still areas of Europe in which the situation was fluid. As the war drew to an end, Churchill was constantly pressing for a rapid advance to capture the key cities of central Europe — Berlin, Prague and Vienna — before the Russians arrived. General Eisenhower's military reservations triumphed over these longer-term political concerns about the post-war settlement. Earlier, at the Tehran Conference, Churchill had failed to win support for his proposal for a simultaneous landing of Western troops in the Balkans and in France in May 1944. As a consequence the Western Allies were deprived of an opportunity to shape political developments in central and south-eastern Europe at the end of the war. Soviet rather than American and British lives were sacrificed for the liberation of the Balkans. The political costs were counted later.

The main substance and greatest problems of the Tehran, Yalta and Potsdam Conferences were provided by the future of Germany and Poland and the issue of German reparations.[23] Even before the Tehran Conference the Soviet Union was very suspicious of any attempt at separate negotiations by the Western Allies with any of their enemies. In particular, they resented their exclusion from armistice negotiations with Italy in September 1943, even though they were kept informed about them. They were quick to use this precedent to exclude the Western Allies from a voice in the administration of Bulgaria, Hungary and Romania in 1945. Poland was, as we have seen, another matter. In the West there was sympathy for the terrible position in which the Poles found themelves as a consequence of double occupation of their country by the Germans and then by the Russians. Britain had gone to war in 1939 over Poland, and the Polish-American lobby was seen as a significant electoral force in the United States (with a presidential election in 1944). The London-based Polish resistance was locked in bitter conflict with the Russians, particularly after the discovery of the massacre at Katyn and the subsequent refusal of the Soviet government in April 1943 to continue to recognize the Polish government in London.[24] The principle that the Soviet Union should acquire the eastern part of Poland and that, as compensation, Poland should receive German territory in the west up to the river Oder was accepted at Tehran, ignoring the views of the Polish government in exile. The matter of Poland's frontiers and the future government of Poland were still key issues at the Yalta and Potsdam Confernces, but the Western Allies were unable to avoid a humiliating outcome. Stalin insisted on the Oder–Neisse line as Poland's western border and would not move from vague statements about free elections in Poland. The Western allies sought to emphasize the provisional nature of this border, and in Article 9 of the Potsdam Protocol the three heads of government agreed that 'the final delimitation of the Western frontier of Poland should await the peace settlement'. Polish elections had to wait until January 1947 by which time the Soviet position had been thoroughly consolidated.

From 1941 onwards the idea of a punitive peace with Germany had gained ground, culminating in September 1944 in the drastic plan of Henry Morgenthau, American Secretary of the Treasury.[25] Stalin had raised the question of reparations as early as September 1941, and dismemberment of Germany was firmly on the agenda. The Morgenthau Plan involved detachment of German territory to its neighbours, the division of the rump into a northern state and a southern state and their conversion into primarily agricultural economies. In the case of this extreme proposal, and of other proposals for dismemberment, analysis of the practical implications of a permanently crippled Germany in the middle of Europe led to its abandonment.[26] The key agreements about Germany and Austria were made before the Yalta Conference by the European Advisory Commission in London.[27] This commission was established by the conference of foreign ministers that met in Moscow in October 1943 and comprised Sir William Strang for Britain and the American, Soviet and (from November 1944) French ambassadors in London. Following on the Moscow agreement of October 1943 that Austria, as the first victim of Hitler, should be reconstituted, the following was agreed and was to prove decisive for the future of Germany:

(1) a proposal for the unconditional surrender of Germany of 25 July 1944, revised at Yalta to incorporate a procedure for the possible dismemberment of Germany, but because of continuing lack of clarity replaced by a short military document when the German *Wehrmacht* surrendered on 7 May 1945 at Reims and on 8 May 1945 at Berlin-Karlshorst;
(2) a protocol on the zones of occupation in Germany and the administration of Greater Berlin of 12 September 1944, and complemented by the agreement of 14 November 1944 which finally defined the three zones (Soviet occupation of the east, British of the north-west and American of the south-west), with eventual agreement on a French zone of occupation at Yalta;
(3) an agreement on the structures and procedures of Allied control in Germany of 14 November 1944, again with agreement at Yalta on a French seat on the Allied Control Council: the three commanders-in-chief were to exercise supreme authority in

Germany on behalf of their respective governments, each in his own zone and all three jointly in matters affecting Germany as a whole.

The fact that these decisions were prepared before French entry into the European Advisory Commission in November 1944, that General de Gaulle was not invited to Yalta or Potsdam, that his provisional government was not recognized by the Western Allies until October 1944, and that that he remembered the lack of respect that he had received in London, not least from the Americans, gave an added dimension to France's post-war concern about obtaining big-power status. Symptomatic of later grand gestures of diplomatic independence was de Gaulle's visit to Moscow in December 1944 where he signed a Franco-Soviet treaty of alliance. The trauma of defeat in 1940 gave an extra dimension also to French concern about security from Germany. Correspondingly, the French veto became another burden on the working of the Allied Control Council. Pointing out that she could not be bound by the Potsdam Agreement, France blocked any moves to establish central administrative bodies in Germany in 1944-6. In particular, de Gaulle argued that settlement of the German problem in the East at Potsdam would turn German vitality and aggressiveness westwards. Symmetry could only be restored to European power relationships if Germany was dismembered.[28]

By the time of the Potsdam Conference in July 1945 dismemberment of Germany was no longer a serious issue for the other three Allied powers. In the eyes of Churchill, dismemberment threatened further to enhance the influence of the Russians in central Europe.[29] On the other hand, Stalin preferred to consolidate the Soviet position in its own substantial zone of occupation rather than become involved in more complex plans for dismemberment that cut across the new zones. Leading figures in the pre-1933 German Communist Party, notably Wilhelm Pieck and Walter Ulbricht, were flown back from their exile in Moscow as soon as the Soviet occupation began. Against the background of communist reminders that left-wing division had helped the fascist cause, the German Communist Party and the Social Democratic Party in the Soviet zone were formed into a new Socialist Unity Party in April 1946. Political priority was given to 'Sovietization' of the eastern zone of occupation. Strategically, the eastern zone — later the German Democratic Republic — was crucial as the western prong of the pincer that held recalcitrant Poland to heel. There were also important economic reasons for the Soviet Union's loss of interest in dismemberment of Germany. The Soviet Union sought hefty reparations, with Stalin suggesting a figure of $10 billion at Yalta. The Ruhr was an obvious source for such reparations, hence the Soviet interest in participating in joint control of the Ruhr. Finally, it was agreed in 1945 that the Soviet Union could take 15 per cent of the industrial capital equipment in the western zones, whilst the Western powers renounced any reparations from the eastern zone. When in 1946 the Americans refused to allow any further dismantling in their zone for reparations, Soviet anger was considerable. They argued that the Western powers were indifferent to the dreadful damage inflicted by Germany on the Soviet Union and that they were more concerned about German than about Soviet recovery. By 1947 the Soviet Union was making German unity dependent on reparations. The Western view was that the Soviet Union was simply interested in aggrandizement of its own power and ignored the tax burden that fell on the West as a consequence of Soviet demands for reparations from current production.

A mix of economic and political reasons informed the Western powers' concept of post-war Germany. Hunger, deprivation and demoralization were to be seen everywhere. In 1947 industrial output was only 27 per cent of pre-war volume. As General Lucius Clay, Military Governor of the American zone (1947–9), commented, 'Western Europe could not recover if there was an economic vacuum left in Germany'.[30] Establishment of the Bizonal Economic Council in 1947, merging the British and American zones, was followed by the European Recovery Programme, better known as the Marshall Plan, after its architect the American Secretary of State General George Marshall, and in 1948 by the German currency reform instituted by Ludwig Erhard. In other words, the foundations of the German economic miracle were laid before the establishment of the Federal Republic of Germany out of the three western zones of occupation in May 1949. A deindustrialized Germany suited the Soviet Union's economic and strategic interests. Such a solution was, by contrast, hostile to Western economic interests and to Western political interests in so far as such a weak Germany would be vulnerable to Soviet pressure. Western political priorities involved a decentralized and 'controlled' process of democratization allied to containment of German heavy industries and any military forces that might be developed. This strategy of containment found expression in the Schuman Plan of 1950, a proposal of the French Foreign Minister to pool coal, iron and steel production in a new supranational authority, established in 1952 as the European Coal and Steel Community; and in the abortive French proposal, the Pleven Plan, for a European Defence Community in which a supranational authority would have to be responsible for an integrated force structure. In inception West European integration was very much about power and interest, specifically about the control of actual and potential German power.

It is important not to underestimate the role of the German problem in the new post-war process of West European integration. The great historic change in French policy in post-war Europe was from simply acting as a break on German power by proposals for dismemberment of Germany, reparations and defensive alliances. France adopted the positive function of providing a politicla motor for West European integration as a means of containment of the German problem by its absorption and control in supranational structures. The aim of security against Germany remained. However, from 1947 onwards this aim was set in the larger and common framework of security against the Soviet Union. The implication was priority to Franco-German collaboration. Bonn and Paris provided the main political axis of the European Economic Community after 1957, and the significance of this axis was underlined by the Franco-German Treaty of January 1963.

As far as strategy for the post-war European order was concerned, the immediate common concern of the Western powers and the Soviet Union was the issue of control of German power in central Europe. Their approaches to post-war Germany were, however, as we have seen, very different. It proved impossible to follow peace with a peace treaty. By May 1945 Churchill was already writing of the Russians that 'an iron curtain is drawn down upon their front. We do not know what is going on behind'.[31] He was to popularise the term 'iron curtain' in his famous speech at Fulton, Missouri, in March 1946. The term 'cold war' was first used by the American statesman, Bernard Baruch, in a speech in 1947. Barometers of the emerging cold war were provided by the meetings of the Council of Foreign Ministers, established by the Potsdam Protocol with the task of preparing 'a peace settlement for Germany to be accepted by the government of Germany when a government adequate for the purpose is established', and by the Allied Control Council in Berlin.[32] Following the two abortive meetings of the Council of Foreign Ministers in Moscow (March–April 1947) and in London (November–December 1947), the Western powers resolved in the so-called London Programme on procedures for establishing a separate West German government and that a new initiative was required to tackle the problems of hunger, squalor and deprivation in post-war Germany. In March 1948 the Russian representative walked out of the Allied Control Council. The Western powers pressed on with the currency reform of June 1948, the economic benefits of which were immediately visible.

Alarmed and angered by this sequence of events (Marshall Plan, London Programme and currency reform), the Soviet Union struck at the weakest point in the Western presence in post-war Germany — Berlin. Berlin was blockaded from June 1948, and the West's response of a massive airlift sustained over a year led eventually to the end of the blockade. The Berlin crisis of 1948–9 confirmed a Western view that it paid to be tough with the Russians. Efforts by the West to normalize relations with Germany were continuously frustrated by a suspicious Soviet Union. Germany's division into zones precluded a separate peace treaty with Germany by the Western allies, whereas a peace treaty with Japan was signed in September 1951 without Soviet ratification. The Western Allies had to be content with 'proclamations' terminating hostilities and later the state of war with all Germany, and with authorizing the heads of the new state governments within their zones to convene a constituent assembly to draft a constitution. In April 1949, on the same day that the military governors approved the Basic Law drafted by the Parliamentary Council, a new Occupation Statute went into effect that still substantially restricted the sovereignty of the new Federal Republic of Germany. Sovereignty was not restored until the coming into force on 5 May 1955 of the Treaty of Termination of the Occupation Regime in the Federal Republic of Germany, signed at Paris on 23 October 1954. As part of the Paris treaties of 1954 the Federal Republic became a member of NATO and the Western European Union. At the same time all NATO members declared that a peace treaty for the whole of Germany and German reunification were fundamental policy aims.

The combination of restoration of sovereignty with the entry of West Germany into the NATO alliance in 1955 was a source of acute anxiety to the Soviet Union. The Warsaw Pact was formed in 1955 as a direct response, just as in 1949 the Soviet Union had established the German Democratic Republic out of its zone of occupation as a complement to the Federal Republic. However, it proved difficult to achieve recognition for the GDR. Bonn, supported by Washington, claimed the right to speak for all Germans in international affairs and in its Basic Law presented itself as a provisional regime pending reunification on the basis of free self-determination by the German people. In the so-called Hallstein doctrine of June 1956 the Federal Republic sought to keep open the door for reunification by threatening diplomatic countermeasures against states which recognized what at the time was referred to as the 'so-called German Democratic Republic' or the 'Soviet Occupied Zone'. In the famous Soviet note of March 1952 the idea of a neutral Germany as the price of reunification had been floated but rejected. As far as Chancellor Konrad Adenauer was concerned, and the Western Allies, Germany was much too important to gamble on its neutrality. They refused to risk a communist takeover and anyway saw the note as a diversionary Soviet move at a time when West German integration into the Western defence system was just coming under discussion. Such a solution was possible for a small state like Austria in 1955, though in the latter case the reluctance of the Western Allies had much to do with the loss of an important land bridge for NATO between the Federal Republic and Italy. In any case Soviet policy was more consistently fixed on consolidation and recognition of the GDR. The internal workers' revolt of June 1953 and the continuing exit to the West of skilled workers from the GDR indicated the scale of the Soviet Union's German problem. Erection of the infamous Berlin Wall in August 1961 was the response.[33]

Conflict about Germany was part of a general divergence of conceptions for shaping the post-war world in Moscow and Washington. The Soviet Union wished to consolidate its wartime gains in Eastern Europe in the form of its own sphere of influence, to make good its own appalling wartime losses and to erect a secure territorial buffer between itself and the 'aggressive' West. Such a policy could be legitimated by the historic role of the Soviet Union as the model of the inevitable transition to communist society. Accordingly, the fraternal relations between it and the other states of Eastern Europe within the socialist community had a special character, summed up later in the 1960s by the Brezhnev doctrine of the limited sovereignty of communist states. The advantageous position of the Soviet Union in Europe at the end of the war, and the clarity and convergence of its strategic and ideological interests, gave it the upper hand in the period 1945–8. In September 1947 an international communist 'information bureau', the Cominform, was established as a successor to the Comintern, which Stalin had dissolved in 1943 as a gesture to his Western allies. By the end of 1948 the Soviet system was being imposed in eastern Germany, Poland, Bulgaria, Czechoslovakia, Hungary and Romania. As far as Moscow was concerned, the culprit was American imperialism, as represented in the Marshall Plan and Western policies towards their zones of occupation in Germany.

Before the end of the Second World War the United States had developed its own vision for the post-war world. In the view of its elites, economic nationalism had been responsible for the slide into political extremism and war in the 1930s. The post-war world required for peace, security and prosperity a 'One World' system, a system of multilateral trade based on the principle of the Open Door and of political and monetary cooperation, represented by such post-war institutions as the General Agreement on Tariffs and Trade (GATT), the International Monetary Fund (IMF) and the World Bank, as well as by the United Nations. As with the Soviet Union, the American vision was congruent with her own ideological principles and economic interests. The corollary was American generosity in the shape of the Marshall Plan and American support for Western European integration. America's search for an interdependent world was reflected in its policies for Germany. As far as Washington was concerned, the culprit was Russian expansionism and self-centredness.

After 1948, once the cold war was firmly established, the initiative slipped to the West. The communists were defeated in Greece after a bitter civil war in 1949. Although Stalin refrained from intervention in accordance with his agreement with Churchill in 1944, Greece formed the background for the enunciation of the Truman doctrine of 1947 which offered American support to 'free people who are resisting attempted subjugation by armed minorities or by outside pressures'. The Marshall Plan provided the economic dimension of the new American containment doctrine. More seriously, Stalin failed to maintain control over the Yugoslav Communist Party. Marshal Tito had virtually liberated his country before the arrival of the Red Army and began to pursue quite independent foreign and economic policies. Yugoslavia was expelled from the Cominform in June 1948, but Stalin's political intrigues and economic pressures on Tito proved ineffective. The Berlin blockade was also ineffective, whilst the American Marshall Plan was a great political and economic success. The formation of NATO in 1949 set the seal on American commitment to the defence of Western Europe, and in 1955 a rearmed Federal Republic of Germany joined NATO. Serious internal problems emerged in the Eastern bloc with revolts in the GDR in 1953 and in Hungary and Poland in 1956. American nuclear superiority was retained throughout the 1950s, taking another qualititative leap when it detonated the first hydrogen bomb in 1952. The GDR remained a pariah state internationally and unloved at home by citizens who looked to the Federal Republic for the promise of the good life. The attempt to engineer another crisis in Berlin in 1958 proved worthless.[34] Then, outside Europe, the Soviet Union faced the prospect of nuclear annihilation in the Cuban missile crisis of 1962. The withdrawal of its weapons under threat was a humiliating experience for the Soviet Union.

The German and European catastrophe of 1945 had given an immense opportunity to the Soviet Union, and it was an opportunity that a masterful power politician like Stalin did not squander. Ideological ambitions and strategic interests were woven into unison; Soviet negotiators knew clearly what they wanted. The circumstances of victory gave few cards to the Western Allies. The

Western powers' essentially realistic approach was refined as they defined more clearly their interests, particularly with respect to Germany and Berlin. With the escalation of tensions into cold war the Soviet Union found itself in a situation of vulnerability, and its strategy became less clearly defined. China became a factor of growing significance in Soviet calculations. Intensification of Sino-Soviet conflicts in the 1960s, culminating in armed clashes on the Ussuri river in 1969, played an important part in Soviet reassessment of its European policies. The beginning of an American search for accommodation with Maoist China during the Nixon–Kissinger period alarmed the Soviet leadership and provided an added incentive to stabilize the situation in Europe by means of agreements. Quite simply, the Soviet Union was losing round after round of the cold war. Its emphasis on aggressive rhetoric and behaviour had consolidated the Western alliance. A change of emphasis in European policies offered at least better prospects of dividing the Western Allies from each other and achieving a cherished goal of the Soviet Union — an uncoupling of Western Europe from the United States. Even then the Soviet Union had to consider whether it would benefit from such a move. The American presence in Europe served to contain Germany. Would its withdrawal open the way for a new German revanchism? Would its withdrawal reduce the credibility of the Soviet's position in Eastern Europe? These questions complicated Soviet strategy.

More concretely, the Soviet Union returned to the task of gaining formal recognition of the territorial arrangements in post-war Europe, particularly for the GDR and the German–Polish frontier. They were, however, to discover that the Western powers were not prepared to translate their political commitment to the post-war division of Europe, which had proved convenient as a means both of clarification and of containing the old centrifugal forces of European politics as well as of controlling German power, into a legal endorsement of Soviet power politics. Post-war Europe continues to live in an absurd situation in which territorial arrangements are seen as permanently provisional. This absurdity can only be understood by reference to the abnormal outcome of the Second World War: abnormal in its scale of cruelty, abnormal in the scale of usurpation of territory, and abnormal in the lack of a peace treaty. The Western powers are prepared to maintain this absurdity because, though the existing arrangements provide stability in Europe, they are based on deep injustice. European peace has been established on the basis of tacit understandings and unspoken rules.

Détente: the ideological and strategic context

The shift from cold war to détente, and then back again to confrontation, is documented and explained elsewhere in this volume. The purpose of this chapter is to put détente policies in their historical, ideological and strategic context: to understand the nature of the rivalry, symbolized by the division of Europe, alongside the imperative of coexistence in the new nuclear age. Détente was about reducing tensions in a divided Europe which, as the Berlin crises of 1948 and 1958, the revolts in the Soviet bloc, and the massive accumulation of conventional and nuclear weaponry indicated, was a grave source of threat to world peace. For historical and strategic reasons there were sharply differing views about the sources of tension in Europe. In the view of the Western powers the problem rested in the way in which Europe had been divided, specifically in the role of Soviet duplicity and coercion and the denial of the right to self-determination of peoples by free elections in Eastern Europe, as laid down in the Atlantic Charter. Some diplomats, like George Kennan, argued that tensions had been greatly aggravated by the political personality of Stalin. His death in 1953 provided at least the prospect of a relaxation of tensions. According to the Soviet Union, the West caused tension by its unwillingness to recognize the post-war division of Europe and the post-war borders. By insisting on the openness of questions like post-war borders the West gave scope to imperialist, revanchist elements in its midst. This difference in interpretation of the source of tensions led to different aims and expectations from détente. The Soviet Union held an essentially static conception of détente. Its aim was to consolidate the post-war European settlement by recognizing the status quo there. The West had a dynamic perspective on détente, seeing it as a means of promoting a different quality in the relations amongst peoples and individuals, based on greater contacts, exchanges and respect for human rights. For the Soviet Union détente was a simple matter of a commitment by governments to recognize post-war realities; for the West it was an educative process, involving domestic political changes as evidence for its reality.

There is no single shared concept of détente that embraces and integrates the policies of the superpowers and the various European states. There is little more in the way of adequate structures and procedures through which détente can be pursued. As we shall see, institutionalization of the détente process is very limited. Right at the heart of détente is the problem of language and the ideological conflicts and motives that this problem reveals. The problem of language in East–West relations is not new. During the Second World War the proclaimed adherence of the Allies to peace, freedom and democracy masked very different interpretations of these terms. Détente proved no different. The Soviet complement to the Western term détente is 'peaceful coexistence'.[35] Peaceful coexistence emphasizes the distinctive and superior quality of relations amongst socialist states and the need to prevent 'internal erosion' from the West's 'psychological warfare' by a controlled flow of information there. Arms control and disarmament depend on Western restraint from 'ideological diversion' in Eastern Europe, in other words from 'interference in the internal affairs' of socialist states. Western insistence on protection of the rights of the individual is an example of such diversion, irrelevant to socialist societies and dangerous to peaceful coexistence. In societies that claim to be eliminating the exploitative relations characteristic of capitalist societies social rights, especially the right to work, take priority. The asymmetry of the Soviet concept of peaceful coexistence stems from the argument that 'ideological struggle' remained a necessary and legitimate function of socialist societies, part of their historic role in the class struggle. Peaceful coexistence was to pave the way for the victory of socialism. Western conceptions of détente were also often oriented to 'system change'. If the Soviets exempted ideological struggle from their definition of peaceful coexistence, the West incorporated in détente its concern to further the cause of human rights. In other words, the West was disillusioned by the Soviet Union's limited conception of peaceful coexistence, whilst the Soviet Union was frightened and defensive about the expansiveness of Western conceptions of détente.

On the one hand, East and West could agree on the need for a code of behaviour to contain confrontation, the dangers of which had been so apparent in Berlin and Cuba. They did this most strikingly in May 1972 in the declaration on the basic rules of détente signed by the Soviet Union and the United States and, as we shall see, in the Helsinki Final Act of 1975, signed by thirty-five European states, the United States and Canada. In 1972 the superpowers could agree four points: to limit arms competition; to intensify cooperation; to recognize each other's security interests; and to refrain from attempts to influence the internal affairs of other states. Yet neither of these two agreements overcame the problem of a lack of rules of the ideological game. Mutual respect and tolerance were most strikingly absent at the ideological level. As long as ideology pointed down a one-way street in terms of historical development, the notion of ideological competition according to certain rules could not take root. Europe was divided by an ideological struggle, its relations conducted to a large extent by what Lord Carrington, the former British Foreign Secretary, called 'megaphone diplomacy', a form of communication perhaps appropriate to those who are condemned to conduct 'a dialogue of the deaf'. Mutual ignorance was functional in ideological terms. At the same time the sheer predictability of the sloganeering in East–West relations placed great premium on the esoteric business of reading signals not just from the type of sloganeering employed at a particular time but from protocol, appointments and dismissals, promotions and demotions, official visits and countries and themes selected for special attention.

Once détente was detached from a historical and ideological frame of reference the dangers of confusion, deception and self-deceit mounted. The aim of convergence of systems by means of détente policies was clearly impractical. Détente had two faces, in other words a Janus-like quality. On the one hand, it involved the search for ways of containing rivalries and managing conflicts and for areas of common interest, not least the shared sense of vulnerability in the new nuclear age. Early examples of steps in this direction were the installation of the 'hot line' between Moscow and Washington (1963), the Nuclear Test Ban Treaty (1963), the Non-Proliferation Treaty (1968) and SALT 1 (1972) which curbed anti-ballistic missile deployments and set a limit to Soviet and American offensive strategic weapon levels. On the other hand, East and West adopted a 'power-game' approach, seeing détente as an instrument to promote bloc and state interests. Peace initiatives under the banner of detente or peaceful coexistence could function as levers to promote certain kinds of change in Europe beneficial to one's own interests. Thus the Soviet Union has pursued the proposals for a system of collective security in Europe allied to a dissolution of the alliance systems. The idea of a collective security system was first put forward in the 1950s as an alternative to Western proposals to integrate a rearmed West Germany into a European Defence Community. It appeals to neutralist and pacifist sentiments in Western Europe and serves to uncouple Western Europe from the United States. Realization of such an idea would be advantageous to the Soviet Union. Moscow keeps thirty-one divisions in Eastern Europe under bilateral treaties that pre-date, and would be unaffected by the disappearance of, the Warsaw Pact. There are no indications that the Soviet Union is prepared to sacrifice its forward deployments beyond its own borders, its 'gendarme' role in policing Eastern Europe or indeed any platform from which it can display its leadership of the 'socialist community'. As the decision to deploy cruise and Pershing missiles in West Germany came closer in 1983, the Soviet Union resorted to the threat of damage to inner-German relations, the major achievement of West German détente policies, to unsettle West German opinion. In reverse the Soviet Union views Western proposals for 'confidence-building measures', like exchange of future plans for maneouvres and exchange of observers at maneouvres, as 'institutionalized spying' and its human rights campaigns as the pursuit of unacceptable and destabilizing political change in Europe. This combination of the search for a European 'peace order' with the interplay of power and interests gives détente its Janus-like character. Détente has alternately an 'offensive' and a 'cooperative' face, an ambiguity that is inescapable. The historical and ideological roots of the tensions and rivalries to which détente is a response, and that accompany détente, go deep. They are so acute that phases of 'cooling' of relations and stagnation of détente are to be expected.

The moral dilemma between pursuit of peace and fear of

aggression, blackmail and intimidation comes out clearly in the complex link of détente and security, both conceptually and institutionally. The institutional link can be seen in the role of the Warsaw Pact and of NATO in the preparation of détente policies in the 1960s and 1970s. From a communiqué of the political consultative committee of the Warsaw Pact in January 1965, through the Bucharest Declaration of July 1966, the Budapest Appeal of March 1969, to the Prague Declaration of January 1972, the Warsaw Pact gave greater precision to its proposal for a European security conference. Security, in the sense of military détente, seemed the central concern of the Soviet Union, and the idea of cooperation in economic, technical and trade matters was only taken on board in 1969. NATO, too, seemed at first to envisage détente in terms of a more political and less military conception of security. This perspective of combining defence policy with political détente found early expression in the Harmel Report, prepared for NATO by the Belgian Foreign Minister in 1967. In its Rome communiqué of May 1970 NATO spoke of a 'conference on security and cooperation in Europe' and in the Brussels communiqué of December 1971 identified economic, scientific, technological and environmental cooperation and human contacts as key themes. In other words, during this period NATO sought to strengthen the diplomatic dimensions of its role.

At the same time the emergence of détente onto the international agenda was associated with a new conception of security. Détente and security were conceptually related. Dictionaries define security (from the Latin *securitas*) as 'freedom from fear and anxiety' or a 'state without danger'. The Russian word *bezopasnost* also means 'without danger'. By contributing to the reduction of tensions détente can enhance security (the Harmel view); by politicizing and broadening the debate about security an important contribution could in turn be made to détente. The latter proposal was taken up particularly in the Palme Commission report *Common Security* of June 1982, and in some of the Western thinking behind the Conference on Confidence and Security Building Measures and Disarmament in Europe, which convened in Stockholm in January 1984. In this view too much weight was being placed on the concept of 'antagonistic security', based politically on the confrontation of two alliances in

East–West relations and expressed in a confinement of debate within military categories. Security is seen as dependent on armed defence *against* the other and *against* the political aims and military capabilities of a potential foe. Such a conception of security seems to undermine the search for détente by sowing seeds of political distrust. It seems also to be self-defeating in that it generates fear and anxiety on which a hideously expensive arms race can thrive. A process of 'threat inflation' is set in motion. This state of 'non-war' through deterrence offers imperfect security. The consequences of human or technological failure in an age of mass-destruction weapons (even if such failure is unlikely) would be so disastrous that a political sense of responsibility for present and future generations calls for all-out efforts at dialogue and negotiation with the political rival and potential foe. 'Common security' can only be achieved by negotiations *with* the political rival and potential enemy and by understanding the reasons for the armed, antagonistic security of the potential enemy. It is in effect détente in military terms: the establishment of mutual confidence and cooperation and the demystification of alleged threats as the basis for efforts at arms control in Europe aimed at a 'balanced' power ratio 'at the lowest possible level'.

The idea of common security seems to have found expression in the policy statements of East and West. From the outset Moscow has emphasized 'military détente', showing a clear preference for a European security conference. Its ideas on 'military détente' were brought together in the Prague Declaration of the Warsaw Pact in early 1983: a non-aggression pact between NATO and the Warsaw Pact; renunciation of first use of nuclear weapons; and establishment of nuclear-free zones in Europe. Western arms control policies have moved beyond the classical elements of arms reduction and disarmament to a new element, confidence-building measures (CBMs). This approach involves small practical steps that aim at concrete achievements to make intentions clearer and help prevent misconceptions and mismanagement (the 'hot line' is an early example of such an achievement). For the West common security required greater transparency of military doctrines, potentials and budgets as well as verifiability. The concept of CBMs found expression in the Helsinki process, with provision in Basket One of the Final Act of 1975 for notice of large maneouvres and exchange of observers. In 1984 these ideas were again taken up by the Stockholm Conference.

As with détente in general, the need for, and urgency of common security in the nuclear age seem obvious; there is a common interest in survival. The question is not so much 'whether' as 'how'. In a world of sovereign states, each defining its own security interests, there can be no generally agreed, and hence generally applicable definition of the term 'security', except within the alliances. The West views the proposals of the Warsaw Pact as declaratory gestures, seeking through 'military détente' to displace the United States from Europe (an aim that is masked) and to achieve a propaganda victory by a 'peace offensive' that identifies the Soviet Union with 'the strengthening of peace and security' and 'the ending of the arms race'. The closed and defensive nature of the Soviet system, rooted in ideological struggle and historical experience, adds two particular and acute problems to common security negotiations, problems that have bedevilled the Mutual and Balanced Force Reduction (MBFR) negotiations in Vienna and the intermediate-range nuclear force (INF) negotiations in Geneva: how to agree about basic data and how to make any agreement verifiable. In turn the Soviet Union sees the common security proposals of the West, with their emphasis on politically binding measures and verification, as attempts to institutionalize spying and undermine Soviet vigilance.

The problematic relationship between détente and security stems not just from the way in which common security proposals are viewed through the lens of the concept of antagonistic security. Even the concept of antagonistic security is interpreted differently. In the West the dominant concept is deterrence with its stress on a war-prevention strategy. 'Mutually assured destruction' (appropriately 'MAD') by means of massive retaliation makes war an unacceptable risk to each side. Effectiveness of deterrence depends on this capability combined with credibility: that is, deterrence depends on a tough political posture. In the face of the Soviet military superiority in Europe as the only European superpower, the deterrence of the other superpower, the United States, is extended to Western Europe. The European theatre is coupled to American deterrence doctrine, with the threat that a Soviet attack on Western

Europe would lead to escalation to a global nuclear exchange between two massively armed superpowers. This notion of 'graduated escalation' became the core of NATO strategy for Europe from the early 1960s. Early use of tactical nuclear weapons would demonstrate the resolve and capability of Western deterrence. At the heart of deterrence doctrine is the idea of a balance of power: and at the heart of West European strategic thinking has been the concern that the American extended deterrence must maintain a balance of power within 'a strategically asymmetrical Europe' in order to deter the Soviet Union effectively. This concern was expressed by West German Chancellor Helmut Schmidt in an influential speech delivered to the Institute of Strategic Studies in London in October 1977. He argued that, whilst superpower parity was being established in the intercontinental-strategic sector, the Soviet Union's Backfire bombers and its SS-20s were, since 1976 and 1977 respectively, gradually confronting Western Europe with a new and mounting nuclear threat: quantitatively (through multiple, independently targeted warheads) and qualitatively (by mobility and pinpoint accuracy). The concern that American extended deterrence would be made ineffectual was behind NATO's famous 'dual-track' decision of 1979 to seek negotiations on intermediate-range nuclear weapons but, failing a satisfactory outcome, to deploy cruise and Pershing in Western Europe from 1983.

Historical experience (particularly of the Nazi invasion in 1941), ideological ambition (fuelled by the fusion of Marxism-Leninism with Russian patriotism), inferiority *vis-à-vis* the United States (illustrated vividly and publicly by the Cuban missile crisis of 1962) and the notion of 'encirclement' combine to give a particularly antagonistic character to Soviet views on security. Moscow rejects the idea of deterrence as imperialist intimidation.[36] Faced by all-round military threat (from northern Europe through the Mediterranean and the Indian Ocean to the Sea of Japan and the Bering Strait) the Soviet Union has developed the idea of 'equal security' rather than just parity of forces with the United States. The Soviet Union argues that it must match Britain, France and China as well as the United States. Especially after 1962 the Soviet Union sought parity with the United States in the intercontinental-strategic sector, leading to an enormous arms build-up that paralleled the maturation of her détente policies. The SALT agreements I and II indicated a Soviet willingness to concede the idea of parity in this sector. Soviet security policy in Europe was, however, a different matter. In the European theatre the Soviet military pursued the aim of guaranteed defence, of ensuring its capability of waging a successful war in which major destruction could be confined outside Soviet territory. This aim set two requirements for Soviet security policy: Soviet military superiority in Europe, geared to rapid offensive conventional drives followed by high priority to INF strikes to counter NATO's idea of 'graduated escalation'; and the elimination of the American extended deterrence by uncoupling Western Europe from the United States, with Soviet INF seen as balancing the British and French deterrents as 'Eurostrategic' missiles. The stress of Ogarkov, Sokolowski and Ustinov on Soviet capability to wage war effectively in Europe is justified by the lack of credibility of Western deterrence doctrine; history is interpreted to show the willingness of 'aggressive' Western imperialists to resort to war and the number of assaults launched on Russia by her Western neighbours.

This obsession of Soviet security policy with Europe is to be explained as much by geography as by ideology and history. The main threat to peace, which must be removed, is American nuclear missiles in Western Europe. In as much as INF weapons like Pershing 2 are capable of reaching targets deep in Soviet territory they are seen as strategic rather than just theatre weapons. As far as Europe is concerned, the Soviet Union has sought absolute security, buttressed by an array of historical, ideological and strategic arguments. In successive arms control talks between the superpowers the Soviet Union has suggested that they should not burden themselves with the complications of the security interests of the smaller European states. Henry Kissinger reports that in September 1972, during negotiations on an agreement for the prevention of nuclear war, the Soviet Foreign Minister Andrei Gromyko and then Leonid Brezhnev urged him to conclude a secret agreement that the Soviet Union and the United States would target their weapons only on each other's allies.[37] Against this background the Soviet Union interpreted NATO's 'dual-track' decision of 1979 as further evidence of intimidation from NATO's deterrence doctrine. It was at the same time given an opportunity by the period of negotiations to exploit the 'inner contradictions' of the West, as evident in the remarkable growth of the peace movement in Western Europe.

The relations between détente and security policies are clearly very complex and made more difficult by the divergence of concepts of security between East and West. In turn, these divergences hide further disputes that exacerbate relations. Within the doctrine of deterrence there are those who argue for 'nuclear sufficiency', a minimum retaliatory capacity, and others who stress avoidance of superiority by the other side; and there are those who adhere to the idea of a graduated and controlled response and others who argue for strategies for a disabling 'first strike'.[38] Within the Soviet military establishment the relative merits of higher INF deployments and modernization of conventional forces in Europe are hotly debated. As we shall see in the next chapter, the refurbishing of American security doctrine with the announcement of the Strategic Defence Initiative (SDI) by President Reagan has further complicated the issues. Underlying these complex disputes of military doctrine is the essential political point that neither side believes that the other appreciates its legitimate security interests. If it appreciates those interests, it is unlikely to be able to accept them anyway. A fair reconciliation of security interests is easier to envisage in Soviet–American negotiations on intercontinental strategic weapons than in negotiations about the European theatre, given the greater divergence of security concepts in the latter region. Resisting the Soviet claim to a higher degree of security for itself than the Kremlin is prepared to allow Western Europe is bound to call for security policy measures that are unpopular, as with INF in the 1980s.

Conclusions

Détente policies in Europe face a paradox, which when put alongside the ambiguity at the heart of détente emphasized in this chapter, help towards an understanding of how the actors in this process have the experience of walking through a hall of mirrors, deceived by their own illusions as well as those of others. On the one hand, the historical, ideological and strategic factors underlying the division of Europe seemed to offer limited prospects for détente. The fundamental Soviet view that East–West relations are of an antagonistic nature was summed up by Brezhnev in *Pravda* on 30 April 1968 against the background of the communist reforms in Czechoslovakia: that as peaceful coexistence progresses, so the class struggle between East and West will be intensified. Leading figures in the Soviet defence establishment have argued that military superiority and 'uncoupling' must remain priorities of Soviet European policy; they seek to remove the threat to Soviet security from Western deterrence in the theatre where they consider the outbreak of war a real possibility, namely Europe. The prime concern of protection of the home territory requires dedication to the ideological struggle, avoidance of war with the United States as an unacceptable risk and capability of winning a war confined to Europe.

On the other hand, détente is attractive to Europeans, and as we shall see Germans in particular, precisely because Europe is both divided and unprecedently dangerous. Europeans live in the shadow of the bomb and experience the existential threat that comes from inhabiting a densely populated continent in which two blocs confront each other with the greatest and most dangerous concentration of arms ever amassed on earth. It is scarcely surprising that European political leaders sought a measure of political insulation from acute tensions elsewhere in the world, like Afghanistan. The American doctrine of linkage as developed under Kissinger — of punishing the Soviet Union in other areas for particular acts of misbehaviour — was accepted with reservations by the Europeans. They tended to favour a broad-based and long-term political strategy for Europe that focused on constructive possibilities rather than just reacted to individual 'outrages'. The radical transformation of Europe caused by its division was accompanied by a second decisive change, the birth and dynamic development of the nuclear age after 1945. By 1985 there were some 50,000 nuclear warheads, nearly all of a power that dwarfs those of Hiroshima and Nagasaki. Exponential growth in capacity for mass destruction was accompanied by delivery systems of ever more extraordinary range, speed and accuracy. Quite simply, it is politically difficult to keep explaining to European publics that the capacity to destroy them in minutes is a guarantee of their security. The political limits of deterrence theory are established by its psychological impact on totally vulnerable populations, creating a dangerous gap between 'the warrior' and 'the victims' of the nuclear age.[39] In economic as well as human and political terms common security policies seemed to make great sense.

Yet the post-war European order associated with Yalta seemed to erect powerful barriers against the development of such policies. For many Europeans, in East as well as West, Yalta was a symbol of a rigid and inert European condition that threatened the peace of the world. It represented the political bondage of a troubled and troublesome Eastern Europe to the Soviet Union. Some 565,000 Soviet troops were required in Eastern Europe not just for forward defence but also as a garrison; about 360,000 were stationed in the GDR alone. Détente appealed to Europeans as a means of overcoming the effects in human and social terms of Yalta. By offering reassurance about the inviolability (though not about the immutability) of post-war frontiers, and by economic and financial inducements, West German *Ostpolitik* (Eastern policy) and *Deutschlandpolitik* (policy for Germany) hoped to achieve a relaxation of attitudes in Eastern Europe and thereby improve conditions of life there. The Helsinki process (CSCE) was important in involving all European states (excepting Albania) in the search for détente, in broadening the agenda to include cooperation as well as the original Soviet concern for security, and in gaining explicit recognition in Principle 7 and Baskets Two and Three of the Final Act that human and interpersonal issues were factors affecting inter-state relations in Europe. Through CSCE the smaller neutral and non-aligned states of Europe (like Austria, Finland, Sweden, Switzerland and Yugoslavia) gained a sense of identity and role in European affairs; whilst, particularly through preparation for negotiations on Basket Two, the system of European Political Cooperation between the nine member states of the European Community emerged as a newly important actor on the European stage. Through détente at bilateral and multilateral levels Europe rediscovered its identity and a sober and pragmatic role in promoting common security and piecemeal human improvements.

Judgements of the problems and prospects of détente differed within both East and West according to perceptions of national interest. As we shall see, détente was associated with deep suspicions within the two blocs as well as between them. Had the détente policies of certain states a hidden face? Was détente serving as an instrument of national power, to enhance national freedom of maneouvre for some unstated purpose? In the 1960s such suspicions were particularly directed at France within the Western Alliance and Romania within the Soviet bloc. In the 1980s they focused on the 'German question' and the motives of the two German states in trying to insulate inner-German relations from superpower confrontation in the wake of Afghanistan, the Polish crisis and the INF deployment crisis.[40] The new Christian Democratic–Liberal coalition government of Chancellor Helmut Kohl in Bonn in 1982 stressed that the German question was still open, reasserting the legal continuity of the German Reich in the borders of 1937. In the federal election of 1983 the neutralist and anti-nuclear Green Party gained representation in the Bundestag for the first time, whilst the peace movement showed its strength in a series of huge public demonstrations. French fears of German neutralism and appeasement of the East were reawakened: was the Federal Republic becoming an unreliable partner? Noting also the abandonment by the West German Social Democrats of their support for INF deployment once in opposition, President Mitterrand made an unprecedented intervention in West German internal politics on this issue just before the 1983 elections in an address to the Bundestag. In 1984, after INF deployment had begun, and the Soviet Union had closed down dialogue with the West, the GDR pursued an intensive programme of contacts with Western leaders, the visits leading to the sort of positive communiqués that had been associated in the past with Hungary and Romania. Was the GDR any longer the Soviet Union's most trusted ally? On 2 August 1984 an unsigned article in *Pravda* catalogued Soviet complaints against the GDR, and in the next month Erich Honecker cancelled his much-heralded visit to Bonn.

The combination of expectation and anxiety associated with inner-German relations in the early 1980s, as with the course of the Polish crisis after 1980, revealed the depth of official opposition in Eastern Europe and the Soviet Union to questioning of the post-war settlement. It revealed two dimensions to Western official responses.

The moral rejection of that settlement was apparent when François Mitterrand wrote in 1980 about 'overcoming Yalta' and when American Vice-President George Bush (in a speech in Vienna in September 1983) and Secretary of State George Shultz (in the opening speeches of the Stockholm Conference in January 1984) spoke of not recognizing the legitimacy of the 'artificially imposed' division of Europe.[41] More typical, however, was concern about the practical political consequences of seeking to 'overcome Yalta'. In short, the West faced a dilemma. It had a moral interest in change in Eastern Europe and believed that unless the Soviet Union responded to these pressures there would be internally generated crises within the Eastern bloc that could threaten the security of Europe. On the other hand, the West recognized that European security depended on stability and predictability in relations. To what extent should the West seek to exploit the potential for instability in Eastern Europe on moral grounds, knowing that the threat to European security was greater there than from any direct East–West conflict? There were in fact some interesting similarities between the British policy towards Eastern Europe developed after 1982 (in the wake of the Polish crisis and the anxieties it caused, and memories it evoked, in Whitehall) and West German *Ostpolitik* as it had developed since the 1960s. Both sought to manage the status quo, to make subtle distinctions in terms of the opportunities available at different times and in different countries, to cultivate a role as interested observers pursuing change through 'quiet diplomacy', to encourage contacts at as many levels as possible, and to prepare for a long and difficult haul. As Andrew Carter indicates in his chapter, the problem of how to manage and respond to change in Eastern Europe is likely to remain the key European problem.

The ambiguities and paradoxes of détente are most clearly apparent to the diplomat. Détente represents a form of dialogue and negotiation amongst independent states that seems particularly congenial to the diplomat. It recalls a period in nineteenth-century Europe when Europe seemed to acquire the characteristics of an international society whose members sought to regulate their relations according to a code of behaviour, 'the public law of Europe'. The age of the Concert of Europe had been born out of the defeat of an earlier European aggressor, Napoleon Bonaparte, and was founded on the concern to control France.[42] It did not survive the new political forces of nationalism and liberalism or the consequences of the rise of German power, and its final vestiges were destroyed by the First World War. The century of 'the old diplomacy' fell into political discredit in the inter-war period. Prospects for a new age of international relations were implicit again in Roosevelt's vision of the 'anti-Hitler' coalition forming the nucleus of 'One World'. They were, however, very short lived. In short, the experience of European diplomacy provides plenty of support for the patient scepticism that it brings to East–West relations and the search to realize a civilized model of inter-state relations.

Détente is less attractive to those who are frustrated and angered by the intractabilities and dangers of East–West relations. To many in the peace movement it appears to be an elite process trapped within the limited and limiting assumptions of bloc politics and of state sovereignty. Its failure to deliver concrete results, particularly in arms control and disarmament, has forfeited public confidence and interest. Only a 'new politics', challenging these traditional assumptions, can make the world safer. Détente is also less attractive to those in the field of security policy, especially in the defence-industry nexus that benefits directly from antagonistic security. They point to the risks of misplaced trust and the speed with which a military imbalance can develop and induce vulnerability and endanger peace. An overzealous commitment to détente can produce an effete Europe, liable to blackmail and even aggression. In short, the peace movement and security policy-makers tend to have less patience with the ambiguities and paradoxes of détente: and, of course, fortunately for the diplomats, they have even less patience with each other.

In so far as European diplomats fail to see the ambiguities and paradoxes of détente they will themselves fall into traps. The opportunities for constructive dialogue to reduce tensions have to be sought and may be very difficult to find at certain times. Détente is a trap once its ideas and policies are divorced from historical, ideological and strategic analysis; and, as the geographer Halford Mackinder emphasized, the besetting sin of liberal democracies is their disposition to neglect strategic factors. The type of analysis pursued in this chapter indicates the powerful constraints on détente policies in post-war Europe. It indicates also how unwise is the rejection of détente. Common security policies are an urgent requirement in an age of mounting potential for mass destruction. Shared vulnerability and shared interest in survival have somehow to be translated into the common political will to achieve significant and verifiable agreements. Security policy-makers would be unwise to ignore public anxieties and the role of détente in making such agreements possible. At the same time the peace movement needs to bear in mind that the 'new politics' that it espouses may make the world a great deal less safe by creating tensions and instabilities, in this case within Western Europe and between Western Europe and the United States. Like the proponents of détente they will need to remember the relation between diplomacy and the power of the states conducting the dialogue. As in the past the question of power, and ultimately of force, is central to the post-war European order. The great historic continuity underlying the division of Europe and bloc politics remains 'the states system' and the capacity of states to use force. Contemporary problems in East–West relations must be seen against the background of this deeper continuity as well as of the more recent origins of the post-war order. Precisely because war in Europe is no longer acceptable the search for solutions is likely to be no easier in the future than in the past. In a period when many Europeans sense a 'historic mutation' it will be even less easy unless careful historical, ideological and strategic judgement is brought to bear on these problems.

Notes

1. Zbigniew Brzezinski, 'The Future of Yalta', *Foreign Affairs*, Winter 1984, p. 295f.
2. Pierre Lellouche, *L'Avenir de la guerre* (Paris: Mazarine, 1985). Franco-German collaboration in the field of military strategy was strengthened substantially during the presidency of François Mitterrand after 1981: former West German Federal Chancellor Helmut Schmidt produced his own plan for defence collaboration in 1984, according to which the Federal Republic would compensate France for extending her nuclear umbrella over West Germany by a substantial improvement of her conventional forces.

3. Hartmut Boockmann et al., *Mitten in Europa: Deutsche Geschichte* (Berlin: Siedler, 1984); Michael Stürmer, 'Kein Eigentum der Deutschen: die deutsche Frage' in Werner Weidenfield, ed., *Die Identität der Deutschen*, (Munich: Hanser, 1983), pp. 83–101; David Calleo, *The German Problem Reconsidered* (Cambridge: Cambridge University Press, 1979).
4. For introductions see Chester Wilmot, *The Struggle for Europe* (London: Collins, 1952) and Herbert Feis, *Churchill, Roosevelt, Stalin: The War They Waged and the Peace They Sought*, (London: Oxford University Press, 1957).
5. Alfred de Zayas, *Nemesis at Potsdam* (London: Routledge and Kegan Paul, 1977). The confusion and misery were vividly portrayed in Victor Gollancz, *In Darkest Germany* (London: Gollancz, 1947). More generally, see Douglas Botting, *In the Ruins of the Reich* (London: Allen & Unwin, 1985). On the Eastern front see John Erickson, *The Road to Berlin* (London: Weidenfeld & Nicolson, 1983); on the holocaust see Martin Gilbert, *Auschwitz and the Allies* (London: Michael Joseph, 1981).
6. For details see M. McCauley, ed., *Communist Power in Europe 1944-49* (London: Macmillan, 1977). On the Soviet Union see Susan Linz, ed., *The Impact of World War II on the Soviet Union* (Tunbridge Wells: Costello, 1985).
7. For the classic statement of this position see E.H. Carr, *The Twenty Years' Crisis 1919-1939* (London: Macmillan, 1948, 2nd edn).
8. Roger Bullen and Margaret Pelly, eds, *Documents on British Policy Overseas: Conferences and Conversations 1945, London, Washington and Moscow* (London: HMSO, 1985).
9. George Kennan, *Memoirs 1925-1950* (Boston: Atlantic Monthly Press, 1967).
10. William Carr, *Poland to Pearl Harbour: Making of the Second World War* (London: Arnold, 1985).
11. Elisabeth Barker, *British Policy in South-East Europe in the Second World War* (London: Macmillan, 1976); Michael Howard, *The Mediterranean Strategy in the Second World War* (London: Weidenfeld & Nicolson, 1968).
12. Winston Churchill, *The Second World War*, Vol. 6; *Triumph and Tragedy* (London: Cassell, 1954), p. 198. He wrote that he 'had never felt that our relations with Rumania and Bulgaria in the past called for any special sacrifice from us' (p. 181).
13. Willy Brandt, *Friedenspolitik in Europa* (Frankfurt: Fischer, 1968); Lawrence Whetten, *Germany's Ostpolitik* (London: Royal Institute of International Affairs and Oxford University Press, 1974); Philip Windsor, *Germany and the Management of Detente* (London: Chatto and Windus, 1971); and William E. Griffiths, *The Ostpolitik of the Federal Republic of Germany* (Cambridge, Mass: Harvard University Press, 1978).
14. Philip Cerny, *The Politics of Grandeur* (Cambridge: Cambridge University Press, 1980); Edward Kolodziej, *French International Policy under de Gaulle and Pompidou* (Ithaca: Cornell University Press, 1974); and Edward Morse, *Foreign

Policy and Interdependence in Gaullist France (Princeton: Princeton University Press, 1973).
15. William E. Griffith, *Superpowers and Regional Tensions: The USSR, the United States and Europe* (Lexington, Mass: Lexington Books, 1982).
16. On the role of history as a political weapon see Hans-Peter Schwarz, 'Geschichtsschreibung und politisches Selbstverständnis', *Aus Politik und Zeitgeschichte*, vol. 36, 1982, p. 14.
17. Most notably in Carl Friedrich and Zbigniew Brzezinski, *Totalitarian Dictatorship and Autocracy* (Cambridge, Mass: Harvard University Press, 1956).
18. Halford J. Mackinder, *Democratic Ideals and Reality* (New York: Norton, 1962; first published in 1919).
19. Winston Churchill, *The Second World War*, Vol. 3: *The Grand Alliance* (London: Cassell, 1950), pp. 393-4.
20. On the concept of 'spheres of influence' and the role of tacit acceptance in post-war Europe (apparent in Soviet intervention in Hungary in 1956 and Czechoslovakia in 1968) see P. Keal, *Unspoken Rules and Superpower Dominance* (London: Macmillan, 1983). For rejection of the view that Yalta endorsed spheres of influence see Boris Meissner, 'Jalta und die Teilung Europas', *Beiträge zur Konfliktforschung*, no. 2, 1985, pp. 85-107.
21. David Reynolds, *The Creation of the Anglo-American Alliance, 1937-41* (London: Europa Publications, 1981); Robert Hathaway, *Ambiguous Partnership: Britain and America 1944-47* (New York: Columbia University Press, 1981).
For details see Chester Wilmot, op. cit., Part 3, 'The Road to Berlin'. As early as 1942 Churchill was writing of 'erecting barriers after the war against communist barbarism': see Pierre Billotte, *Le Temps du choix* (Paris: Laffont, 1950).
23. John Wheeler-Bennett and Anthony Nicholls, *The Semblance of Peace: The Political Settlement after the Second World War* (London: Macmillan, 1972); Herbert Feis, *Between War and Peace, the Potsdam Conference* (Princeton: Princeton University Press, 1960); Alexander Fischer, ed., *Teheran, Jalta, Potsdam* (Köln: Verlag Wissenschaft und Politik, 1968); William Hardy McNeill, *Survey of International Affairs, 1939-46* (London: Oxford University Press, 1953); Daniel Yergin, *Shattered Peace* (Boston: Houghton Mifflin, 1977). The United States had a particular concern with the war with Japan and with the Soviet role in the Far East. See William Carr, op. cit.
24. For a passionate account from a former prime minister of the exiled government see Stanislaw Mikolajczyk, *The Rape of Poland* (New York: McGraw-Hill, 1948). For a different perspective see George Sanford, *Polish Communism in Crisis* (New York: St Martin's Press, 1983). As early as Tehran it was agreed that Poland's frontier with Russia should be 'the Curzon line', proposed by the British Foreign Secretary in 1920, and not the frontier of 1939, which had been fixed in 1921 after the Russian-Polish war.
25. Henry Morgenthau, *Germany Is Our Problem* (New York: Harper, 1945). For a

similar British view see Lord Robert Vansittart, *Bones of Contention* (New York: Knopf, 1945). Strong opposition came from Harry Hopkins, Roosevelt's special adviser, Cordell Hull, Secretary of State, and the British Foreign Secretary, Anthony Eden. See Cordell Hull, *The Memoirs* (London: Hodder and Stoughton, 1948), Vols. 1 and 2.
26. J.H. Backer, *The Decision to Divide Germany* (Durham: Duke University Press, 1978).
27. A. Sharp, *The Wartime Alliance and The Zonal Division of Germany* (Oxford: Oxford University Press, 1975).
28. Alfred Grosser, *French Foreign Policy under De Gaulle* (Boston, Mass: Little, Brown, 1965), pp. 2–5.
29. Herbert Feis, op. cit., p. 619.
30. Herbert Mayer, *German Recovery and the Marshall Plan* (New York: Atlantic Forum, 1969), p. 1.
31. Winston Churchill, *The Second World War*, Vol. 6: *Triumph and Tragedy*, p. 498.
32. Michael Balfour, *Four-Power Control in Germany and Austria* (London: Oxford University Press, 1956); Boris Meissner, *Russland, Die Westmächte und Deutschland* (Hamburg: Nölke, 1953).
33. Hans-Werner Richter, ed., *Die Mauer oder der 13. August* (Hamburg: Rowohlt, 1961) describes the reactions of shock.
34. Hans Speier, *Divided Berlin* (New York: Praeger, 1961) traces this crisis.
35. W. Bruns, *Friedliche Koexistenz* (Hamburg: Landeszentrale für Politische Bildung, 1976); Peter Klein and Stefan Doernberg, *Friedliche Koexistenz in Europa* (Berlin: Institut für Internationale Politik und Wirtschaft der DDR, 1977) and A. Kuballkova and A. Cruickshank, *Marxism-Leninism and the Theory of International Relations* (London: Routledge and Kegan Paul, 1980).
36. Gerhard Wettig, 'The Essence of the Soviet Threat Dialectic', *Aussenpolitik*, no. 1, 1984, pp. 31–43; Gerhard Wettig, 'The Soviet Union and Arms Control', *Aussenpolitik*, no. 1, 1985, pp. 25–36. For Soviet views on deterrence see John Erickson, 'The Chimera of Mutual Deterrence', *Strategic Review*, Spring 1978, pp. 11–17, and John Erickson, 'The Soviet View of Deterrence', *Survival*, November–December 1982, pp. 242–51. For Soviet views on INF see W.V. Garner, *Soviet Threat Perceptions of NATO's Eurostrategic Missiles* (Paris: Atlantic Institute for International Affairs, 1983) and S.M. Meyer, *Soviet Theatre Nuclear Forces* (London: International Institute of Strategic Studies Adelphi Papers 187 and 188, Winter 1983–4). More generally, see Keith B. Payne, *Nuclear Deterrence in US–Soviet Relations* (Boulder: Westview Press, 1982).
37. Henry Kissinger, *Years of Upheaval* (London: Weidenfeld & Nicolson, 1983), pp. 236–9.
38. The nature of the debate can be gathered from Michael Carver, *Policy for Peace* (London: Faber, 1982); Colin Gray, *Strategic Studies and Public Policy* (Lexington: University of Kentucky Press, 1982); Lord Cameron, ed., *Diminishing the Nuclear Threat* (London: British Atlantic Committee, 1984);

and George Kennan, *The Nuclear Delusion: Soviet–American Relations in the Atomic Age* (New York: Pantheon Books, 1982).
39. Freeman Dyson, *Weapons and Hope* (London: Harper and Row, 1984).
40. Eberhard Schulz and Peter Danylow, *Bewegung in der deutschen frage?* (Bonn: Forschungsinstitut der Deutschen Gesellschaft für Auswärtige Politik, 1985, 2nd edn).
41. François Mitterand, *Ici et maintenant* (Paris: Fayard, 1980), p. 209.
42. On 'concert diplomacy' see Alan Palmer, *The Chancelleries of Europe* (London: Allen & Unwin, 1983); F.R. Bridge and R. Bullen, *Great Powers and the European States System 1815–1914* (London: Longman, 1980); and Harold Hinsley, *Power and the Pursuit of Peace* (London: Cambridge University Press, 1963).

2 Détente and East–West relations: American, Soviet and European perspectives

Andrew Carter

Mikhail Gorbachev's accession to power in the Soviet Union in 1985 gave rise to hopes of radical new departures in Soviet foreign and domestic policy. These hopes were entertained in some parts of Eastern Europe as well as in Western countries. Gorbachev, who was only 54, could look forward to perhaps some twenty years in power. Unlike his two immediate predecessors, Andropov and Chernenko, he seemed to have time to develop and implement a coherent long-term strategy. Some Western commentators were eager to see him as a man of determination and vision, and at the same time of realism. They believed that one of his priorities would be to reverse the decline in the rate of Soviet economic growth and that, in order to release resources for this aim, he might show more flexibility in relations with the West. There could, for example, be a renewed Soviet commitment to an arms control agreement with the West; such an agreement would permit defence expenditure, or at least its rate of increase, to be reduced. Two questions arise. First, why have such high hopes been attached to Mr Gorbachev? And second, what likelihood is there that these hopes will be fulfilled?

The answer to the first question was to be found in the profound apprehension on both sides of the Iron Curtain at the extensive breakdown of dialogue between the superpowers in the early 1980s, especially in the field of arms control. The causes of this new cold war could be sought in both East and West. In the United States the invasion of Afghanistan in 1979 transformed President Carter's perceptions of Soviet policy. Subsequently, President Reagan rebuilt American self-confidence by giving priority to the expansion of American military power; the United States defence budget increased by 40 per cent in real terms during Reagan's first term of office (1980–4). In the East, the invasion of Afghanistan and the imposition of martial law in Poland in December 1981 were followed by a period of defensiveness and overinsurance as the deadline (1983) for Western deployment of cruise and Pershing missiles, in response above all to the earlier Soviet build-up of SS-20's, drew nearer, and as first Brezhnev, then Andropov and Chernenko, were prevented by illness from exercising sustained and effective leadership. The answer to the second question was that in Gorbachev's first months in power it was imprudent to expect too much from him in terms of substance as distinct from style. Any new figure coming to power against a background of superpower hostility and paralysis of Soviet leadership would inevitably become the focus of hopes for improvement. Yet it is also legitimate to ask whether a resurgent and confident Soviet Union would necessarily suit the interests of the West more than the relatively inefficient and unimaginative power of recent years. A short look in greater detail at the background to the present state of East–West relations may help to illuminate the future prospects for détente.

Origins, motives and achievements of détente

The origins of détente, in the sense of efforts by both sides to reduce political and military tension and to promote a measure of cooperation, can be traced back to the thaw that followed the death of Joseph Stalin in 1953. Détente found expression in the 'spirit of Camp David' after the summit between Khrushchev and President Eisenhower in 1959. However, it was the Cuban missile crisis of 1962, during which there was an unprecedented and since unsurpassed risk of nuclear war, that brought home to both superpowers their common interest in self-preservation. The efforts undertaken thereafter to stabilize the superpower relationship bore fruit in the Partial Test Ban Treaty of 1963 and the Non-Proliferation Treaty of 1968. Moves towards a more constructive and safer superpower relationship were, nevertheless, strictly limited in scope. They were based on the simple self-interest of both sides in avoiding nuclear annihilation. There was little sign of more positive cooperation, of an expansion in trade, or of greater restraint in foreign policy. The United States continued its involvement in Vietnam and intervened elsewhere, as in the Dominican Republic in 1965. Also the Soviet-led invasion of Czechoslovakia in August

1968, and the ensuing repression of the aspirations of the Czechoslovak people for 'socialism with a human face', blighted the still tender shoots of growing East–West détente. The enunciation of the Brezhnev doctrine, of the limited sovereignty of socialist states, which sought to legitimize interventions by socialist states to preserve Soviet-style systems under threat, showed that the Soviet Union was prepared to act ruthlessly whenever what it considered to be its vital interests were at stake, regardless of the price in political or economic terms. Yet while memories of the repression in Czechoslovakia were still fresh, moves towards détente were resumed and accelerated. This paradoxical development reflected different but strong pressures in the Soviet Union, the United States and Western Europe.

After the Cuban missile crisis the Soviet Union determined never again to be vulnerable to such humiliation and embarked on a large-scale military build-up that aimed at achieving parity with the United States. This development was a clear departure from previous policy which had emphasized the sufficiency of a minimum nuclear deterrent force. The military 'coming of age' served not only to increase Soviet confidence but also to give the Soviet Union an interest in reaching agreements with the United States that would limit the need for yet further military expenditure at the cost of other Soviet economic priorities.

A second Soviet motive for improving relations with the West was the ever-deepening Sino-Soviet split. Although originally deriving from Mao's resentment at Khrushchev's ideological departure from the principles of Stalinism, the dispute became increasingly strategic as China revived territorial claims against the Soviet Union and acquired a military dimension with Sino-Soviet clashes on the Ussuri River in March 1969. The threat of a military confrontation with China, and signs after 1969 that the Nixon administration was set on improving relations between Washington and Peking, strengthened the Soviet interest in improving relations with Western Europe and even with the United States as an act of insurance.

A third Soviet motive for détente was economic. Declining growth rates in the late 1960s demonstrated the difficulty, in a centrally planned economy, of achieving high productivity and a suitably diverse range of agricultural and industrial products of high quality adapted to the requirements of the defence sector, industry and the consumer. The need to increase economic efficiency and raise living standards was also central to the problem of consolidating the political stability, and claims to legitimacy, of the regimes in the Eastern European socialist countries. Yet developments in Czechoslovakia in 1968, 'the Prague Spring', showed how vigorous and easily released were the heterodox pressures lying beneath the surface in socialist societies. An attractive alternative, and one that seemed less dangerous from a political point of view, offered itself: an expansion of trade with the advanced capitalist economies which, in the days before the first oil-price shock in 1973, were still booming. Increased access to Western technology could give the planned economies a short cut to modernization that would lessen the need for structural reform. Such imports of technology, in the form of licences, finished machinery or complete turnkey projects, could be paid for, if not by existing industrial or agricultural products from the East, then by exports of energy and raw materials, or eventually of the products of the newly installed technology.

The American impulse towards détente was partly a reaction to developments in Soviet policy and partly generated by domestic factors. The Americans had to take cognizance of the increase in Soviet military power and could only share the desire to lessen the economic burden of military competition. More important, however, were the domestic political strains induced by weariness with the responsibilities of being the world's premier superpower, as well as the repeated blows to national confidence administered by the Vietnam War. There is a striking contrast between the generous confidence of the United States at the start of the 1960s, personified by President John Kennedy, and the growing national disunity and lack of moral confidence as the Vietnam tragedy unfolded. As national consensus on foreign policy issues declined, and domestic pressure to withdraw from foreign obligations grew, there was a clear incentive to try to reach some sort of accommodation with the Soviet Union. To this extent exhaustion and uncertainty were motives for détente. However, as we shall see, as the process of détente developed it acquired a positive thrust and aimed at encouraging the Soviet Union to cooperate in constructing a more stable world order.

In Western Europe the impulse for détente originated mainly in France and the Federal Republic of Germany. After the establishment of the Fifth Republic in 1958 and the withdrawal from Algeria in the early 1960s, President Charles de Gaulle perceived an urgent need to re-establish French national pride and self-confidence as a step towards bolstering internal stability. His chosen method was to assert France's unique character and total national independence. In the mid-1960s he distanced himself from his NATO allies, withdrew France from the integrated military structure of the Alliance, developed the independent French nuclear deterrent (*force de frappe*) and embarked on a highly idiosyncratic foreign policy. To the consternation of France's friends and partners in the West, de Gaulle adopted the theory of defence in all directions ('*à tous azimuths*'). Part of de Gaulle's policy involved the cultivation of special relations with the Soviet Union and the countries of Eastern Europe. His approaches found a ready response from a Soviet Union that was always anxious to take any opportunity to drive wedges between major Western countries.

In the Federal Republic of Germany the Social Democratic Party, under the influence of Willy Brandt and Egon Bahr, was increasingly concerned by the *de facto* consolidation of the division of Germany after the construction of the Berlin Wall in 1961. This dramatic event had led not only to the blocking of the last remaining emigration route for discontented GDR citizens but also to a revival of the East German economy and to the beginning of the growth of a form of national self-confidence in the German Democratic Republic as people decided that, if they could not leave, they might as well make the situation at home as tolerable as possible. The Social Democrats' ideas, summed up in the slogan 'change through rapprochement' (*Wandel durch Annäherung*), acquired practical political force when the SDP entered into the grand coalition with the Christian Democrats, the CDU/CSU, in 1966. In NATO new ideas on the management of East–West relations found expression in the Harmel report of 1967. It argued that a strong defensive posture and a readiness for dialogue with the East should be seen not as contradictory but as complementary pillars of a coherent policy.

At the outset, therefore, détente was not a new institutional or procedural mechanism agreed between East and West for the safer management of relations. It resulted from the coincidence of a series of largely unrelated pressures on both sides. Each of the main actors had a different conception of the meaning of détente; these differences led later to misunderstanding, resentment and accusations of bad faith. Despite certain rhetorical emphases by the leadership, for the Soviet Union détente was in practice limited and compartmentalized in scope. The aims of détente were to minimize the risk of nuclear confrontation, to regulate the arms race and to gain the time and means for economic progress. Détente did not mean any diminution of the ideological or political competition between the two blocs, capitalist and communist, or any slackening of support for national liberation movements in the Third World. The aim of the Soviet Union's policy of 'peaceful coexistence' was still to shift the correlation of forces in favour of the socialist camp.

For the United States under President Richard Nixon and Dr Henry Kissinger, on the other hand, the concept of détente evolved into a comprehensive philosophy for the management of East–West relations. Kissinger's thinking had been profoundly influenced by his study of classical nineteenth-century European diplomacy, and especially of the achievement of the Austrian Chancellor Metternich and of the British Foreign Secretary, Castlereagh, who had constructed after the Napoleonic wars a European security system based on balance between powers of roughly equal size. In particular, in the light of his study of the efforts of the European powers to control the dynamism and aspirations of revolutionary France, Kissinger saw the need for a strategy to induce the Soviet Union to accept a responsible role in an international order of which each actor acknowledged the legitimacy. He perceived the dangers that flowed from the differences between the ideology of the Western powers, which aimed at preserving equilibrium, and that of the Soviet Union, which was revolutionary and dynamic and aimed at achieving socialist and eventually communist transformations on a world-wide scale. Kissinger envisaged not so much a bipolar world dominated by the United States and the Soviet Union, as a multipolar world system accommodating other centres of power such as China, Japan and Western Europe. In such a multipolar world the Soviet Union would perceive that its record in one sphere of activity or part of the world would have direct impact upon its interests elsewhere; there would be rewards, both economic and political, for restraint in the exercise of Soviet power and ambition. Evidence that the Americans planned a consistent and long-term strategy, rather than piecemeal reaction to individual events, was provided by the fact that within months of the invasion of Czechoslovakia, President Nixon was speaking, in his inaugural address in January 1969, of a move away from the 'era of confrontation' towards an 'era of negotiation'.

The West European concept of détente was similar in many respects to that of the Americans, although, especially in the case of the Federal Republic, it had more strictly practical and humanitarian aims. The West Germans hoped that a policy of the outstretched hand towards Eastern Europe would reduce the obsession of the Soviet Union with maintaining strict and exclusive control over the area. They wished to preserve and expand direct contacts between the two German states and to create a climate that would facilitate the emigration of German ethnic minorities from the Soviet Union, Poland, Romania and elsewhere. To this end the Federal Republic was prepared to offer economic incentives and also diplomatic rewards, of which the greatest was the abandonment of the Hallstein doctrine of non-recognition of any state that recognized the GDR. The practical results of *Ostpolitik* in the late 1960s and early 1970s were spectacular, including a treaty with the Soviet Union, the establishment of diplomatic relations with the East European countries, the recognition of the GDR (although in a manner that stopped short of treating the East German state as a foreign country) and the entry of the two German states into the United Nations. The Four-Power Agreement on Berlin of 1971 was concluded by the United States, Britain, France and the Soviet Union as powers with continuing responsibilities for Germany as a whole. It improved greatly the practical circumstances of life for Berliners and access to the city from the Federal Republic, while preserving the special legal status of the city as a whole. Despite conflicting interpretations of the terms of this agreement, and associated diplomatic wrangles, its great achievement was that Berlin ceased to be a major point of potential conflict between East and West.

The achievements of the heyday of détente, which lasted until the mid-1970s, were considerable. There was a substantial increase in

East–West trade, and progress in arms control negotiations, leading to the conclusion of the SALT I agreement (strategic arms limitation) between the superpowers and other agreements to reduce the risk of military confrontation. On the political front, agreements such as that on the Basic Principles of Relations between the United States and the Soviet Union were believed to symbolize at least a willingness to seek stability and predictability in their relationship. The Conference on Security and Cooperation In Europe (CSCE), long sought by the East as a means of legitimizing the post-war political arrangements, was conceded by the West, which insisted however both on the participation of the United States and Canada and on the inclusion in the agenda not only of wide-ranging political principles but also of measures relating to human rights, human contacts and the increased flow of information across the East–West divide. The West secured also, as an effective quid pro quo, Eastern agreement to negotiations on Mutual and Balanced Force Reductions (MBFR) in central Europe. It is ironic that the outcome of these two sets of negotiations has been different from that expected by the participants at the outset. The 1975 Helsinki Final Act, which embodied the results of the CSCE, has no binding treaty force, although it is a document of great political importance. It acknowledges the inviolability of frontiers in Europe, while providing for their change through peaceful means and by agreement. The Soviet Union and its partners achieved a measure of what they wanted, albeit in static and qualified form. On the other hand, the human rights and contacts provisions are dynamic and have given the West a point of reference on the basis of which to press repeatedly, at review conferences in Belgrade and Madrid as well as at other meetings, for improvements in Eastern performance. The MBFR negotiations have, by contrast, made no effective progress, largely because within the framework of those negotiations the West has little to offer to induce the East to reduce its substantial preponderance in conventional forces in central Europe.

The decline of détente

The reasons for the decline of détente in the mid- and late 1970s were complex and derived mainly from the different concepts of détente outlined above. Two factors deserve emphasis. The first was the Soviet view of détente as compartmentalized, as not extending to any abandonment of support for national liberation movements in the Third World. This view amounted to a rejection of Kissinger's ideas of comprehensive détente, linkage and restraint. Thus the Soviet interventions, directly or by proxy, in Angola, Mozambique and later in the Horn of Africa, were seen by the American administration as evidence of Soviet bad faith. However, American national self-confidence had been badly shaken in the wake of the Vietnam War and the Watergate affair, and there was no longer a consensus on basic foreign policy goals between Congress and the administration. In particular, the withdrawal of Congressional support from the pro-Western guerrilla groups in Angola, and the curbs placed on the activity of the CIA, sent confusing signals to Moscow about the resolve and priorities of American policy.

The second factor was the shift of emphasis in American policy away from the creation of realities and inducements, to which the Soviet Union could respond without loss of face, towards the setting of public preconditions, for which the Russians would receive rewards only after compliance. The main example of this shift was the Jackson–Vanik amendment of 1974, which made trade concessions by the United States contingent upon Soviet facilitation of Jewish emigration from the Soviet Union. The Soviet Union refused to bow before such public pressure. Nevertheless, this tactical tendency in policy was strengthened under the Carter administration after 1976. Kissinger's policy had been based less on moral considerations than on the realities of the balance of power. As noted above, he wished to create a world in which the Soviet Union would perceive that there would be rewards for conforming to the rules of a legitimate international order and penalties for revolutionary adventurism. Under Carter the priorities were changed. Moral considerations, and especially those relating to human rights, became a dominant factor in foreign policy decision-making. Secret diplomacy was replaced on occasion by negotiation through public pronouncements. The emphasis on the concept of rewards and penalties gave ground to attempts to gain from the Russians concessions in advance, in areas defined by the West, before the Soviet Union could hope to enjoy the benefits of détente, especially those of economic cooperation with the United States. Such conditionality, when publicly expressed, involved Soviet prestige directly and had little chance of success.

The countries of Europe, both East and West, could not remain unaffected by the deteriorating climate between the superpowers. Nevertheless, the urge to preserve the benefits of détente remained strong. Trade relations continued to develop as, initially at least, the East European countries were relatively insulated from the effects of the oil-price shock of 1973 and the Western world, as it moved into a period of inflation and recession, saw opportunities in the relatively stable markets of the East. But here, too, there were disappointments. Progress in improving the relationship between the two German states was slow and subject to setbacks. The hopes that had been raised by the signing of the Helsinki Final Act for a real improvement in observance of human rights and contacts in Eastern Europe were not fulfilled; indeed, the Charter 77 activists in Czechoslovakia, who required no more than that their government should respect its own constitution and international obligations, and the unofficial groups in the Soviet Union and other East European countries which attempted to monitor observance of the Helsinki Final Act, were subjected to repression. Moreover, economic cooperation ran into difficulties. Certain countries, such as Poland, Romania and Hungary, had invested heavily in Western technology and taken substantial Western loans in the early 1970s in the expectation of paying their debts in large measure through export of the products of that technology. But it proved difficult, if not impossible, for centrally planned economies to make full and efficient use of the new technology; and inflation and recession in the West as a result of successive oil-price rises meant not only that interest rates rose, thus increasing the size of East European debt, but also that their economies were less able to absorb manufactured products from Eastern Europe. The problem was further compounded when certain countries, especially Poland, resorted to borrowing hard currency in order to finance consumption rather than investment.

The final blows to superpower détente came at the end of the 1970s. The Soviet intervention in Afghanistan — the first post-war deployment of the Red Army outside the socialist bloc — seemed to prove, at least to the American Right, that the Russians were unregenerate in their determination to expand their influence whenever and wherever they could, stopping short only of a direct confrontation with the United States. This Soviet action finally set the seal on the unwillingness of the American Congress to ratify the SALT II agreement, which in turn evoked strong Soviet resentment. The deployment of Soviet SS-20 missiles, with their enhanced capability to strike NATO targets in Western Europe, seemed to confirm that even if, as in the 1970s, the West relaxed its military build-up, the Soviet Union continued to press for unilateral advantage. In the words of the American Defence Secretary Harold Brown: 'We build, they build: We stop, they build'. After the NATO 'twin-track' decision of 1979, to deploy cruise and Pershing missiles in Western Europe as a counterbalance to the SS-20s unless successful negotiations made this unnecessary, the Soviet Union showed a distinct and protracted reluctance to return to the negotiating table. They resorted instead to threats of yet further deployments and to a large-scale propaganda effort aimed at deflecting the governments of Western Europe from their commitment to accept the basing of cruise and Pershing missiles on their territory. Finally, the imposition of martial law in Poland in December 1981 and the suppression of the Solidarity free trade union movement, against the background of a Soviet military threat to Poland, seemed to demonstrate that the Russians would under no circumstances permit the erosion of Soviet-style systems in Eastern Europe.

Of course, none of these issues was clear cut. If the East European countries had been unwise in seeking to mitigate the basic inefficiency of their system through massive borrowing in the West, the Western response in pouring money into the area went far beyond the bounds of normal financial prudence. Harold Brown's dictum quoted above is an oversimplification. It is possible to argue that the Soviet SS-20 deployment was the fruit of a modernization programme initiated many years previously, and that the United States made substantial progress in the 1970s in refining the accuracy and sophistication of its nuclear arsenal, as well as laying the foundations for several of the programmes that are bearing fruit today, such as the B-1 bomber and the MX missiles. In Poland the escalating and increasing political demands of Solidarity, and the fragmentation of authority within the union, were accompanied by a steady weakening in the effective power of the government to administer the country and reform an economy that was in a catastrophic state even before the creation of Solidarity. It could be argued that if Solidarity had shown sufficient restraint to limit its demands and build on the achievement of the Gdansk agreements of August 1980 it might still exist today and Poland might have been spared the trauma of martial law.

At the start of the 1980s East–West relations had dropped to a low point, characterized by some as a new cold war. Lacking firm and consistent leadership, the Soviet Union retreated into insularity and defiance in the face of the resurgent confidence of the United States under the leadership of President Reagan. Negotiations on the limitation of intermediate-range nuclear forces in Europe and on the reduction of strategic arms made no progress and, following the first cruise and Pershing deployments, were broken off. This state of affairs, and events such as the Soviet shooting down in September 1983 of a Korean airliner that strayed into Soviet airspace, led to growing fears, especially among Western European governments, that the absence of dialogue and contact between the superpowers could have potentially disastrous consequences. In Eastern Europe certain governments showed concern that the superpower confrontation could directly affect their own interests and the stability of their societies which, despite all difficulties, continued to need a measure of economic cooperation with the West. We should now examine the present state of affairs, and future prospects, from the points of view of the main actors: the Soviet Union, the United States, Western Europe and Eastern Europe.

Present and future prospects for détente: the Soviet Union and the United States

The second question posed at the start of this chapter concerned the likelihood of realization of the hopes reposed in Mr Gorbachev. Some signs were positive. Gorbachev was a man of relative youth and undoubted intellectual vigour and ability. His early statements as leader showed that he inherited the mantle of his patron Andropov, that he is determined to combat corruption, inefficiency and debilitating social problems such as alcoholism, and that he is prepared to move younger men into positions of authority and demand that they accept responsibility. A note of caution was, nevertheless, in order. Gorbachev was a product of the existing Soviet system. Despite great personal prestige, he remained surrounded by powerful representatives of previous regimes. He was still subject to consensus in the Politburo. Moreover, it would require more than penalties for corruption or more energetic management to overcome the intractable structural problems of the Soviet economy. And any profound structural change would threaten the interests of the numerous and privileged *nomenklatura* class and risk releasing unpredictable political pressures, as was demonstrated in Budapest in 1956, Prague in 1968 and Warsaw in 1980.

One touchstone of the policies of the new Soviet regime was the arms control talks in Geneva. At the time of writing the prospects for early success did not seem good. The negotiations were of unprecedented complexity, since they concerned not only the limitation or reduction of strategic and intermediate-range nuclear arsenals but also the question of anti-ballistic missile weapons in space, which as yet exist only in rudimentary form or as a gleam in the scientist's eye.

The question of space weapons seemed likely to be the most sensitive issue in East–West relations, as well as in relations within the Western Alliance, in the near future. The Soviet Union had developed a somewhat crude capability to attack satellites, and the Americans had no equivalent capability. However, in what has become known as his 'Star Wars' speech of March 1983, President Reagan outlined plans for research into a strategic defence initiative (SDI) which, if successfully developed and deployed, would give the Americans the ability to destroy incoming Soviet ballistic missiles before they reached their targets. Experts in many countries are still struggling to come to terms with the implications of SDI. Critics argue that it undermines the threat of mutual assured destruction which, through a balance of terror, has, however imperfectly, created a form of stability and prevented war between NATO and the Warsaw Pact for decades. To deploy weapons developed under the SDI would breach the anti-ballistic missile treaty of 1972 which was specifically intended to limit the capability of the two superpowers to develop systems to protect their military assets and territory. SDI could thus start to unravel the limited achievements of the arms control process. It is further argued that it is unlikely to be possible to develop technology that could defend Western Europe, which could be struck by Soviet missiles in a very few minutes, and that SDI would therefore subject NATO to intolerable strains. Finally, it is argued that SDI would not, as its advocates claim, render nuclear weapons obsolete because of the many ways that exist to deliver a nuclear weapon other than by means of a ballistic missile. On the other hand, those sympathetic to the concept argue that, at the very least, research should proceed because of indications that the Soviet Union has for some years been engaged in similar research. Moreover, the advocates argue, the concept of the balance of terror is an unsatisfactory way of seeking to preserve peace if it means the accumulation of ever larger quantities of sophisticated weaponry. It would surely be a step forward, they argue, if it were possible to develop technology that would render a great part of the strategic arsenals of the superpowers unusable. Furthermore, it should be more difficult for peace movements and other objectors to criticize research into a system that has no hostile capability, but is purely defensive in nature. Finally, they point out that President Reagan has not excluded the possibility of sharing the technology with the Soviet Union, if the research is successful.

At present, despite continuing misgivings of principle in the capitals of Western Europe, a degree of consensus seems to have emerged among major participants in the NATO military structure that research into the SDI should go forward, particularly if the Europeans are able to participate and benefit from the economic and technological spin-off. But there is still no agreement about whether eventual deployment would be in the interests of NATO. The Soviet Union has tried rather unconvincingly to represent SDI as a further escalation of the arms race. More convincingly, it has stated that it would be prepared to make the necessary sacrifices to increase its offensive capability so as to overwhelm any eventual space-based defensive system. The Russians are perhaps unlikely to break off the

Geneva negotiations over the issue of SDI, having suffered a propaganda defeat after their walk-out from the INF and START negotiations in 1983. But there are other options open to them. They could attempt to play on Western European fears that an eventual system could not satisfactorily defend the European territory of NATO, and would simply mean that a fortress America would be tempted to leave Western Europe to its fate. Alternatively, the Russians could decide to play for time in negotiations that will, in any event, be complex and protracted, in the knowledge that in a year or two the American negotiating hand will be weakened by the prospect of the 1988 presidential election. The Russians will also be aware of the possibility that the next few years might bring changes of government in the Federal Republic, Britain and France.

In other areas the Soviet Union faced a range of formidable problems. We have noted the difficulties that Mr Gorbachev confronts in his attempt to revitalize an economy that, despite enormous resources and underlying strength, is moving towards stagnation and is falling further behind the West in all areas except that of military technology. In 1984 and 1985 there were increasing strains in the relationship between the Soviet Union and its Eastern European partners. Clearly the Soviet Union is still able and willing in the last resort to impose its will on its allies. Examples of this capability were the cancellations in 1984, at the last minute and evidently under protest, of planned visits to Bonn by the East German leader Erich Honecker and the Bulgarian leader Todor Zhivkov. The main reason for this intervention seems to have been frustration at the failure to prevent INF deployment and fear of the political implications of the development of close relations between the Federal Republic of Germany and East European countries at a time of tension between the superpowers. Admittedly, consistent with his policy of relative independence in foreign policy, the Romanian leader Nicolae Ceauşescu did visit Bonn, although even he seems to have taken account of Soviet sensitivities. He took a hard line in discussion, no communiqué was agreed, and the practical benefits of his visit were few. But there was further evidence of strain between the Soviet Union and its Eastern European clients. Four examples illustrate this point. First, as discussed more fully below, there are clear differences of perception about the importance of political and economic relations with the West. Second, the outcome of the CMEA (Council for Mutual Economic Assistance) summit held in Moscow in June 1984 was inconclusive: little practical progress was made towards removal of the obstacles to greater efficiency in that organization. For instance, no progress was made on the establishment of a genuinely convertible currency which would be vital for the stimulation of multilateral trade within the CMEA, as distinct from bilateral barter. Certain Eastern European countries, notably Hungary, defended successfully the basic principle of freedom of national maneouvre in economic and trade matters. Third, there was official acknowledgement of public disquiet in Czechoslovakia and the GDR, hitherto unquestioningly loyal supporters of Soviet policy, over the decision to deploy Soviet nuclear missiles in those countries in response to the deployment of cruise and Pershing in the West. Fourth, it proved impossible to conceal the resentment in Eastern Europe, especially in a country of outstanding athletic achievement such as the GDR, over the need to fall in with the Soviet decision to boycott the Los Angeles Olympic games in 1984.

In wider perspective the Soviet Union can have derived little satisfaction from foreign policy developments in the early 1980s. The Russians failed to disrupt INF deployment or to make significant inroads into NATO unity on this issue. Despite American setbacks, they had little success in taking over the initiative in the Middle East, and the phenomenon of Muslim fundamentalism emanating from Iran posed a growing threat to the stability of the Muslim republics of the Soviet Union with their rapidly growing populations. The pragmatic domestic course adopted by China under Deng Xiaoping and the prospect of significant Chinese economic progress, coupled with the improvement in political and economic links between China and the West, could give little comfort to the Soviet Union, whose own relations with Peking still lacked warmth and whose image in the world risked suffering by comparison with China as an example of a dynamic, reforming socialist system. Japan was likely to develop its political and perhaps even military cooperation with NATO countries following Mr Nakasone's expression of support for Western security aims at the Williamsburg economic summit. In Afghanistan the Soviet Union seemed as far as ever from achieving a decisive military victory over the mujaheddin and world-wide condemnation of Soviet conduct in that country continued unabated. The Soviet gains in Africa that caused such concern in the West in the 1970s looked increasingly hollow, given the realization in the affected countries of the limitations on Soviet ability to give any aid other than in the military and security fields. Finally, it remained a fact that there was no country in the world in which a freely elected government had chosen to enter into alliance with the Soviet Union.

Compared with the problems facing the Soviet Union, the position of the United States appeared relatively strong. The presidential election of 1984 demonstrated President Reagan's personal domination of the domestic political scene. Reagan's rhetoric of strength helped to restore national self-confidence. The economy appeared to have recovered strongly, and the American military posture had been substantially strengthened, for example through the confirmation of such controversial programmes as the B-1 bomber and, despite Congressional limitation, the MX missile. The Americans gained propaganda advantage from the Soviet walk-out from the INF arms control negotiations in 1983 and could claim that the policy of building up American strength had induced the Russians to return to the negotiating table. The Grenada affair of 1983, when American troops occupied that Caribbean island, reminded the Soviet Union and Cuba of the risks of misjudgement, especially in Central America. The fact that NATO countries withstood successfully the strains that preceded INF deployment, and seemed likely to support at least research into SDI, indicated that the Alliance was in reasonably good shape and had recovered from the tendencies, both visible in recent years, first to accuse the Americans of lack of leadership and then to complain of a domineering American attitude and lack of consultation.

There were also negative features. Pressures were mounting that could both threaten Western unity and undermine the capacity of the United States to conduct a constructive dialogue with the East. The first such strain derived from the conduct of American domestic economic policy in the 1980s. The rapid recovery of the American economy increased the demand for imports and thus helped other countries to emerge from recession. At the same time the United

States continued to operate a massive budget deficit that could be financed only by offering very high rates of interest. As a consequence capital was sucked in from abroad and interest rates in her trading partners were forced higher than was otherwise necessary. The high interest rates in the United States led also to difficulties in certain areas of the American economy itself, for example in agriculture and even banking. There was increasing agreement that the contradictions in American economic policy could not be sustained in the longer term. The question was how a return to a more rational policy could be achieved without provoking either a slump that would affect all the economies of the free world or a collapse of confidence in the dollar that could engender yet higher interest rates. So far the steps taken towards reconstructing a stable international financial order, and resisting tendencies towards protectionism, were only tentative. Yet it was in the economic field, just as much as in the military, that the United States was called upon to exercise both leadership and understanding, if the prosperity and ultimately the security of the free world was to be preserved. Interdependence is a reality that applies also to the United States.

Present and future prospects for détente: Eastern Europe and Western Europe

In Eastern Europe, governments and peoples looked forward, in hope or apprehension, to a period of change over the next few years. In the GDR, Czechoslovakia, Hungary and Bulgaria the national leaders were well into their seventies and, however discreetly, had to be planning their succession. Although Romania's President Ceauşescu is only in his sixties, economic mismanagement led to such hardship for the people, especially during the hard winter of 1984–5, that there were signs of real discontent even among the traditionally docile Romanian people. In Poland, although General Jaruzelski succeeded in restoring order with what, by East European standards, was only a moderate degree of repression, he showed little sign of being able to solve any of the country's deep-seated social, political or economic problems and the situation in the country remained unstable.

Yet perhaps the most important point about contemporary Eastern Europe, apart from Soviet readiness to intervene with force to preserve the communist system there, is that the governing elites have now to recognize that internal stability can be strengthened only by acknowledging and reflecting national interests, and the aspirations of the people, even when these are not identical to, or even directly compatible with, those of the Soviet Union. The days when the key to survival for East European leaders was unconditional loyalty to the Soviet Union, or bleak repression, are past. Nationalism is once again a potent factor. Given the centuries-long history of conflict and suspicion between the peoples of the area, resurgent nationalism was not necessarily an exclusively positive development. However, although historical antipathies are alive beneath the surface, nationalism seems at present to take the form more of a realization that the socialist system must be adapted to reflect the unique identity of each nation, and the need of the people not only for security but also for prosperity and consumer satisfaction. Because of the limitations of the CMEA, this reassessment suggested cooperation not only with socialist partners but also with the wider world. Increasingly Eastern European politics was a matter of preserving the basic structures and achievements of the socialist system — the leading role of the party, full employment, a wide range of at least basic social services and access to education — while improving the efficiency of the economic system. Such a development raised a fundamental dilemma. According to Marxist theory, progress towards communism should involve a decline in political activity, since politics is defined as the clash of class interests. Yet economic reform, aimed at stimulating efficiency by devolution of decision-making authority to a wide range of wealth creators, seemed destined to bring with it a repoliticization of society, as different economic interests regained the ability to compete with each other.

This dilemma was clear in Hungary. The economic reform process there has been applied, with interruptions, since 1968 and achieved relative success. However, it is still at an early stage when judged by the criteria of economic efficiency. Despite the success of Hungarian agriculture, and the reduction of the role of central planning to the setting of broad guidelines, there was still a long way to go before a real devolution of authority in industry was achieved. There were, for example, very few bankruptcies of inefficient enterprises. The comparison with the achievements of Hungary's neighbour and historic partner Austria demonstrated the extent to which the economic system inhibited still the natural talent and enterprise of the Hungarian people.

The dilemma was even clearer in Poland. Despite the experience of martial law, there were still many features in the country that made it the most liberal in Eastern Europe. The Church, the embodiment of national pride and traditions, was stronger than ever, and had preserved most of the gains of recent years, as measured for instance by church building, the numbers of priests, and access to the media. Agriculture was still overwhelmingly in private hands, although a persistent lack of trust and cooperation between the farmers and the authorities condemned it to relative inefficiency. Despite restrictions in recent years, the press was still lively by East European standards, and intellectual and cultural life was vigorous. However, each successive political crisis reduced the prospects of building real trust and confidence between the rulers and the ruled. There were few signs that General Jaruzelski would succeed any more than his predecessors at building a national consensus. Although the military element of the party restored and maintained order, the civilian element was still divided between advocates of economic and political reform and those who, through fear for their own position or of the social and political implications of relaxing control, resisted reform. Even if one gives credit to the Polish authorities for such actions as the trial of the secret policemen responsible for the murder of Father Popieluszko, the positive impression was diluted by renewed arrests of dissident intellectuals and Solidarity supporters, and by evidence that local party and police chiefs were still willing and able to resort to crude repression on their own authority. The outlook for Poland was one of uneasy calm, continued failure to realize the country's economic potential, and popular apathy and resentment. It would be uncharacteristic of the Poles if the situation did not at some future stage lead to a renewed period of overt unrest.

Taking Eastern Europe as a whole, four main features emerge. First, there remained great diversity in the area. Internal politics ranged from the harsh internal controls and cult of personality in Romania to the relative freedom of expression that existed still in Poland and the attempts being made both there and in Hungary to revive popular interest in the political process by providing a wider, if still controlled, participation in local and parliamentary elections. In economic policy the spectrum encompassed traditional centralised control in Czechoslovakia and relative responsiveness to market forces in Hungary. In foreign policy there was a striking contrast between the genuinely independent gestures of Romania (which for example maintained relations with Israel, developed links with China, had a UN voting record comparable with that of non-aligned Yugoslavia, and refused to allow Warsaw Pact troops or maneouvres on its territory) and the predictable conformism of Bulgaria.

Second, the key to social peace in these countries, and the best hope of strengthening the still fragile legitimacy of the rulers, was economic success. The majority of the Eastern European states resisted successfully Soviet attempts to make the CMEA a supranational mechanism of control. However, intra-CMEA trade was still hampered by the inefficiency and limited scope of its operations. The growth in CMEA bureaucracy since the early 1970s did not lead to full exploitation of the potential for mutually beneficial exchange of goods and services. Most Eastern European countries saw an unavoidable need to increase economic links with the West if their economies were not to fall further behind the world leaders. It will, nevertheless, be difficult to meet this need in the next few years. Certain countries which ran up high levels of hard-currency indebtedness, such as the GDR, Hungary and Romania, successfully reduced outstanding obligations, but only at the cost of restricting imports and thus compromising prospects for future economic progress. Despite the gradual emergence of the West from recession, there were still limits to the quantities of Eastern European goods that it could absorb, especially if these were agricultural products or industrial products of relatively low quality, unadapted to Western market demands. The accession to the European Community of Spain and Portugal, which in some respects have a level of economic development comparable to the East European countries, might further decrease the ability of East European countries to penetrate the important West European market, and force them to concentrate their activities in the Third World.

Third, there was increasing concern in Eastern European capitals that their countries might be made hostage to, and suffer from, Soviet policy priorities and Soviet–American tensions. We have noted concern in Czechoslovakia and the GDR over Soviet missile deployment, and the resentment over the Olympic boycott. It is worth noting how skilfully President Ceaușescu exploited his decision that Romania should attend, both to underline his independence and to benefit his own position from the patriotic upsurge with the welcome given to the returning athletes. Hungary and the GDR, as well as Romania, stressed the need for East–West dialogue at times of tension; even the Czechoslovaks and the currently self-absorbed Poles spoke in similar terms.

Fourth, the ability of the Soviet Union to halt fissiparous tendencies among its allies seemed limited. Clearly, the Brezhnev doctrine continued to apply. But how was the Soviet Union to resist challenges that stopped short of a threat to one-party rule and membership of the Warsaw Pact? There were limits to the extent to which the ailing Soviet economy could prop up several other countries at once; evidence is provided by the rise in Soviet raw material export prices, by Soviet demands for higher-quality manufactures from Eastern Europe, and by the only limited help that the Soviet Union has given to those of its allies with debt problems. The Soviet authorities must take account of their own people's awareness that in most cases the Eastern Europeans enjoy already a higher standard of living than Soviet citizens. The Eastern European leaders could argue that internal reform and increased contact with the West defuse internal tension and reduce the requirement for Soviet assistance. However, they are then faced with the question of how far reform can be permitted without threatening the interests of the communist ruling class and the stability of the system itself.

If there have been strains in Eastern Europe the same phenomenon was certainly to be found in the Western half of the continent. Since the mid 1970s the Western Europeans have had to contend with shifts in American policy away from the 'balance-of-power' détente of Nixon and Kissinger to the 'remoralized' policies of Carter and then to reassertion of American power under Reagan. After a decade in which increased trade had been seen as a major contributing factor to a more stable East–West relationship, the Western European governments found no alternative, under pressure from their own public opinion as well as from the United States, to resorting to the traditional method of economic sanctions against the Soviet Union and Poland to mark disapproval of the invasion of Afghanistan and martial law in Poland. Indeed, the Reagan administration sorely tested the cohesion of the Alliance by attempting to insist that West European contracts with the Soviet Union for the supply of technology and equipment for the exploitation of Soviet gas reserves should not be honoured. The United States took a hard line also over the broader question of the transfer of technology to the East. Strains emerged over the conduct of the INF negotiations and the best way to handle the domestic challenges of the peace movements. Pressures on defence budgets increased, with calls from across the Atlantic for the Europeans to provide more resources, and at least to meet the agreed NATO target of 3 per cent annual real increases in defence spending. Warnings of the possible consequences of a failure to respond came from the American Senate in the form of the Nunn Amendment, which called for the withdrawal of a proportion of American troops from Europe unless European performance improved.

Some of these pressures could be contained. Alliance unity was preserved over INF and other tricky issues, such as coordinating alliance policy towards Poland's debt problem. The pressures from the peace movements diminished. Intensive consultations within the Alliance have improved understanding and created a degree of consensus on technology transfer and related issues. The procedures and criteria to be applied in COCOM, the body in which most NATO countries and Japan coordinate a policy of restraint of the export of sensitive technology to the East, have been improved. There were tentative signs of progress towards reviving the Western European Union (WEU) and finding it a role in strengthening the European pillar of the Western Alliance. This organization has the advantage of involving France in consideration of defence policy. Increased European spending on defence infrastructure went some way towards meeting the concerns that lay behind the Nunn Amendment. In particular, it seemed to be better understood in

Washington that close consultation and coordination of foreign policy within the Alliance need not presuppose that the policies of all member states will be identical. A measure of diversity, reflecting national interests and priorities, can be a sign of strength rather than weakness. Moreover, there was a reaffirmation of the policy of differentiation towards the countries of Eastern Europe. This policy should be seen as an attempt not to drive wedges between members of the Warsaw Pact, but to seek imaginatively for opportunities to develop contacts and cooperation, and to be ready to respond to signs of Eastern European interest in détente. These opportunities will vary from time to time or from country to country, and may variously include a more intensive political dialogue, or economic cooperation, or cultural and academic exchange, or sport or tourism.

Conclusions

What then are the prospects for East–West relations in the immediate future? The course of United States policy is not yet clear. At the start of his second term, during which, with no prospect of re-election, he will increasingly become a 'lame duck' President, President Reagan seemed to have lost his sureness of touch. The failure to secure Congressional support for the 'Contra' guerrillas fighting the Sandinista regime in Nicaragua, the public relations disaster over plans to lay a wreath at a German war cemetary during a state visit to the Federal Republic, and Congressional votes to freeze or even reduce defence spending, were signs of this development. There was tension within the administration between those who believed in dealing with the Soviet Union from a position of uncompromising strength and saw little chance of progress at the arms control negotiations in Geneva, and those who believed that the start of the Gorbachev era provided an opportunity to seek a relationship with the Soviet Union based, if not on trust, at least on mutual respect and restraint. Little agreement was possible between those who saw the world in terms of unremitting superpower confrontation, deriving from Soviet efforts to extend their hegemony, and those who took a more complex and sophisticated view, arguing that problems in the Third World that seemed to threaten American interests could arise from domestic causes, and need not always derive from, or be susceptible to exploitation by, Soviet pressure. This dichotomy was reflected in President Reagan's statements: he perceived clearly the need to temper his instinctive anti-communism not only for domestic reasons but also out of concern for Alliance unity and respect for the views of major allies such as the Federal Republic of Germany.

Similarly, it is too early to predict with confidence the nature of Mr Gorbachev's policies. It is unlikely that the traditional Russian and Soviet instincts to resort to overinsurance, to compensate for a deep-seated sense of inferiority with displays of military might, and to seek to capitalize on developments anywhere in the world that are unfavourable to Western interests, will disappear overnight. In domestic policy, Gorbachev's early actions seemed intended to make the existing system work better through the promotion of younger and energetic personnel, rather than to initiate root-and-branch reform. Despite the promotion of younger men to the Politburo, it will still take him time to spring-clean the bureaucracy in accordance with his own ideas. In foreign policy, the initial emphasis seemed to be on declaratory propaganda rather than conceptual innovation: conciliatory tones have been juxtaposed uneasily with traditional anti-imperialist rhetoric.

It is perhaps in Eastern Europe that the possibility of change, although limited, is greatest. The area remains unstable, and is an actual or potential source of political and economic difficulties for the Soviet Union. The Soviet Union could be said to have three policy options. The first would be to attempt to re-establish the isolation and autarky of the area by cutting back on economic and other contacts with the West, and reinforcing a wide spectrum of internal controls. It must be doubted whether this option is feasible or would be seriously considered in Moscow. Such a policy would confirm Eastern Europe's relative economic backwardness, and stimulate social pressures such as those that led to the Solidarity era in Poland. Despite repeated efforts and some limited success, CMEA has proved inefficient as a means of securing all-round economic developments in the area. Even Soviet resources could hardly prop up a whole range of ailing economies, or repress simultaneous outbreaks of unrest in several countries. The Soviet Union could, of course, exploit the latent antipathies between the Eastern European states by the techniques of divide and rule. However, as was noted above, the ruling elites in these countries are anxious to preserve their dominant position and might no longer see their interests as best served by servility towards Moscow.

The second option would be for Moscow to conclude that, in the era of ballistic missiles, it is no longer so important to have a buffer zone of reliable states between Soviet territory and that of NATO. Controls over Eastern Europe could be relaxed to the extent that these countries could go their own way, at least as far as a form of neutralism and economic independence. This policy option seems also unlikely, since Eastern Europe does provide at least some economic benefit to the Soviet Union, in particular as a supplier of manufactured goods and as a collaborator in the development of Soviet energy and raw material reserves. Moreover, the shock to Moscow's claim to be the leader of a socialist system that will eventually encompass the world would be too great. It is not too fanciful to speculate that the abandonment of Eastern Europe would encourage latent fissiparous tendencies within the constituent republics of the Soviet Union itself.

The third and most likely option is a continuance of the situation that has evolved in recent years, in which the Eastern European countries are permitted a measure of latitude to find their own ways towards socialism, and develop contact with the West, provided that certain basic minima, such as the exclusive rule of the communist party and membership of the Warsaw Pact, are preserved. The granting of a degree of freedom could in fact reinforce prosperity and stability in these societies, through a process of gradual and controlled evolution.

There are opportunities for the West to develop a consistent and coherent long-term policy based on this third option. Despite its crucial importance, arms control is too narrow a subject to carry the whole weight of East-West contacts. As noted above, it is necessary to broaden the basis of understanding and to seek areas in which cooperation might be possible. These opportunities would differ from country to country. There is also a need to re-establish consistency and stability in economic relations. The recent use of both the carrot and the stick created resentment and uncertainty and damaged Western economic and political interests. There is little evidence that such sanctions work. In future, Western countries could be guided by three principles. The first is realism. The West should avoid risking an enhancement of Warsaw Pact military power, or undermining its own technological lead; it should avoid excessive dependence on the East in any area or commodity. The West should not let East European countries exploit the monopoly power of the state-trading system to play off one Western country against another to secure economic benefits. The second principle is flexibility. The West should accept that a tightly coordinated Western policy, covering the whole range of trade with the East, would be difficult if not impossible to achieve, and concentrate on key areas, e.g. through COCOM. The West should also acknowledge the diversity of the Eastern European economies. Trade policy should be adaptable, and the West should look for opportunities to encourage liberalization and structural reform. Third, the West should exercise prudence, not extending unilateral advantages, while avoiding protectionism and opening markets wherever possible to Eastern European goods. Finally, by respecting the specific character of Eastern European states, the West should seek to encourage existing trends in the area towards a distinctive, even if internally diverse, central European identity. Such a policy must be suitably gradual, and take account of legitimate Soviet security interests, if it is not to arouse suspicion and become counterproductive. But the West must at the same time stress its belief in the right to independence for all the countries in the area, and their right to pursue their own interests.

3 The Conference on Security and Cooperation in Europe: Europe before and after the Helsinki Final Act

Kenneth Dyson

After some ten years of intensive discussions and negotiations the heads of government of thirty-three European states (only Albania was not present), and of the United States and Canada, gathered in Helsinki to sign the Final Act of the Conference on Security and Cooperation in Europe (CSCE) on 1 August 1975. The Helsinki Final Act has come to form the central reference point for an ongoing process of multilateral diplomacy — 'the Helsinki process' — with a series of 'follow-up' meetings in Belgrade, Madrid and Stockholm (and Vienna in 1986) as well as expert meetings. Though these meetings had achieved precious little by the time the foreign ministers of the signatory states assembled in Helsinki ten years later to celebrate the Final Act, and in consequence the Western media gave them little if any attention, the Final Act — and the famous 'Baskets' into which it is divided — achieved symbolic importance to both East and West. For the Soviet Union the Helsinki Final Act was a 'historic milestone', a substitute peace treaty that sealed the post-war frontiers of Europe. The Act recognized formally 'political realities'; détente was 'irreversible'. For the West the Final Act kept open the possibility of peaceful change and was novelly significant because it recognized that the treatment of individuals by their government was of direct relevance to the quality of international relations. Violation of human rights was contrary to the Final Act and thus hostile to the spirit of détente. Hence in his speech, which concentrated on such violations, at the tenth anniversary meeting in 1985 the American Secretary of State, George Schultz, refrained even from using the term 'détente'.

CSCE was to provide a common institutional framework for a

general European dialogue, a basis for a return to normalcy in the relations amongst European states.[1] The Helsinki Final Act was to be the first step in a process of refining a code of conduct, involving renunciation of force and the threat of force, promotion of cooperation in various fields, and acceptance that in a system of sovereign states different ideological, political and social systems must coexist. In practice the Final Act added nothing to international law. It did not change the political map of Europe; and it did not provide a solution to any specific and pressing problems. Neither in form nor in language was the Final Act like an international treaty. There were no provisions about its ratification and coming into effect. It was not a peace treaty. There was no reference to the Second World War and its political and legal consequences. In that sense it could not be interpreted as akin to the Potsdam Protocol of 1945. The Helsinki Final Act was more like a communiqué issued at the end of an international conference. It was more important in defining a broad agenda for East–West dialogue, for cataloguing outstanding problems and for establishing an institutional procedure of 'follow-up' meetings to review implementation of principles and make further progress.

If the Final Act was understood to be the start of a long process, it was also always clear that the process would not be self-contained. In the words of the foreign minister of the host country, Finland, the Helsinki process was 'a major tributary to the main river'. It paralleled a range of international negotiations, notably between the superpowers directly, like SALT (held in Geneva) and the MBFR negotiations on conventional force reductions in central Europe (held in Vienna). The Helsinki process was bound to be 'open-ended' and indeterminate, evolving in accordance with the problems and possibilities of international life and all too easily jeopardized or superseded by events. The impacts of the INF, Afghanistan and Polish crises were to underline the fundamental truth of this observation.

The particular interest of the Helsinki process as a tributary to the main river of East–West relations derived from its peculiar character and the opportunities that stemmed from this character. First, its agenda combined security with cooperation. The breadth of this agenda stimulated the interest of European states, particularly those, like the Federal Republic of Germany, in or close to central Europe. Michael Clarke's chapter shows how discussion of cooperation gave a new role to the EEC states in East–West relations. Second, the Helsinki process was the only pan-European negotiation. It was important because it recognized the constitutive role of the two North American allies in European affairs. It was also important because it gave equal formal status to the smaller European countries, notably the neutral and non-aligned (NNA) states. The sovereign equality of the participants was symbolized in the consensus rule. On the one hand, decision-making was bound to be laborious; on the other, the NNA states were given a new opportunity to bring their good offices to bear as 'go-betweens' and mediators. The smaller European states were to particularly welcome the Helsinki process as a means of diffusing influence on European affairs, and of overcoming the rigidities of bloc politics.

Two events help to put the Helsinki process in perspective. In January 1984 the Stockholm meeting on 'security and confidence-building measures and disarmament in Europe' opened despite the fact that at the end of 1983 the Soviet Union had walked out of the INF talks and the START talks and postponed recommencement of the MBFR negotiations. The polemics at the opening session, addressed by the foreign ministers, underlined the extent to which the Helsinki process functioned as a barometer of East–West relations; and the slow progress in the first year indicated the effects of the wider political context on CSCE. On the other hand, along with inner-German relations, Stockholm functioned for a time as 'the only show in town'. This element of continuity in Stockholm and in Bonn and East Berlin indicated just how central these two fields of activity were in the politics of European détente and the strengths of the interests supporting them.

A second illustrative event was the tenth anniversary meeting in 1985. This celebration, like the continuing Stockholm meeting, was very much in the background to the new Geneva arms talks (begun in March 1985) and the proposed summit meeting between President Reagan and Gorbachev in November. Disappointment and frustration with the Helsinki process were apparent on all sides. Shultz spoke against the 'artificial' division of Europe, as in January

1984 in Stockholm, and raised the specific cases of the incarceration of Dr Yuri Orlov and Anatoly Shcharansky and the internal exile of Dr Andrei Sakharov as evidence of Soviet indifference to the Final Act and the spirit of détente. The Polish Foreign Minister pointed to the forces of *revanchisme* in the West, reflecting the fact that the Soviet Union had achieved no substantial progress in consolidating its position in Eastern Europe after the Final Act.[2] The NNA states appealed to the superpowers to show greater responsibility and sensitivity in their conduct of East–West relations. Ambivalence towards the Helsinki process was perhaps best summed up by the lack of an agreed final communiqué coupled with endorsement of the need to continue the process.

CSCE is important above all as a process of multilateral diplomacy and as an umbrella for bilateral relations in Europe. By the end of 1985 one could not speak of its substantive results as significant. Accordingly, this chapter deals with CSCE as a case study of the politics of East–West relations. CSCE indicates the conditions under which a process of détente becomes institutionalized, helps us to understand the politics of détente and tells us something about the impacts on political relationships and prospects of détente.

The origins of the Helsinki process: dialogue by communiqué

The initiative that led to the Helsinki process can be traced to the Soviet Union and its Eastern European partners.[3] During the Berlin Four-Power Conference of Foreign Ministers in 1954 the Soviet delegation submitted the draft of a 'General European Treaty of Collective Security in Europe', to be open to all European powers, including the two German states as equal participants 'pending the creation of a united, peace-loving and democratic German state'. The idea of a system of collective security in Europe figured in the second paragraph of Article II of the Warsaw Treaty of May 1955:

> Should a system of collective security be established in Europe, and a General European Treaty of Collective Security concluded for this purpose, for which the contracting parties will unswervingly strive, the present Treaty (of

Friendship, Cooperation and Mutual Assistance) will cease to be operative from the day the General European Treaty enters into force.

The Soviet idea of multilateral negotiations on European security did not die. It was revived in a speech of the Polish Foreign Minister, Adam Rapacki, before the UN General Assembly in December 1964 (earlier in October 1957 he had submitted a plan for a demilitarized zone in central Europe) and by a meeting of the Consultative Committee of the Warsaw Pact in January 1965. France's withdrawal from the military wing of NATO in March 1966 provided the Soviet Union with a new partner for its plan of solving the problems of the continent in a European framework without American participation. The joint Franco-Soviet declaration of June 1966 was followed in July 1966 by the 'Bucharest Declaration' of the Warsaw Pact. In the latter the Warsaw Pact sought to catalogue the principles on which European security must rest: respect for national sovereignty, non-interference in internal affairs, renunciation of force or the threat of force, territorial integrity, peaceful arbitration of disputes.

If France provided a diplomatic opportunity for the Soviet Union, Romania's behaviour indicated the threats to its own control unless the détente process was steered in careful detail. Romania used the new room for maneouvre to open diplomatic relations with the Federal Republic of Germany in January 1967. Thereafter interest in bringing about a European security conference took second place to preventing further political successes of the West Germans in Eastern Europe. A network of bilateral treaties between the socialist states followed, with the aim of constraining the room for maneouvre of individual states in future détente negotiations. In particular the crisis in Czechoslovakia in 1968 — the 'Prague Spring' — served to hold up the momentum of Soviet policy. Brezhnev's doctrine of 'the limited sovereignty' of socialist states indicated the paramount importance that the Soviet Union gave to the unity of its bloc as a condition of European détente.

The Budapest Appeal 'to all European countries' of March 1969 showed a new flexibility, taking on board the theme of cooperation as well as security and indicating the importance of improvement in inner-German relations. 1969 was to be a year of important events:

the new Nixon administration was considering accord with China, a threatening development for the Soviet Union that suggested the need to seek opportunities to stabilize relations in Europe; de Gaulle, with his vision of national independence and 'a Europe from the Atlantic to the Urals', left power in France; and the new Social Democratic–Liberal coalition government of Willy Brandt (Chancellor) and Walter Scheel (Foreign Minister) in Bonn indicated that *Ostpolitik* would be pursued with new vigour. Moscow was more prepared to encourage Bonn, which achieved even greater significance in Moscow's *Westpolitik*. The Prague Declaration of October 1969 accepted the Finnish Memorandum of May 1969, suggesting Helsinki as the location for a possible conference, and spelt out the interest of the Warsaw Pact in economic, technological and trade cooperation. In the Budapest Memorandum of June 1970, now five years after the first declaration, the Warsaw Pact accepted the idea of American and Canadian participation, supported the idea of a succession of conferences — a 'process' — and took on board the themes of culture and environment. By the time of the Prague Declaration of January 1972 the emphasis on military issues had been dropped; whilst, in the Soviet view, the signing of the German–Soviet Treaty in August 1970 had consolidated its position in Europe and provided both a model and a catalyst for further bilateral détente in Europe, notably the German–Polish Treaty and the Basic Treaty between the two German states.

The Soviet Union's desire for a European security conference had to contend with more than just the problem of unity in its own bloc. NATO's reactions to its proposals were cautious and slow to emerge. The emphasis in NATO was on careful preparation and prior agreement before talks. Some states — like Belgium and Denmark — had close links with Eastern Europe and were keen to see NATO take a stronger initiative. Others — like Italy, the Netherlands, and not least the United States — were sceptical. The Soviet proposal for a European collective security system was seen as a ploy to achieve Soviet domination of Western Europe. Accordingly, it was essential to maintain the American presence and, if the latter was in doubt, to move ahead with political unification of Western Europe prior to any such negotiations with the Soviet Union. Belgium's role was apparent in the so-called Harmel Report of 1967 on the future tasks of the Alliance, prepared for NATO by its foreign minister. The report emphasized the need to combine defensive efforts with the search for détente. In its Reykjavik communiqué of June 1968 the North Atlantic Council stressed that 'the opportunities for rapid progress towards general détente should not be over-rated' and the need for a step-by-step approach; at that time there was anxiety about the situation in Czechoslovakia. In April 1969 a meeting of NATO ministers in Washington agreed to establish a special committee to study the prospects for negotiation. Its work took some two years. Meeting in Brussels in December 1969, the NATO ministers indicated that détente must embrace more than simply a *rapprochement* amongst states. Their call for 'freer movement of people, ideas and information' was to become basic to Western proposals for Basket Three of the Final Act. NATO's Rome communiqué of May 1970 reiterated the emphasis in the 'Reykjavik Signal' of 1968 on mutual and balanced force reductions in Europe. For the first time it mentioned 'a conference on security and cooperation in Europe'. Also, it indicated that such a conference would be dependent on concrete progress in ongoing talks, notably about Germany and Berlin and in SALT. A test of Soviet good intentions was a prior condition. The results of the work of the special study group emerged finally in the Brussels communiqué of December 1971. The proposed conference would have to cover four areas: military and non-military aspects of security (the latter including the principles governing relations amongst states); 'freer movement'; cooperation in economic affairs, applied science and technology and pure science; and cooperation on environmental improvement.

The turning point was reached in 1972: the SALT I documents were signed by President Nixon in Moscow in May; a satisfactory solution to the Berlin talks was reached in June; and a treaty between the two German states followed in November. MBFR negotiations remained the outstanding issue; the Warsaw Pact wished to see such negotiations follow an all-European conference, whereas NATO wanted them before or in parallel (reflecting its concern about Soviet superiority in conventional forces in central Europe). In September the superpowers agreed on a staggered arrangement, with CSCE beginning just before MBFR but with no organic link between them.

They had no particular wish to subject their security policies to negotiations in an all-European forum.

The eventual decision to convene a conference on security and cooperation in Europe in 1973 was the outcome of years of dialogue by communiqué. By the time of NATO's Rome Declaration of May 1970 and the Warsaw Pact's Budapest Memorandum of June 1970 the two security pacts had developed a broad diplomatic role, conveying their developing views to other interested parties in Europe and acting as channels for the growing number of bilateral diplomatic contacts by which each side sought to refine its understanding of the other. Momentum was maintained, above all, by the desire of the Soviet Union to achieve recognition of the status quo in Europe, in particular of the immutability of frontiers and of the GDR. A common security system was seen as the best guarantee of the post-war settlement. The limits were provided by bloc unity. There were clear differences in the motivations and expectations of East European states. However, after 1968, with the exception of Romania, the Soviet bloc maintained a striking solidarity throughout the Helsinki process. Romania was closer to the approach of Yugoslavia, a non-aligned state, in insisting on the importance both of sovereign and equal partnership in a Helsinki process that was valued for its 'bloc-free' character and of more intensive bilateral relations as a precondition for negotiations. Under Ulbricht the GDR argued that its own recognition must be a precondition of the Warsaw Pact for negotiations. From this vantage point the German–Soviet Treaty of 1970 was a disappointment. Ulbricht did not get his way: instead the GDR got a more flexible and less defensive leader in Honecker. Hungary saw in the Helsinki process an opportunity to develop its model of economic reform by means of closer regional cooperation amongst the 'Danube states' of Austria, Czechoslovakia and Hungary. The Hungarian line de-emphasized polemics in favour of a businesslike cooperation and greater flexibility of approach within the Warsaw Pact.

As far as NATO was concerned, France was a special case after 1966. France sought to reactivate its bilateral relations with Eastern European states, with for instance the joint declaration on friendship and cooperation with Poland in October 1972. France was one of the strongest supporters of CSCE, which it saw as a means of strengthening the independent identity and effective sovereignty of individual European states, in East as well as West, and of getting away from bloc politics to greater flexibility in Europe's political relations.[4] It opposed NATO's priority to MBFR as attacking the symptoms rather than causes of East–West tensions. France emphasized cooperation, especially in the economic field. By contrast, Helmut Schmidt, as Social Democratic Minister of Defence in the Brandt government, argued with success that MBFR must play the central part in NATO's initiative on détente. For the Bonn government CSCE was a logical extension of its own *Ostpolitik* and *Deutschlandpolitik*, a necessary multilateral umbrella for its bilateral policies. Whereas Denmark, Norway and Belgium were closely engaged in discussions about a prospective all-European conference, Britain's position was — as Phil Williams emphasizes — one of scepticism and reservation: reservation about Soviet intentions (especially about its security proposals) and scepticism about the value of declarations of principle. In the key period 1970–3 a new Conservative government in London was preoccupied by the redefinition of its relations with Western Europe, implicit in negotiations about entry into the EEC. Like the British the Americans emphasized the need for concrete substance to the negotiations. The United States was particularly concerned that CSCE negotiations should follow rather than precede its own agreements with the Soviet Union. In other words, a broader European détente was conditional on superpower détente. The final agreements on the Helsinki negotiations followed the Nixon–Brezhnev summit of May 1972. Resentment about America's subordination of CSCE to its own bilateral relations with the Soviet Union was a further source of conflict within NATO. In the end, however, all NATO countries — with the exception of France — judged that a delay in European détente was a price worth paying for the maintenance of Alliance solidarity.

Even before the Helsinki Conference convened in 1973 three sets of significant actors were emerging, in addition to NATO and the Warsaw Pact. Already the NNA states had seen CSCE as an opportunity to exercise greater influence on international affairs in Europe. Their emergence as an identifiable and active grouping was to be one of the most striking political phenomena of the Helsinki process. In the earliest stages Finland was the most active catalyst in preparations for the conference; whilst Sweden and Austria emphasized the importance of security discussions within the new framework. Secondly, against the background of its geopolitical situation and the position of a divided Germany in a divided Europe, the Federal Republic of Germany was able to act as a pacemaker for multilateral diplomacy. In its bilateral *Ostpolitik* and *Deutschlandpolitik* the Federal Republic stressed consultation and solidarity with NATO. In his first declaration of government in May 1974 Chancellor Helmut Schmidt, who had been Defence Minister during the main phase of *Ostpolitik* negotiations (1969–72), stressed the crucial role of CSCE in building confidence against the background of a 'necessary balance of power'. The creation of a special interministerial working group (IMAG) in 1972 reflected the importance attached to an active and integrated approach to CSCE. Political control of CSCE negotiations was much closer than in Britain; indeed there was a division of labour, with the Chancellor's Office specializing in *Ostpolitik* and inner-German relations and the Foreign Ministry in CSCE. A pessimistic assessment of CSCE by the opposition Christian Democratic Union (CDU) was complemented by harsh criticisms from its Bavarian sister party, the Christian Social Union (CSU), whose leader Franz-Josef Strauss was later to compare the Helsinki Final Act to the Munich Agreement of 1938. Up to the decisive election victory of Brandt in 1972 the internal German dimension of European détente remained problematic: although it was never clear that the opposition, pledged in its own view more loyally than the government to the Western alliance system, had any real alternative. Thirdly, as Michael Clarke's chapter shows, the new machinery of European Political Cooperation (EPC) emerged from 1972 as the centre of operational work on CSCE for the nine (from 1973) member states of the EEC. EPC was the product of the work of the original six at the Hague summit of December 1969, of the subsequent Davignon report of July 1970 and of final political decision in October 1970. By institutionalizing cooperation in foreign policy EPC was to help promote a clearer European identity. CSCE was one of the first two big issues on the agenda of EPC (the Near East was the other). In February 1971 a working group on CSCE was established, followed in May by an *ad hoc* group on economic issues (later Basket Two) with representatives of the

European Commission present. Despite the reservations of Italy and the Netherlands about CSCE, and of France about too much cooperation in EPC, a coordinated EPC position for the first phase of CSCE had emerged by January 1973. The EEC states were well aware that their divisions could be exploited by the Soviet Union; they were also aware of the scepticism of Henry Kissinger about CSCE. They could, therefore, make common cause to ensure their collective strength through developing a role for themselves as main actors in CSCE. 1973 was also Kissinger's 'Year of Europe' and of his abortive 'New Atlantic Charter', in which Western Europe was to make concessions on monetary and trade matters for continued American military assistance. Tensions between Washington and Western Europe were to reach a high point with the new Arab–Israeli war of October 1973, particularly when the Nixon administration declared a world-wide alert of American forces without consulting its NATO allies.

The Helsinki Conference and the Final Act

A fascinating paradox of the Helsinki Conference was between the size and time-scale of the conference and public interest in its existence, let alone its proceedings. The representatives of thirty-five states met in Helsinki for a first phase (July 1973); in Geneva for a second phase (September 1973–July 1975); and in Helsinki for the final phase on 30 July 1975, with the heads of government signing the concluding document on 1 August. In total some 500 delegates were registered (on average 200–300) for more than two-and-a-half years of negotiations: the West with 218, the East with 147 and the NNA states with 128. At the beginning the West German delegation numbered over thirty. Yet even in the Federal Republic there was little public interest.[5] Not even one in five West Germans knew what was meant by CSCE; only one-third thought that the Final Act represented 'a decisive step to secure peace'.

The paradox is not surprising. The Western countries approached the Helsinki Conference in a cautious and reserved manner. Even neutral countries like Switzerland emphasized the importance of not expecting too much. Far more exciting in implications during this period seemed the Arab–Israeli war and the oil crisis, the Turkish invasion of Cyprus, the resignations of President Nixon as a consequence of the Watergate scandal and of Chancellor Brandt as a result of a spy scandal in his own office, the death of President Pompidou of France, and the collapse of dictatorship in Portugal.

The phase of 'multilateral preparatory talks', or the so-called 'Helsinki Consultations', from November 1972 to June 1973, was to be important not just for the Conference but for the whole future of the Helsinki process. Here the Romanians supported the NNA states in their call for the principle of the sovereign equality of all participants. As a corollary, a rule of consensus was adopted (which meant a right of veto for every participant on any issue), along with open access to all working groups and the idea of rotating chairmanships. The 'Blue Book' that emanated from these consultations gave CSCE its definitive name as well as its operating procedure. It accepted the Western proposal for a 'follow-up' system after the Helsinki Conference, conditional on agreement at later meetings, rather than a permanent commission as sought by the Eastern bloc. Implementation of agreements and further progress would be left as a matter for these later meetings. The Austrian delegation introduced the idea of ordering all proposals into 'Baskets'; whilst the Swiss were given the task of providing synopses as the basis for discussing the problems in the three major Baskets: security, cooperation in economic, scientific and technological affairs, and cooperation in humanitarian and other fields. The particular contribution of the NNA states was already apparent.

In the business of the Helsinki Conference itself the bloc character of diplomacy was in fact always apparent. There was close consultation between EPC and NATO over details. Both divided up the management of its relations with the NNA states skilfully: the Federal Republic of Germany maintained special contacts with Austria, whilst Denmark (for EPC) and Norway (for NATO) took care of relations with Finland and Sweden. Numerous bilateral state and party agreements bound the East European countries firmly to the Soviet position. Regular meetings of Communist Party chiefs and heads of party central committee divisions (especially those for ideological and international affairs) paralleled the Warsaw Pact (in whose Political Consultative Committee the party general secretaries participate) and the Council for Mutual Economic Assistance (CMEA). Despite this bloc pattern the NNA states were able to have an independent impact on the process, especially through the informal 'open-ended' meetings organized by Austria, Finland, Sweden and Switzerland in the rooms of their delegations. Though these four states were closer to the NATO and EPC positions on Basket Three (human rights), they were able to effect compromise here: for instance, in July 1974 when their idea of a package deal linking Basket One (the Soviet priority) with Basket Three (the Western priority) was accepted. Throughout the conference Finland and Switzerland provided the secretariat.

The Helsinki Final Act has four Baskets, each with a preamble, and a short introduction and conclusion. As a wide-ranging and comparatively brief document, the Final Act is susceptible to diverse interpretations. Thus the Warsaw Pact countries regard the principles of Basket One as 'directly applicable law'; Baskets Two and Three are 'recommendations' based on Basket One. With significant amendments these principles were incorporated in the new Soviet constitution of 1977. In the view of the Western countries the Final Act is not a legally binding document. It is a carefully balanced political document in which each part is of equal value. Because the Final Act has become such an important reference point in political relations in Europe, it is necessary to go into some detail about its contents.

Basket One

Basket One deals with security in Europe in its non-military dimension (the ten principles on the relations between the participating states) and its military dimension (confidence-building measures and certain aspects of disarmament).

Principle 1, on sovereign equality, contains the provision, so important to the West, that frontiers can be changed by peaceful means and by agreement.

Principle 2, on the renunciation of the threat or use of force, repeats Article 2 of the UN Charter but specifically applies it to the mutual relations between CSCE signatories. Reference to the 'indirect' use of force here was particularly wanted by Romania and

Yugoslavia as a means of countering Brezhnev's doctrine of the 'limited' sovereignty of socialist states.

Principle 3, dealing with the 'inviolability' of frontiers, was a key element for the Soviet and Eastern European delegations and perhaps the most controversial and difficult issue. As was clear in the Prague Declaration of 1972, they sought legitimation for the territorial status quo in the form of the 'immutability' of frontiers. The West insisted successfully on the term 'inviolability', a term referring specifically to the non-use of force, rather than 'immutability' with its more definitive meaning. The West continued to emphasize that peaceful change of frontiers was permitted under Principle 1, whilst Principle 8 acknowledged the 'self-determination' of peoples.

Principle 4, on the territorial integrity of states, was most strongly supported by Romania again and by Cyprus (with its recent experience of the Turkish invasion).

Principle 5, on the peaceful settlement of disputes, did not go beyond the UN Charter. Neither new procedures nor new sanctions were devised. This omission was especially disappointing for the Swiss, who had been active in promoting a treaty on an obligatory European system for the peaceful resolution of conflicts.

Principle 6, on non-interference in internal affairs, was, along with Principle 3, central to the Soviet Union. It offered a means of opposing Western efforts to liberalize the East on the basis of Principle 7 and of Basket Three. Principle 6 was to become the major reference point for the Soviet Union in 'follow-up' meetings. The West saw Principle 6 as relevant to military activities but of little relevance in a world of growing interdependence through modern means of communications. Interestingly, Romania and Yugoslavia regarded this principle as a useful instrument with which to oppose the Brezhnev doctrine.

Principle 7, on respect for human rights and basic freedoms, including freedom of thought, conscience, religion and belief, was of key importance to the Western and NNA delegations. This establishment of a clear relationship between respect for human rights and freedoms and the quality of inter-state relations was seen as a novel feature for an international agreement.

Principle 8, on equality of rights and self-determination of peoples, was of particular significance for the West, and especially for the Federal Republic of Germany. This principle could be used against the Brezhnev doctrine, though in this case Yugoslavia was aware that it might encourage separatist tendencies amongst its own ethnic minorities. The West stressed that Principle 8 referred to peoples and not to states; whilst the Soviet Union saw it as relevant to problems of the Third World rather than to political relations in Europe.

Principle 9, on cooperation between states, went further than the Soviet bloc's emphasis on contacts at the level of states to encompass the Western view that more comprehensive contacts and exchanges should be developed. As far as economic and technological cooperation was concerned, Romania and Yugoslavia tended towards the Western view.

Principle 10, on fulfilment of duties in international law in good faith, was another victory for the West. Here it is clearly stated that all the principles are of fundamental importance and each must be read alongside the others. In the Western view this provision guarantees the balance of static and dynamic elements in the détente process.

The second part of Basket One dealt with the military dimension of security. Here the conceptions of the three main actors diverged sharply. The Warsaw Pact sought an end to the system of alliances in Europe, a renunciation of the deployment of nuclear weapons on foreign territory and the creation of nuclear-free zones. The NATO countries saw decisive strategic advantage for the Soviet Union in the realization of such proposals. With the exception of France they viewed force reductions in Europe as the central issue for any European security conference. Once it was clear that MBFR and CSCE would be parallel processes, NATO emphasized confidence-building measures (CBMs). The NNA states saw disarmament as the basic issue and had wanted to bring MBFR negotiations within CSCE so that their political impact could be increased. The outcome of negotiations on this aspect of Basket One disappointed all sides. The Warsaw Pact made no progress with its proposals; the NNA states, frustrated over MBFR, focused on CBMs; whilst the West's emphasis on CBMs produced small results. The overriding problem of CBMs was the openness and publicity required from the Soviet

Union. It was finally agreed on prior notification (twenty-one days) of large military manoeuvres (of more than 25,000 troops) up to a distance of 250 km from the frontier of a neighbour; and on an exchange of observers at such maneouvres. The NNA states (and Norway in NATO) were especially dissatisfied by the large size of notifiable maneouvres; armies below a size of 25,000 could be a threat to them.

Basket Two

Basket Two deals with cooperation in economic, scientific, technological and environmental affairs. In negotiations on this Basket the GDR and Hungary played the most active role on behalf of the Soviet bloc, and the EEC was central in the coordination of Western positions. The proposals from the Soviet bloc stressed comprehensive European cooperation based on the principles of equality and preferential treatment. In this context the customs union and Common Agricultural Policy of the EEC were discriminatory mechanisms. Particular stress was placed on cooperation in large projects of common interest, especially in energy and raw materials. By contrast, the EEC gave priority to the principles of reciprocity and openness in trade, transport and technology. Cooperation had to be based on mutual concessions and found its limits in the EEC's interest in its own further development. In particular, the EEC pressed for practical measures to ease commercial contacts and exchange more economic information. The preamble sought to reconcile the two positions by combining reference to 'the equality of partners' with reference to 'mutual satisfaction of the partners'.

Yugoslavia and Romania pleaded the case for the North–South problem to be recognized on the CSCE agenda, and it was agreed that cooperation encompassed global problems of development and not just Europe. Questions of security and cooperation in the Mediterranean were also incorporated in this Basket, with Malta and Yugoslavia taking the initiative. Throughout the CSCE process Malta continued to express virulent criticism of the failure of CSCE to take the problems of the Mediterranean region seriously enough.

Basket Three

Basket Three, on cooperation in humanitarian and other fields, was at the centre of the concerns of NATO and the EEC. Dissident movements in Eastern Europe and the cases of prominent Soviet dissidents like Alexander Solzhenitsyn were the subject of wide public concern in the West, as symbols of injustice and oppression. This concern was bound to surface and to aggravate proceedings, and the NNA states, themselves closer to the West in this field, had great difficulty in helping to devise compromise formulae. For the West respect for human rights and opening of human contacts were indispensable for the security of Europe; they were also essential if trust was to be built between East and West. Without liberalization Eastern Europe would remain unstable. The Soviet bloc denied the relevance of such demands to a socialist community whose rationale and achievement was the guarantee of social rights, like the right to work. In the Soviet view, unemployment and criminality were indicators of the West's denial of rights.

In practice the language of the four sections — on human contacts, information, cooperation and exchange in cultural affairs, and cooperation and exchange in educational affairs — has more to do with intentions and possibilities than with duties. The details are left to the discretion and good will of governments. One cannot speak of much concrete success for the West. The most specific statements were made in the declaration of intent on family contacts, family reunions, marriage and the activities of journalists. Basket Three had to contend with the basic refusal of the Soviet bloc to include the field of ideology in the détente process. 'Internal erosion' by an 'uncontrolled flow of ideas and information' was, in the Soviet view, contrary to Principle 6 on non-interference in internal affairs.

Basket Four

Basket Four dealt with the consequences of the Helsinki Conference and reflected mainly the Western position that the Helsinki process should not be too institutionalized. It should be periodically reviewed in the light of experience. A review meeting was to be convened in June 1977 in Belgrade, where there would be a discussion of progress in implementation of the Final Act and an opportunity to take new initiatives to continue the CSCE process. Stress was placed on the importance of bilateral agreements to implement Baskets Two and Three (e.g., cultural agreements); and on the role of the UN Economic Commission for Europe for implementation of Basket Two and of Unesco for Basket Three.

The 'follow-up' process: Belgrade, Madrid and Stockholm

Until the final stages of the negotiations at the Helsinki Conference the American government displayed limited interest and expectations. In the view of Henry Kissinger, the Soviet Union's desire for a European security conference was useful in providing the West with a bargaining lever on Berlin and MBFR. The Helsinki Conference itself was of little value. According to Kissinger, European security depended on guarantees from the two superpowers; whilst the belief that détente could further societal change through an emphasis on human rights was actually a threat to European security. The Helsinki Final Act became a factor in the Ford–Carter presidential election campaign of 1976. The Republican Right labelled it as a Soviet victory, a viewpoint that was to become politically significant with the election of President Reagan in 1980. Meanwhile, the new Democratic administration of President Jimmy Carter saw the Final Act as an important weapon in its new campaign for human rights. This campaign had the support of powerful domestic lobbies and deep roots in the idealism and optimism in American attitudes to foreign affairs. As a consequence, the Belgrade meeting of 1977–8 was marked by a new high-profile American role, a less visible role for EPC, a less effective role for the NNA states, and new tensions between Western Europe and the United States. The American delegation under Arthur Goldberg drew heavily on the work of the Congressional Commission on Security and Cooperation in Europe about implementation to conduct a 'full and frank' review, focusing on prominent Soviet dissidents like Ginsberg, Orlov, Sakharov and Shcharansky.[6] This tough moralism of American policy, played heavily to an attentive media, offended Western European countries who wished first and foremost to test the opportunities for further practical negotiations and to emphasize the opening of human contacts as the prime purpose of CSCE. The Western European preference for a low-key approach of quiet diplomacy, aimed at practical results, was lost from view as the American delegation directed a sharp eye at media impact and the presidential commitment to human rights.[7]

The change in the character of American engagement in CSCE was paralleled by a more negative attitude from the Soviet Union. This negativism was encouraged by the American position but had other roots. The Soviet Union was worried about the specific contents and effects of the CSCE process, particularly the dynamic elements inserted by the West. Instead of underwriting the status quo (the aim of Soviet policy) the Final Act seemed to have handed the West an instrument with which to mobilize public opinion, in East as well as West, against the Soviet Union. Charter 77 in Czechoslovakia was a worrying indicator. Western ideological confidence was further fortified by the fall of European authoritarian regimes in Greece, Spain and Portugal in the period 1974–6. Meanwhile, the Soviet Union was worried by the phenomenon of Eurocommunism. The Spanish Communist Party's leader attacked the Soviet system, the Italian Communist Party committed itself to staying in NATO, and the French Communist Party abandoned the concept of the dictatorship of the proletariat. The Soviet Union was further concerned about Eastern Europe's continuing trade imbalance with, and growing indebtedness to, the West. Closer economic relations threatened to make Eastern Europe dependent on the West. Finally, détente was threatened from another quarter. The Soviet Union's continued arms build-up coincided with American military retrenchment, provoking new fears in the West about Soviet intentions. Hesitancy in Washington about strategic decisions (the decision to cancel B-1 bomber production was followed by doubt about, and later postponement of, production of the neutron bomb) may have convinced Moscow that it had a new opportunity to adopt a tough approach. Soviet negativism at Belgrade was in turn a source of disappointment to Eastern European countries that felt that they had much to gain from closer economic and technological cooperation with the West.

The bitter polemics and rigid postures at Belgrade, and the meagre and empty final document, indicated that the multilateral promise of the Helsinki process had been submerged in bloc politics.[8] At Belgrade the NNA states were able to have little impact either as independent actors or as mediators. The motivations behind the approaches of the two superpowers to CSCE had changed, whilst dialogue between Moscow and Washington had already begun to break down. Against this background little more could be agreed at Belgrade than to continue CSCE with a further 'follow-up' meeting in Madrid in 1980 and, meanwhile, to hold three 'expert meetings' on specific topics: the scientific forum in Bonn in June–July 1978, the Montreux meeting on the peaceful settlement of disputes in October–December 1978, and the Valletta meeting on the Mediterranean in February–March 1979.

Expectations of the Madrid meeting were limited, not least because of the absence of significant results from the expert meetings.[9] More dramatic, of course, was the Soviet intervention in Afghanistan in 1979 and subsequent American sanctions and boycott of the 1980 Olympic games in Moscow. The Madrid meeting was scheduled to end in March 1981. In fact it lasted for three years. After a succession of harsh and bitter debates — beginning with Afghanistan and in February 1982 reaching a climax over the situation in Poland after the declaration of martial law — a concluding document was eventually agreed in September 1983. Even then the atmosphere of the closing session was poisoned by the Korean airliner tragedy. The West focused attention once again on such issues as misuse of psychiatric treatment, the state's behaviour towards Helsinki monitoring groups, use of internal exile, failure to award exit visas, and the treatment of Jews, the Baltic peoples, Tartars and Ukrainians. At first the Soviet bloc countered by appealing to Principle 6 of the Final Act; later it turned to the attack with denunciation of Western violation of human rights, citing as evidence high unemployment figures, organized crime, racial discrimination, anti-Semitism and the treatment of trade unionists. The West responded by pointing out that it, unlike the Soviet bloc, welcomed debate on such matters.

The international context of the Madrid meeting was even harsher than that of Belgrade, with a number of breaks of proceedings: the fact that a concluding document was agreed seems remarkable. This document was once again a success for the West. By being patient the West was able to exploit the attachment of the Soviet bloc to the idea of a European disarmament conference. France's proposal of May 1978 for a European disarmament conference was to have an important impact on the agenda at Madrid. Another factor was that the European allies of both superpowers, as well as the NNA states, were keen to keep CSCE alive. In the concluding document the Soviet emphasis on 'military' détente was brought together with the Western emphasis on human rights. An expert meeting on human rights was planned in Ottowa in May 1985, and an expert meeting on human contacts for Bern in April 1986. The Soviet Union was given its European security conference, to be convened in Stockholm in January 1984, but essentially on Western terms. Somewhat disillusioned with CSCE, the Soviet Union would have preferred such a conference outside CSCE. The conference agenda gave primacy also to the CBMs that were so desired by NATO and the NNA states. It was agreed in Madrid that the Stockholm meeting — with the title 'Conference on Confidence and Security Building Measures and Disarmament in Europe' — would seek to reduce the threat of military confrontation in Europe by concrete and effective steps to create trust and security. The next review meeting, in Vienna in November 1986, would then judge whether sufficient progress had been made for disarmament talks to begin.

Once again the Stockholm meeting opened with low expectations, for reasons outlined earlier in this chapter.[10] The West sought to reduce military threat by greater transparency, openness and calculability, building on the measures in Basket One of the Final Act. These latter measures had been expected to be implemented on a voluntary basis. In practice the Soviet Union had only invited observers to its maneouvres in exceptional cases and then very selectively. It had also argued that maneouvres on its own territory fell outside the scope of the Final Act. A key achievement of the West was to extend discussions of CBMs at Stockholm to incorporate Europe up to the Urals, that is the whole European territory of the Soviet Union. The West sought agreement on measures that would be militarily significant, politically binding and verifiable; the Soviet bloc emphasized declaratory aims like non-aggression pacts (the West cited the history of their failure to contain aggression) and the renunciation of the first use of nuclear weapons. By 1985 negotiations focused on two groups, as proposed by the NNA states: *A* dealing with new proposals (like a non-aggression pact), and *B* handling the CBMs. The NNA states gave special emphasis to CBMs, both to serve their own security as small states confronted by great powers and to help close the gap between the MBFR talks (which were geographically limited to central Europe, and thus of limited use for instance to Finland and Sweden) and CSCE.

Some conclusions

The Helsinki process is a monument to the paradox of détente: on the one hand, each side wishes to keep the game of European détente going, having learnt from the cold war period and the escalating arms race the risks in its abandonment; on the other hand, CSCE has itself been a learning process about the limits of détente, the conditions that make it viable and the difficulties of insulating European détente from developments and events elsewhere in the international system. Since the Helsinki negotiations of 1973–5 the Soviet Union has not had the same incentive to negotiate. Indeed it learnt from American use of the Final Act the dangers of the concessions that it had already made. The open question in 1985 was whether Soviet concern about the lethargic performance of its own economy will prove as powerful an inducement to negotiate for a 'cooler peace' in Europe as concern to legitimate the political status quo earlier. By 1985 the new Soviet leadership under Gorbachev was beginning to take Western Europe more seriously as an independent actor, with Gorbachev stressing the potential importance of negotiating formal links between the EEC and CMEA (reviving Basket Two?) and paying closer attention to relations with London and Paris at a time when prospects for progress with the Reagan administration seemed limited. In the context of Soviet priority to greater economic efficiency and organisational changes in the economy, and to bilateral links with Western Europe, the Helsinki process had continuing value as a multilateral umbrella and facilitator.

The Helsinki process continues because no state or grouping wishes to incur diplomatic odium or loss of negotiating leverage by breaking up the game. At the same time it is important that no state or grouping appears to be a complete loser from the process. Despite accusations from the American Republican Right that the Helsinki Final Act constituted a betrayal, the Soviet Union has come closest to being the loser. In Basket One the Soviet Union gained recognition of the post-war frontiers, but it did not get its full position on the territorial status quo in Europe. The negotiations, particularly on Baskets Two and Three, gave new political vitality to the EEC as an international actor. Perhaps of greater significance, Basket Three portrayed a European society based on Western rather than Soviet values; it rested on a Western conception of détente as a dynamic process altering the quality of East–West relations by internal political change. In order to gain the summit to which its leaders had become deeply committed, the Soviet Union inflicted this wound on itself late in the negotiations.[11] Finally, the West was successful in actually shaping the Helsinki process. The Eastern bloc's proposal for a permanent consultative committee, to act simply as a clearing house for bilateral and multilateral consultations, was rejected in favour of the West's step-by-step approach of review meetings through which the Final Act could be used to bring pressure to bear on the Soviet Union. However, though the United States gained an important political instrument in the Final Act, it had little prospect of bringing about implementation of Principle 7 and Basket Three. Hence in Belgrade and Madrid both superpowers were uncertain supporters of CSCE. Keeping the process going had become a major achievement; translating the process into substantive results of any significance seemed an ongoing problem.

In the context of the resurfacing of a tough bloc politics in CSCE after the Final Act the NNA states have emphasized the need to search for areas, however small, in which cooperation can be developed. Although their role as independent actors and mediators has been less effective, they have continued with some success to stress the need for a patient, businesslike and long-term approach to CSCE and the importance of CSCE for promoting a European identity.[12] The common vested interest of the NNA states, and of other European states, in CSCE as a forum for security issues is not to be underestimated: many are excluded from MBFR, and all were excluded from SALT, INF and the later comprehensive Geneva arms talks.

What in concrete terms has the CSCE achieved? Clearly post-war Europe has come a long way from the Berlin blockade of 1948 to the Final Act of 1975. On the other hand, CSCE was the product of this process rather than its driving force. The Quadripartite Agreement on Berlin, the bilateral treaties between the Federal Republic of Germany and the Soviet Union, Poland, the GDR and Czechoslovakia, and the superpower accords were more significant in this respect (see the chapters by Schulz, Stürmer and Carter respectively). By 1975 Berlin had already been transformed into a symbol of détente in the very heart of Europe. The real achievement of CSCE lay in the nature of the process. CSCE was something completely new, involving not just the representatives of the main alliances but also the NNA states in a multilateral framework characterized by the formal equality of the participants. It symbolized the search for a reality other than the sharp division of post-war Europe, a quest that had many silent as well as vociferous friends in East and West. Yet reference to a common European cultural heritage and to shared responsibilities was unable to overcome the realities of a divided Europe grounded in the facts of concrete power. CSCE was overshadowed by concern about the balance of military power between East and West and the role of the two superpowers as guarantors of European security (as Kissinger had well understood). In the late 1970s the coincidence of, and asymmetry between, Soviet expansion of her military presence in Eastern Europe, with SS-20s and Backfire bombers, and American military retrenchment struck at the basis of CSCE. The Harmel report on the link between military balance and détente continued to form the basis of NATO thinking, and not least of Chancellor Schmidt's thinking. Schmidt, who was viewed in Washington as a proponent of continuing regional détente in Europe, emphasized that the security from détente could not be prior to, or a replacement for, the security of a balance of power. Accordingly, CSCE was a fragile growth, prey to setbacks from new developments and events. Secondly, CSCE was overshadowed by the problems of political stability in Eastern Europe.[13] The course of the Polish crisis in 1981–2 indicated that CSCE had contributed little if anything to the improved management or containment of crises there. Western policy remained caught in a dilemma: overdue change in Eastern Europe could precipitate a crisis that could rapidly be transformed into an East–West confrontation; on the other hand, challenging or subverting the Soviet position in Eastern Europe could toughen the Soviet position and frustrate change. If peaceful change in Eastern Europe was in the best interest of West European security, how best to proceed? In practice the provisions of the Final Act were used more to conduct ideological struggle than to seek leverage through more businesslike economic cooperation. Basket Three took precedence over Basket Two. The best interests of West European security were not perhaps well served by this emphasis.

The British view of CSCE, expressed in the opening speech of the Foreign Secretary to the Helsinki Conference in July 1973, struck an apt note. The Helsinki Conference was not concerned to establish peace, like the Vienna and Versailles conferences. It was there to create 'a better peace' by 'practical measures'; its success depended on 'quiet diplomacy'. In July 1975 the West German Foreign Minister said of the Final Act that it represented a further step towards a 'policy of limited progress' that was to be judged by what was 'actually possible today'. Such pragmatism was reflected in the NNA states which were even more concerned about the impact of the abstract advocacy of human rights. They favoured giving attention to the concrete and practical aspects of Baskets Two and Three in a spirit of 'realistic cooperation'. Like other West European states, notably the Federal Republic of Germany, the NNA states were particularly anxious that criticisms of violations of human rights should bear in mind 'overall effects'. The great danger was that necessary contacts across the East–West divide (necessary for security and liberalization) would be sacrificed either to abstract advocacy of human rights or to individual cases of prominent intellectuals. Human rights must be placed in the context of security and of practical measures to promote cooperation. In the Western view violation of human rights does not promote security and is hostile to détente. On the other hand, destabilization of the East undermines security and jeopardizes détente. Faced with this dilemma, Western European states are prone to identify a European interest in forbearance.

In the field of economic relations and human rights it is difficult to identify much direct impact of CSCE. Basket Two did little more than ratify long-standing Western European interests in using economic relations to build bridges in a divided Europe, to create through a complex and expanding web of cooperation a common interest in containing crises, and to bring about change in Eastern Europe by subtle and long-term means. The West German–Soviet trade treaty of 1978, with its long-term programme for cooperation, seemed to herald a success for 'the spirit of Helsinki'. In fact, it did no more than develop a trade treaty policy between the two countries that dates back to the late 1950s.[14] Nevertheless, numerous East–West bilateral trade treaties were concluded between 1972 and 1975 in parallel with the Helsinki Conference.

Western Europe tended to give greater importance than the United States to Basket Two. Thus, as governing mayor of West Berlin, Richard von Weizsäcker, wrote in *Die Zeit* on 30 September 1983: 'We Germans have been given the task of making Basket Two the keynote of East–West relations.' The United States was, by contrast, more prepared to sacrifice long-term trade cooperation to its containment policy: insisting on a tougher approach by COCOM on sensitive strategic exports, pursuing a policy of sanctions under President Carter (with the American grain embargo imposed in January 1980 after Soviet intervention in Afghanistan), and clashing with the Western Europeans over the 'natural gas for pipelines' deal (with the American government in June 1982 imposing sanctions on companies in Western Europe fulfilling pipeline contracts, on which it could exert pressure via American licences or capital). Whereas the proposed American–Soviet trade agreement of 1974 collapsed as a consequence of the Jackson–Vanik Amendment (a Congressional amendment making the grant of American trade concessions dependent on exit visas for Soviet Jews), the Western Europeans, especially the Germans, continued to insist on the value of maintaining the economic bases of détente — particularly as a lever for change and as a means to build up a web of cooperation in order to enhance security.[15]

Political conflicts about East–West trade were further fed by economic developments: protracted recession in the West, competition from newly industrializing countries of the Third World, and rising costs of credit led to high indebtedness to the West, rescheduling problems and import curbs in Eastern Europe. The trauma of Poland's insolvency in 1981, the illiquidity of Romania and the credit problems of Hungary created a confidence crisis about the CMEA bloc within the Western banks, not least when it became clear that the Soviet Union was not prepared to keep a protective umbrella over CMEA countries.[16] At the end of 1981 total CMEA debt to the West stood at an estimated 91 billion dollars (Poland accounted for 23–26 billion). Hungary became a member of the IMF and joined the World Bank in 1982. Within CMEA Hungary became the chief spokesman for an 'outward-looking' approach and joined Romania and Bulgaria in seeking higher agricultural prices within CMEA (to increase their return on the food they sell to the Soviet Union). In practice, as a consequence of the economic developments mentioned above, economic interdependence between East and West Europe did not materialize. Bilateral ties between West Germany and the Soviet Union continued to be the main pillar of East–West trade. However, West German trade with Eastern Europe in the 1980s sank to the level of the early 1960s. East–West trade has always been less significant for the West than for the East. Since the Helsinki Final Act, up to the mid-1980s, East–West trade declined in terms of overall trading activity by OECD countries.[17] The proportion of the total trade of OECD accounted for by the six Eastern European countries fell from 2 per cent in 1970 to 1.5 per cent in 1981; the proportion accounted for by the Soviet Union rose from 1.2 per cent to 2 per cent. The proportion of Eastern European trade accounted for by OECD countries fell from 27.2 per cent in 1970 to 22.4 per cent in 1982; the proportion of the Soviet Union's trade rose from 24.3 per cent in 1970 to 33.7 per cent in 1982. In short, though Western European governments hoped to exploit Basket Two to intensify economic relations, they found their scope for influence limited by market and structural factors as well as by the systemic differences between Eastern and Western European economies. In the decade after the Final Act there was the complicating political factor that both superpowers watched economic relations between Eastern and Western Europe with suspicion.

As far as human rights were concerned, the West had little

leverage. It was not clear that the West could, or would be prepared to, offer anything by way of an 'adventurous' détente policy that could persuade the Soviet Union to pay a high political price in terms of human rights. Focusing on particular cases, and bringing individuals out of the Soviet Union and Eastern Europe, could do nothing to change the nature of the regimes. Little has changed in the working conditions of Western journalists in the Soviet bloc, the practice of jamming Western radio broadcasts or the availability of Western newspapers and magazines. Cultural exchange has continued to be hindered by the very different organizational structures of the two systems. Emigration from the East has not shown a rising trend since 1975.[18] The peak year for Jewish emigration from the Soviet Union was 1979 (with over 51,000); by 1984 the figure had fallen back to that of the 1960s (with less than 1,000). As Schulz shows in his chapter, ethnic Germans were helped to leave for West Germany: thus some 125,000 left Poland between 1976 and 1979; some 30,000 left the GDR in 1984. However, these figures have more to do with bilateral relations than with the CSCE process itself. Though the Final Act was important in encouraging unofficial monitoring groups in the East, with domestic costs there, the Soviet bloc was able and willing to meet this challenge. By 1982 the Moscow group had disappeared.

CSCE has been a learning process within the wider context of East–West relations. The lessons from substantive progress have been that very limited expectations are appropriate; that patience and a flexible long-term approach are needed; and that means have to be found to go beyond simply cataloguing the numerous problems of East–West relations in Europe. It is necessary to delimit the agenda, in order to ease the procedural problem of consensus, and to agree a long-term strategy that is designed to discipline the short-term political temptation to play to particular domestic audiences.[19] Détente is above all policy for the long term. Such a strategy needs to seek out a very few common and complementary interests as the basis for constructive negotiations. The common general interests in security and cooperation must be continually reaffirmed. However, from the point of view of negotiations complementary interests are perhaps more important. Each side must have or develop certain practical aims, however limited, that require concessions from the other side. In other words, each must offer some bargaining power to the other so that the game is worth playing. It is the task of creative European diplomacy to clarify the existence of such bargaining power; without it CSCE will continue to be moribund. Such bargaining power may be found in the discussions on the military dimensions of security in Stockholm. It may also be found in economic relations, in which case the EEC may be able further to develop its political interest in European détente, in helping to spin a web of cooperation that gives all Europeans a greater practical incentive to contain crises.

Notes

1. The best documentation and analysis is, not surprisingly, available in German, notably: *Sicherheit und Zusammenarbeit in Europa: Dokumentation zum KSZE-Prozess* (Bonn: Auswärtiges Amt, 1984); Hans-Adolf Jacobsen *et al. Sicherheit und Zusammenarbeit in Europa (KSZE)*, 2 vols (Cologne: Verlag Wissenschaft und Politik, 1973 and 1978); and Helga Haftendorn, ed., *Verwaltete Aussenpolitik* (Cologne: Verlag Wissenschaft und Politik, 1978).
2. S.M. Terry, ed., *Soviet Policy in Eastern Europe* (New Haven: Yale University Press, 1984).
3. The period of 'dialogue by communiqué' is analysed in Timothy Stanley and Darnell Whitt, *Détente Diplomacy: The United States and European Security in the 1970s* (New York: Dunellen, 1970); Karl Birnbaum, *Peace in Europe: East–West Relations 1966–1968 and the Prospects for a European Settlement* (London: Oxford University Press, 1970); Michael Palmer, *The Prospects for a European Security Conference* (London: Chatham House, PEP, 1971); Johan Galtung, ed., *Cooperation in Europe* (New York: Humanities Press, 1970); Zbigniew Brzezinski, 'America and Europe', *Foreign Affairs*, no. 1, October 1970, pp. 11–30; and Hans-Peter Schwarz and Helga Haftendorn, eds, *Europäische Sicherheitskonferenz* (Opladen: Leske Verlag, 1970).
4. On France see André Fontaine, 'Détente, Entente, Cooperation' in F. Alting von Geusau, ed., *Uncertain Détente* (Alphen aan den Rijn: Sijthoff and Noordhoff, 1978).
5. For details see Jacobsen *et al.*, op. cit., Vol. 2, p. 510.
6. *Implementation of the Final Act of the Conference on Security and Cooperation in Europe: Findings and Recommendations Two Years after Helsinki* (Washington: Report by the Commission on Security and Cooperation in Europe, 1977) — the so-called Fascell's report.
7. Richard Davy, 'The United States' in Nils Andren and Karl Birnbaum, eds, *Belgrade and Beyond: The CSCE Process in Perspective* (Alphen aan den Rijn: Sijthoff and Noordhoff, 1980).

8. For an excellent study of 'Belgrade 77' see Andren and Birnbaum, op. cit. Also Per Fischer, 'Das Ergebnis von Belgrad', *Europa-Archiv*, no. 8, 1978; and Tessa Solesby, 'Helsinki to Belgrade — and Beyond', *NATO Review*, no. 3, 1978. For American reactions see *The Belgrade Follow-Up Meeting: A Report and Appraisal* (Washington: Report by the Commission on Security and Cooperation in Europe, 1978). For a different West German perspective see J. Delbrück, N. Ropers and G. Zellentin, eds, *Grünbuch zu den Folgewirkungen der KSZE* (Cologne: Verlag Wissenschaft und Politik, 1977).
9. On the Madrid meeting see J. Sizoo and R. Jurrjens, *CSCE Decision-Making: The Madrid Experience* (The Hague: Martinus Nijhoff, 1984).
10. Horst Pusch, 'Die Stockholmer Konferenz — ein neuer Anfang?', *Beiträge zur Konfliktforschung*, no. 1, 1984, pp. 5–24. See also F.S. Larrabee and D. Stobbe, eds, *Confidence-Building Measures in Europe* (New York: Institute for East–West Security Studies, 1983).
11. This point was made by an experienced American negotiator: see Gerard Smith, 'Negotiating at SALT', *Survival*, no. 3, May–June 1977.
12. On the role of the NNA states see Hermann Volle and Wolfgang Wagner, eds, *KSZE, Beiträge und Dokument aus dem Europa-Archiv* (Bonn: Verlag für Internationale Politik, 1976).
13. See Terry, op. cit. Also Richard Löwenthal and Boris Meissner, eds, *Der Sowjetblock zwischen Vormachtkontrolle und Autonomie* (Cologne: Markus Verlag, 1984).
14. Jürgen Nötzold, 'Political Preconditions of East–West Economic Relations', *Aussenpolitik*, no. 1, 1985, pp. 37–54. See also Hanns-Dieter Jacobsen, *Die Ost-West-Wirtschaftsbeziehungen als deutsch-amerikanisches Problem* (Ebenhausen: Stiftung Wissenschaft und Politik, 1983).
15. Friedemann Müller et al., *Wirtschaftssanktionen im Ost-West-Verhältnis* (Baden-Baden: Nomos, 1983).
16. Klaus Schröder, 'Rescheduling the Debts of CMEA Countries', *Aussenpolitik*, no. 2, 1983, pp. 135–44.
17. For statistical information see the UN Economic Commission for Europe, *Economic Bulletin for Europe*, especially no. 4, 1984, p. 435 and no. 36, 1985, p. 254. See also Daniel Franklin, *The Prospects for East–West Trade* (London: Economist Intelligence Unit special report no. 154, 1983).
18. My thanks to Geoffrey Edwards for these figures.
19. On procedural reforms of CSCE see Sizoo and Jurrjens, op. cit.

4 Berlin, the German question and the future of Europe: long-term perspectives

Eberhard Schulz

Like all its predecessors the West German government of Chancellor Helmut Kohl after 1982 adopted the official position that the German question was 'open'. This position is not readily comprehensible to non-Germans. After all, forty years have passed since the end of the Second World War. Are there not today two German states — the Federal Republic of Germany and the German Democratic Republic — each of which pursues policies completely independent of the other? It is not impractical and dangerous for the Germans to continue to insist that the German question is open?

A central, indeed decisive feature of post-war Europe is the existence of two German states on the territory of the German Empire; their possession of most of the attributes of sovereignty; and their ability to pursue their own interests in international affairs with some success. The Federal Republic and the GDR belong to opposed alliance systems (NATO and the Warsaw Pact respectively), and by now every German has realized that the division of Europe, which passes through the middle of Germany, cannot be overcome in the foreseeable future. The overwhelming majority of Germans recognize also that 'a solution to the German question' cannot mean a return to the situation before the Second World War. The German question must be viewed in its Europe-wide, indeed global, political context.[1] Only then are its long-term dimensions made clear. At the same time it becomes apparent that the German question involves highly topical and, unfortunately, exceedingly complex aspects for Germans, their European neighbours and the United States and the Soviet Union.

Berlin and the German question

A vivid example of the complexity of the German question is provided by an unimportant incident that was not noticed at all in the international press outside Germany. In the autumn of 1984 the GDR closed the Glienicke bridge in Berlin without warning; before the end of the same day they reopened the bridge. What had happened? The Glienicke bridge connects an island in the territory of West Berlin with the town of Potsdam in the territory of the GDR. This bridge is not available for the use of Germans; it serves only for the traffic of Allied personnel between the Western military missions in Potsdam and West Berlin. For that reason a flag of the Soviet Union, as well as one of the GDR, flies at the GDR's end of the bridge. The bridge had been in need of repair for a long time. West Berlin's half of the bridge had already been completely renovated, and the costs borne by the Senate of West Berlin. On behalf of the three Western occupying powers (Britain, France and the United States) the Senate of West Berlin asked the GDR to have the necessary repairs undertaken on its side. The representatives of the GDR rejected this request. They argued that the GDR had no interest in the bridge because its citizens did not make use of it. Hence the Senate of West Berlin should pay all the costs of renovation. The Senate rejected this argument. In any case the people of West Berlin were also not permitted to use the bridge. Then the GDR took action. One morning the flags of the GDR and the Soviet Union were taken down, and the bridge was barricaded. Lively diplomatic activity began behind the scenes. As a consequence the bridge was reopened in the evening. And when, by chance, on the same day the mayor of West Berlin, Eberhard Diepgen, visited the Soviet ambassador in East Berlin, Vyacheslav Kochemasov welcomed him with the news that the problem of the bridge had been long since fixed. The detailed chain of events is not public knowledge. Clearly the representatives of the three Western powers protested to their Soviet counterparts, and after a brief 'to and fro' the latter instructed the GDR authorities to reopen the Glienicke bridge. West Berlin paid the price in the sense that it had to bear the cost of DM 2 million for repair of the bridge.

This simple example illustrates the lack of sovereignty of the two

German states. In questions that affect 'all Germany and Berlin' final responsibility continues to rest with the four victorious powers of the Second World War. As early as the Yalta Conference of February 1945 the four Allied powers had agreed on joint control of defeated Germany from Berlin. And in the London protocols of September and November 1944, in which they defined the zones of occupation, they decided that the area of Greater Berlin *(Gross-Berlin)* was not to be allocated to a zone of occupation but to be governed jointly with the aid of the Allied Control Council located in Berlin. When the two German states were established in 1949, the three Western powers refused to endorse the incorporation of 'the state (*Land*) Berlin' into the Federal Republic of Germany and suspended the relevant passages in the Basic Law of the Federal Republic and in the constitution of (West) Berlin.[2] Yet West Berlin was unable to become politically and economically viable on its own. The three Western powers were, therefore, prepared to tolerate more limited efforts by the Federal Republic to draw West Berlin *de facto* into its political sphere. In this way there emerged a distinctive legal 'grey area' that was not even to be clarified by the Quadripartite Agreement on Berlin in 1971. The four powers confirmed that, on the one hand, 'the ties between the Western Sectors of Berlin and the Federal Republic of Germany will be maintained and developed' but that, on the other hand, 'these Sectors continue not to be a constituent part of the Federal Republic of Germany and not to be governed by it'.[3]

Elements of the original quadripartite administration for the whole of Berlin exist still: namely, the prison for war criminals in Spandau, where Rudolf Hess remains interned, and the Allied air traffic control centre for the area of Greater Berlin. Also, the Western powers continue to place great value on the regular dispatch of military patrols to East Berlin as a means of displaying and confirming that they maintain their original rights of occupation. The Soviet Union takes great care, however, no longer to appear as an occupying power in East Berlin. The asymmetry between the two parts of the former imperial capital is clear: one half is factually the capital city of the GDR, the other hangs suspended, is — to use a pun — 'an island in the red sea', which means that it forms an enclave in the territory of the GDR and its capital city East Berlin.

The incident at the Glienicke bridge, which otherwise is only mentioned in the international press when spectacular exchanges of spies take place on it, throws light on a broader political context:

1. A durable solution for the German question has not yet been found. With regard to their political organization the Germans continue to find themselves in a provisional status. This fact forms the basis of the statement that the German question is still open.
2. Despite their otherwise sharp divisions about East–West relations the four victorious powers of 1945 agree on two matters: neither of the two German states is absolutely sovereign (although the Soviet Union would never admit that publicly in relation to 'its' German state, the GDR); and Germany must not be allowed to become the site for a military conflict between the four powers.
3. The German question has a dual character. For the Germans it means the desire to regain security and freedom for the whole nation. For the other powers it means the desire to control the Germans in order to prevent a disruption of the peace in central Europe, which could be unleashed by the Germans.
4. The Federal Republic of Germany is prepared to pay a fair political and financial price for the maintenance of the provisional status (the 'openness' of the German question until a permanent peace settlement is agreed) and for the reduction of tensions in East–West relations as a prerequisite. However, this price cannot include the sacrifice of the greatest political achievement of post-war Germans, political freedom for the people of the Federal Republic and West Berlin.

The special German interest in the CSCE process

The preamble of the Helsinki Final Act of 1975 contains a notable passage whose real meaning is probably not appreciated by most readers: 'Determined . . . to give full effect to the results of the Conference and to assure, among their states and throughout

Europe, the benefits deriving from those results . . .' Why 'among their states and throughout Europe'? The answer is that, though Europe is a system of states, there is a territory whose affiliation to a state is controversial — Berlin. Nobody doubts that East Berlin belongs to the GDR, even if the Western powers, along with the Federal Republic, do not recognize its character as the capital city of that state. Yet, in contrast to the Federal Republic, they are agreed that West Berlin is not part of the Federal Republic of Germany. West Berlin does not, of course, form a separate state. Nikita Khrushchev had no success in 1958 when he demanded that West Berlin should be transformed into 'a special political unit', in effect into a third German state. The formula in the Helsinki Final Act makes clear that West Berlin is supposed to be covered by the terms of the Final Act despite its unclear status within the system of European states.

The Quadripartite Agreement on Berlin of 1971 is probably the most remarkable agreement in international history, because its parties were unable to agree about the object of the treaty. In his diplomatic note of 27 November 1958 Khrushchev claimed that the Western powers had grossly violated the Allied agreements and thus forfeited the right to maintain their regime of occupation in Berlin and the whole of Germany. Therefore, the Soviet Union regarded the London Protocol of 12 September 1944 on the definition of the zones of occupation and the supplementary agreements as no longer operative. Khrushchev threatened that the Soviet Union would draw practical conclusions from this statement unless within six months the Western powers were prepared to enter into a new treaty relationship.

The Soviet Union was not able to maintain this tough position, and in the preamble of the Quadripartite Agreement of 3 September 1971 she conceded the following statement '. . . Acting on the basis of their quadripartite rights and responsiblities, and of the corresponding wartime and postwar agreements and decisions of the Four Powers, which are not affected . . .' However, whereas the Western powers insisted that the object of the agreement must be Greater Berlin, the Soviet Union wanted to limit the negotiations to West Berlin. The result was the strange compromise that leaves the question open and speaks about 'the relevant area'. Only Part II contains the provisions that affect the Western sectors of Berlin. The Western powers draw the logical conclusion that the Western sectors are clearly only a part of 'the relevant area', to which the rights of the four powers apply, namely Greater Berlin.

The fact that the Quadripartite Agreement came about despite the opposed legal positions of both sides, and their firm adherence to these positions, indicates that there are higher interests that are common to the four powers or at least run in parallel. Obviously these interests involve the avoidance of military conflict between the nuclear powers in a highly armed central Europe. This fact permits also another conclusion: that the viability of West Berlin can only be secured by keeping East–West tensions in tolerable limits. If a military conflict were to break out in central Europe, West Berlin would certainly be affected immediately. It is also worth noting that the Quadripartite Agreement provides only for a *modus vivendi*. Because of the irreconcilable opposition of interests and legal positions a durable regulation was not possible. The *modus vivendi* keeps conflicts below the military level, conflicts that might arise out of the frictions between the two German states. It calms the situation at the point in Europe where military conflict could most easily arise. This pacification is decisive for the survival of West Berlin. In a nervous climate necessary commercial investments are not forthcoming and inhabitants emigrate. The population of West Berlin has tended to fall steadily since the end of the Second World War. West Berlin is thus dependent on a minimum of détente in East–West relations; only in this way can the *modus vivendi* be maintained.

The German question has yet another aspect that is of topical importance. The security of the Federal Republic of Germany is guaranteed by the deterrence of the Atlantic Alliance. Under the protective umbrella of this alliance the Federal Republic has the possibility to maintain its political system based on 'the free democratic basic order' and to shape its own development. The Germans in the GDR are largely denied this possibility. In addition, the policy of *Abgrenzung* (of political 'fencing off') by the GDR leadership threatens the cohesion of the German nation. The Soviet leadership holds the view that the security of its own state can only be guaranteed by erecting a broad buffer zone or cordon of states in Eastern Europe dependent on itself. For that purpose the Soviet

Union needs also 'its own' part of Germany: on the one hand, because in this way the restless Poles can be encircled and contained; on the other hand, because the largest and, for the Soviet Union, the most dangerous nation in Europe is thereby divided.[4] In order to secure her ascendency in Eastern Europe the Soviet Union imposed her own Marxist-Leninist system on the states there, thereby denying a free political development to the Germans in the GDR as well as to the Poles and other Eastern European nations.

Experience shows that the Soviet Union attempts to tighten the reins in Eastern Europe as soon as the climate in East–West relations deteriorates. The effects are felt only by people in the Soviet sphere of influence, not by those in the Western countries — with the exception of the Germans, because a part of the German nation is subordinated to Soviet domination. Hence when, in a period of mounting East–West tensions, repression increases in the Soviet bloc and the policy of *Abgrenzung* is tightened, the German nation is threatened by the danger that consciousness of common nationhood will evaporate with the limitation of direct contacts. Though all West European countries protest against the infringement of human rights in the Soviet bloc, the only nation in Western Europe that is directly affected is the German.

It may be that the sense of common national identity declines so far in the two German states that it loses its political importance in favour of stronger emotional attachments to the respective German state.[5] History is littered with examples of parts of nations that are separated and develop into independent nations. Such a phenomenon is not necessarily a catastrophe. However, history provides also examples of the opposite development, namely of nations that rebel against external violation and rally in force to defend themselves. If this type of development were to occur in the middle of Europe in the nuclear age, the consequences would be incalculable.

These difficulties and uncertainties form the basis of the fundamental interest of the Federal Republic of Germany in a reduction of tensions in East–West relations. They provided the main motives for the Federal Republic's bilateral *Ostpolitik* (Eastern policy) in the 1970s. They are the reason why the West German federal government insists on a continuation of the multilateral CSCE process, which represents the logical extension of bilateral

Ostpolitik. In the early 1980s, with mounting tensions between the two superpowers, there was no other level of negotiations between East and West that even approximated in political importance to the CSCE process. This statement requires elaboration.

The main elements of German special interests *vis-à-vis* the East

For reasons already outlined, the Federal Republic is above all interested in promoting what the Helsinki Final Act calls 'freedom of thought, conscience, religion or belief'. It is, however, not simply a matter for self-congratulation to say that this interest is embodied in the Final Act and indeed earlier in the UN Covenant on Civil and Political Rights of 1966. In the Soviet bloc the Marxist-Leninist ideology is authoritative. This ideology requires, for instance, the struggle against 'religious prejudices' and other 'remnants of bourgeois ideology'; indeed it demands that the population must be compulsorily indoctrinated, even if in other Eastern European states the work of the party in this field has gradually lost momentum. However, in the mid-1980s Soviet leaders expressed the view that the shock to communist rule in Poland in 1980 from the unofficial trade union Solidarity, like the earlier periods of weakness (the GDR in 1953, Hungary and Poland in 1956 and Czechoslovakia in 1968), would not have happened if the indigenous Communist Party had not neglected its role of ideological indoctrination. In complete contrast to the Western understanding of the Helsinki Final Act the Soviet leadership demanded an intensification of ideological work in the 1980s. It is possible that the consequences for other Eastern European countries will not be as unpleasant as on earlier occasions in the post-war period. Nevertheless, the situation that faces millions of people in Eastern Europe is that their career prospects can only be guaranteed as long as there are no doubts about their ideological reliability.

A special feature of the German situation is that the people of the communist-ruled GDR speak the same language as those in the Federal Republic of Germany. Some three-quarters of the inhabitants of the GDR are regular viewers of West German television and throughout the GDR West German radio stations can be heard, even if West German newspapers are almost unobtainable. According to the Basic Law of the Federal Republic, the citizens of the GDR count as 'German citizens' *(Staatsbürger)*. Consequently, if they ask for a passport of the Federal Republic of Germany, the authorities of the Federal Republic must provide one. Citizens who are politically persecuted in the GDR and who succeed in leaving do not need to ask for asylum in the Federal Republic. Full rights as a citizen are automatically granted to them on request.

Scattered remnants of the German population are to be found in most East European states. The Federal Republic is obliged to show solidarity with them. When, for instance, people who are Germans or identify as Germans seek an exit visa and are as a consequence arrested, the consular representatives of the Federal Republic in the particular country take an interest in them. Over more than twenty years the Federal Republic has 'bought freedom' for more than 100,000 political prisoners from the GDR. It has exploited the GDR's pressing need for foreign currency in order to make possible the exit of opponents of the regime to the Federal Republic and thereby protect them from further political persecution.

A few figures will indicate the importance of human contacts within the German nation across the borders of the two states.[6] In 1984, 2,500,000 citizens of the Federal Republic travelled to the GDR and East Berlin for more than one day; an estimated 1,100,000 West Germans stayed for a day in East Berlin; and 343,000 West Germans made use of the bilateral agreement between the Federal Republic and the GDR on the possibility of visits to the border area of the GDR. The government of the GDR did not permit comparable opportunities for travel to its own citizens; normal citizens of the GDR cannot travel to the Federal Republic or to West Berlin. Exceptions exist for pensioners, of whom 1,546,000 visited the Federal Republic in 1984, and 'in pressing family circumstances' for those citizens of the GDR who are not counted as amongst the numerous 'holders of secrets'. Of this latter group, 61,133 were allowed to visit the Federal Republic in 1984, some 5 per cent less than in 1983, but 50 per cent more than in 1982. Additionally, there were some 21,800,000 transit travellers in 1983 between the Federal Republic and West Berlin in both directions; this figure includes foreigners.

Over the years the number of trips between the two German states has varied greatly, and the trends are very interesting. The importance of the Quadripartite Agreement about Berlin is reflected in the way in which the number of West Berliners who travelled to East Berlin increased by 150 per cent between 1971 (the year in which the agreement was made) and 1972. The number reached its highest level in 1977. Then it fell to half the 1977 level by 1981, when the GDR increased the minimum exchange rate drastically. The other visits mentioned above have not been affected by political tensions to the same degree.

Telephone communications are another important indicator of the cohesion of the German nation. Whereas neither travel nor telephone links are possible between the two Korean states, these forms of communication between the two German states have never wholly died away). In 1969 there were 34 telephone links between the Federal Republic and the GDR. This figure rose to 860 in February 1984. No telephone lines existed between West Berlin and the GDR in 1969; their number had risen to 657 by 1984. 500,000 telephone calls were made from the Federal Republic to the GDR in 1969; there were 23,200,000 in 1984.

The comparison with the situation in Korea raises the question of whether, and to what extent, the GDR is interested in the development of a minimum level of friendly relations with the Federal Republic. During the period till 1971, when Walter Ulbricht led the Socialist Unity Party (*Sozialistische Einheitspartei Deutschlands* (SED)), it seemed that the GDR's leadership was seeking to sever all links to the Federal Republic. Ulbricht had to resign because he did not wish to be forced by the Soviet Union to assent to the Quadripartite Agreement on Berlin and the inner-German agreements. His successor Erich Honecker too could not afford simply to open the borders to the Federal Republic of Germany. However, there are two main reasons that encourage him to permit communications with the Federal Republic in a carefully prescribed form. The first reason is that the GDR derives financial advantages from agreements with the Federal Republic. The so-called 'swing', an interest-free technical credit, was already available for inner-German trade to the GDR under Ulbricht. Its importance for the external trade of the GDR declined somewhat in the early 1980s, but it provides still the simplest opportunity for the GDR to overcome short-run bottlenecks in its liquidity position *vis-à-vis* 'hard-currency' states. In addition, since the 1970s a series of agreements has provided the GDR with regular income. Perhaps the most prominent examples are the lump-sum payments of the Federal Republic for the transit passengers to and from West Berlin and the postal charges that are the product of the imbalance of mail between the Federal Republic and the GDR. Finally, there is a technology transfer, albeit limited, from the Federal Republic to the GDR, and the GDR's leadership is anxious to maintain this transfer.

Much less well known is the other reason why Honecker is concerned to prevent a decline in relations with the Federal Republic below a certain level: the mood of his population. An authoritarian government like that of the GDR is not orientated towards the consent of its population to the same extent as a democratic state. Yet the GDR's leadership cannot be indifferent to the popular mood. With the start of deployment of new American intermediate-range nuclear weapons in the Federal Republic after 1983, and of new Soviet nuclear weapons in the GDR and Czechoslovakia, anxiety about the possibility of war grew visibly in various sectors of the GDR's society. The leadership of the SED thought that it would be opportune to distance itself in a cautious manner from the mounting and threatening rhetoric from the Kremlin. Honecker seemed to attempt to project himself to his population as a sort of prince of peace who wages everything to ensure that the tensions between East and West do not lead to military conflict and to contribute to reducing antagonisms on the level of the smaller European states. On occasion this behaviour drew criticism of Honecker from the Soviet Union. On the other hand, however, the Kremlin had to recognize that in the final analysis the domestic stability of the GDR was in the Soviet interest.[7]

The end of the Second World War marked the close of an epoch in international political history. Since the Renaissance in the fifteenth and sixteenth centuries the peoples of Europe had extended their influence over almost the whole world. The eventual consequence was the emergence of powerful colonial empires centred on Europe. The two world wars during the first half of the twentieth century drained the energies of the European countries to such an extent that not only their colonial rule collapsed but also they were simply no longer able to shape their own history. International politics, and the fate of Europe itself, fell under the controlling spell of the two 'flanking' powers, the Soviet Union and the United States. This phenomenon is well known and needs no further explanation. At the same time, however, the collapse of the German Empire in 1945 meant the end of another historical epoch, that of the 'German colonization of the East'. For more than 700 years the Germans have spread out over eastern and south-eastern Europe — partly by peaceful settlement of underpopulated areas, partly by the trade of the cities of the Hanseatic League, partly by armed conflict in the early form of the Teutonic order. As a consequence of the two world wars some of the eastern European peoples achieved independent statehood. German settlements in their countries were now felt to represent a threat to their national cohesion as states, all the more so when they were faced by Hitler's policy, which aimed to suppress them or even physically annihilate them because of their supposed racial inferiority. The counteroffensive was now directed against the Germans in eastern Europe, and within a few years most of those who had not already fled were expelled from their areas of settlement to the German heartland. Hundreds of thousands had in fact to remain behind — partly because the national groups had intermixed over the course of centuries and, consequently, German national identity could not be clearly established, partly because the Eastern European governments did not want to lose their expertise or because they had not understood in time the real extent of the historical transformation.

By means of more or less formalized agreements with the Eastern European states the Federal Republic of Germany succeeded in gradually making it possible for the greater part of those Germans left in the East to leave or to be reunited with their families living in the West. The public in the other Western European states allied with the Federal Republic took very little interest in this policy compared with the passions aroused by the fate of dissidents or Jews in the Soviet Union and the other states of Eastern Europe. This coolness is understandable in the wake of the crimes of National Socialism. At the same time it reveals little understanding of the national concerns of an allied partner. The federal government could do no other than stand by fellow countrymen in Eastern Europe, for the Federal Republic has the only government in Germany that rests on the legitimacy of free elections and has a corresponding moral duty to assist those Germans who are denied the same freedom. There is another factor. During the period of the Third Reich the government of Hitler had deprived thousands of Germans of their citizenship, leaving them abroad without protection. When German statehood was re-established with the creation of the Federal Republic in 1949, it was accepted as a moral imperative (and written into the Basic Law) that in future no German could again be denied his citizenship.

This problem played a special role in the relations of the Federal Republic of Germany and Poland.[8] In the context of the German–Polish treaty of December 1970 the Polish government opened to people of 'incontestably German nationality' in principle the possibility to leave for the Federal Republic. Five years later the Helsinki Final Act confirmed in a general form that all Europeans were to be given the right to leave their country without hindrance if they so wanted. The question for German policy is which of the two principles — that of nationhood or that of general human rights — promises the best practical results. Both have their advantages and disadvantages. With respect to German nationhood, some of the Eastern European states are very sensitive in the wake of their experiences of the Germans after the First World War and in the Nazi period. At the same time they tend to reject the Western interpretation of general human rights because along with the Soviet political system some of them have taken on board the principle of sealed borders (Poland and Hungary are exceptions) and because they do not wish to admit — partly on grounds of ideology, partly of national pride — that citizens need to leave their country. Additionally, the Helsinki Final Act is not in the strict sense a treaty that creates international law and can be reliably invoked by individuals. Even so it ought to be possible for the Federal Republic to mobilize more support for its aims from Western public opinion by invoking the Helsinki Final Act than by simply appealing to ethnic principles.

In this connection it should be noted that in the second phase of the CSCE negotiations in Geneva the West was able to extract quite remarkable concessions from the Soviet Union and its allies. As the Soviet leadership had determined that the principles of Basket One must be anchored in a multilateral agreement whatever the circumstances, and as Brezhnev had committed himself to signing the Final Act personally, the West found itself in an unusually favourable negotiating position. How was that position to be used? Basically the West had two options. The West could exploit the Soviet Union's political needs and press for maximum concessions from the Soviet side. These concessions could then be embodied in precise provisions of the Final Act and thus block the loopholes that the Soviet Union would have so liked to keep open. The other option was to recognize the special character of the Soviet system and to exploit Soviet interests where they ran parallel with Western interests. This latter option would have meant that the West did not exert heavy pressure on the Soviet delegation in order to force concessions that were basically incompatible with its system. The emphasis would have been on the Soviet interest in cooperation with the West and on efforts to achieve trust and a relaxation of tensions. Past experience had shown anyway that in the final analysis the Soviet Union did not abide by agreements that it judged to be a threat to its security. With this second option the West would have opted for a gradual process and for a long-term change of the Soviet system.

The West agreed finally on the first option. In ever more new rounds of negotiations the Western delegations pressed with great success the case to make more and more precise the contents of the Final Act in so far as they affected alleviation of the human condition or human rights. In this way the West established a text that could create the impression that the communist-ruled states had taken on board the ideals of the Western constitutions. In reality nobody could hope that these states would adhere to these texts, all the less so after the West itself insisted that the Final Act should not have the authoritative status of international law — partly out of fear that existing international law might be weakened by new formulations, partly because of the danger that a treaty with the status of international law would not be ratified by every parliament. So in the end the Helsinki Final Act had only the character of a declaration of intent. In practice little was lost as a consequence. It could not have been expected that the Soviet government or other communist governments would have submitted to a proceeding before the International Court of Justice. In any case the protection of human rights, as agreed in the Helsinki Final Act, remained dependent on the extent of détente in East–West relations. In other words, the situation for human rights deteriorated as tensions revived.

In the review meetings of Belgrade (1977–8) and Madrid (1980–3) the West attempted by means of vehement protest to stop this unfavourable development. Past experience seemed to suggest that firm protest in even less favourable circumstances could at least bring amelioration for prominent personalities who were suffering from communist persecution. Meanwhile, however, the large-scale deployment of new SS-20 rockets by the Soviet Union had ruined détente. The West took political and military countermeasures, which had, however, the secondary effect of weakening the protection that the West had to a degree been able to provide for opponents of the Eastern European governments. Helmut Schmidt's Social Democratic–Liberal coalition in Bonn played a central role in the NATO decision to rearm,[9] only to find itself under mounting pressure from the peace movement and from within the Federal Chancellor's own Social Democratic Party. The new conservative-liberal federal government in 1982 proclaimed 'a new era' (*Wende*). The effects were not to be seen in *Ostpolitik*, in which Chancellor Kohl continued the policy of his predecessor. A substantial difference from the Social Democratic-Liberal coalition was that in the new federal coalition government the rhetoric about the German question and German legal arguments were deployed with new persistence.

The substance of the German question

What is at the heart of the German question? The two main aspects have already been mentioned: the desire for freedom and security for the whole German nation, which is stressed by the Germans; and the need to control reliably the excessive potential of Germany, which is the concern of the political elites in her neighbouring countries. Both aspects can be traced back historically, at least into the seventeenth century. The German nation is located in the centre of Europe. There is no clear boundary to the areas of German settlement, indeed historically changes have been constantly taking place — not only in the West towards France but also in the East towards Poland and the other Eastern European nations.

An additional important dimension is that Germany has never had a strong central power as France had both under Louis XIV and his successors and in the nineteenth and twentieth centuries. As a consequence the German nation was unable to develop as distinct an identity as the French who were transformed from a diffuse multitude of people, by means of pressure from above, into a group with a specific profile. On the one hand, the boundaries of the German area of settlement were fluid; on the other, there were strong regional differences and constantly changing external influences, which also found expression in treaties like the Treaty of Westphalia in 1648 or the Holy Alliance of 1815. For the Germans these treaties had the character of public law as well as international law. In 1648 foreign princes acquired rights to influence German affairs, whilst in 1815 the foundation of the German Confederation was an integral part of the wider European solution at the Congress of Vienna. Examples of comparable importance do not exist for any other European nation.

Against this background it seems sensible to ask the question whether there is really a German nation that can be clearly defined. As German borders have constantly changed and the subjects or citizens have changed, and as there is no distinct and pronounced national profile, it is difficult to apply either the French criteria for the nation, namely a common political consciousness, or the ethnic criteria, which are for instance so influential in Poland today. Neither on political, ideological or religious grounds nor on ethnic grounds is it easy to distinguish the Germans from their neighbours.

In these circumstances it is not at all surprising that a German nation state did not emerge till 1871 so that Germans have been called 'the delayed nation' (*verspätete Nation*).[10] The establishment of Bismarck's Empire was also very controversial within the German intelligentsia. The German Empire that was formed in 1871 was more an extension of Prussian ambitions for power and hegemony than an all-German state, for the Austrian component, with the seat of the former Emperor in Vienna, remained excluded, whilst non-Germans were absorbed into the new Empire against their will. However, the nature of the dilemma that had been produced by the national development of the Germans only became clear with the Treaty of Versailles in 1919. In the eyes of her neighbours Germany remained too strong; in the eyes of pan-Germans she had become unaccceptably small.

This national dilemma of the Germans provided a powder-barrel for the whole of Europe. The principle of the nation-state, which shaped the structure of Europe from the end of the eighteenth century, could not be properly applied to Germany. Hence the peace in Europe was constantly in danger. There seemed only one solution to this problem — European unification. Far-sighted Europeans had recognized this solution as early as the turn of the twentieth century. In the inter-war period more Europeans became aware of the need for European unity. Yet only with the Second World War did the European movement achieve clear political forms and in the 1950s achieved its first practical results — paradoxically at a time when the problems of European nation-states were being overshadowed by those of the bilateral East–West confrontation.

Against a background of antagonisms between East and West the West needed the territory of the Federal Republic as a glacis and its potential as an effective instrument of Western defence. At the same time the presence of American troops and nuclear weapons in the Federal Republic represented a guarantee that the much feared neutralist tendencies amongst the Germans could not triumph. On the other hand, the GDR is locked into the Soviet bloc. The Germans of the GDR are the real losers of the Second World War, for unlike the West Germans they were not able to gain freedom with the collapse of the Hitler dictatorship in 1945. The more fortunate Federal Republic of Germany is obliged to show solidarity with the other part of the German nation. The Federal Republic cannot simply leave the other Germans to their own fate. Here, alongside the special difficulty of Berlin, lies the topical importance of the German question.

The present condition of Europe will not last for ever. The continuation of the antagonism between the two blocs can only be expected to last for a transitional period. It would be rash to assume that the United States will be prepared to maintain the presence of its troops in Europe for an unlimited time. Who would have predicted in 1945 that forty years later American troops would still be stationed in Europe? Even the Soviet ascendancy in Eastern Europe will not go on for ever. In recent years there have been growing signs of a decline of the Soviet Union's capacity for political leadership in Eastern Europe. This statement is not directed at the military potential of the Soviet Union; the Soviet Union is a superpower and will continue to be in the position to control Eastern Europe militarily. The growing problem for the Soviet Union is its capacity to maintain its claim to leadership in the political, social and economic development of the East European states. Increasingly the Russian political culture in these countries proves itself to be a foreign body that is unsuited to their Western tradition. Yet nobody can predict the consequences of this fact for the actual course of events in Europe.

Long-term perspectives of the CSCE process

The high political tensions between the two blocs in the first half of the 1980s meant that modest expectations were associated with the Stockholm Conference on Confidence and Security Building Measures and Disarmament in Europe, which was convened in January 1984 after the bitter CSCE review meeting in Madrid. It seemed that the era in which agreements about arms control could be negotiated and embodied in treaties was coming to an end. A major factor in its demise was that rapid technological development was producing a complex variety of weapons systems that are difficult to control. At the operational level arms control policy faces mounting difficulties in trying to tie up equitable and verifiable package agreements that cover a sufficient range of weapons systems in order to prevent a diversion of the arms race into new areas. Nevertheless, the CSCE process, to which the Stockholm negotiations belong, remains the only pan-European level of negotiation that still functions and that ought to be maintained at almost any price.

The CSCE process needs to be maintained not least because of the open German question. Officially the Federal Republic of Germany represents the view that the German question will remain open till there is a freely agreed peace settlement with a freely elected all-German government. But how could such a peace settlement come about and how would it look? Can one really assume that an all-German state can be formed before the beginning of negotiations? Can one further assume that the government of such a state would be in the position to negotiate a peace settlement freely as an equal amongst equals with the former victorious powers? Can it be in the German interest to confront all other governments alone in such negotiations and thereby risk changing present allies back into former enemy powers?

On the other side, the Western powers would be preoccupied with the need to ensure that the Western values, which they had pushed through in Germany after 1945, were maintained. They would not permit a return of the Germans to an authoritarian regime. In addition, the Western powers would place great stress on integrating into a European structure the power potential of the Germans, for the latter continues to exceed that of its neighbouring countries. Finally, the Western powers would not allow a situation in peace negotiations in which they stood once again opposed to the Germans. How then can there be a peace settlement that will transform a present German situation whose conditions cannot be maintained over time into a state of affairs that will be acceptable to all and thus durable?

It is a function of the weak historical consciousness of the age that scarcely anyone has thought of a long-term use of the CSCE mechanism for a regulation of the German question. A preliminary condition is, of course, that the tensions between East and West are first reduced by degrees. This process might be achieved all the more quickly the sooner public opinion is freed from its fixation on the idea of disarmament. Only when the tensions are reduced are there any prospects for a slowing down of the arms' race; the opposite route is scarcely practicable. In connection with the CSCE process one might also consider how the European nations can be integrated in structures that will subdue the uncontrolled nationalism of the period before the Second World War. The CSCE process could also serve to canalize the eventually unavoidable disengagement of the

United States and the Soviet Union (which is unlikely to become apparent at the same time) so that a power vacuum or the outbreak of a conflict is avoided. In this context the need might also arise to find a framework for the regulation of the German question. It is sensible at this point to draw on experience from the past. The treaties of 1648 and 1815 did of course spring from quite different conditions, and they contained many elements whose return, even if possible, ought to be avoided. But they had one thing in common that ought to be striven for in a future German peace settlement: they were pan-European agreements.

Notes

1. As to role of the European Economic Community in the German question see Eberhard Schulz, 'Unfinished Business: the German National Question and the Future of Europe', *International Affairs*, Summer 1984, pp. 391–402. The broader context of the role of the German nation in Europe is discussed by the same author in *Die Deutsche Nation in Europa*, Schriften des Forschungsinstituts der Deutschen Gesellschaft für Auswärtige Politik e.V., (Bonn: Europa Union Verlag, 1982).
2. The BK/O(50) 75, issued 29 August 1950, on the Berlin Constitution, states: 'In approving this Constitution . . . the Allied Kommandatura makes the following reservations: . . . (b) Article 1, Paragraph 2 and 3 are suspended. (c) Article 87 is interpreted as meaning that during the transitional period Berlin shall possess none of the attributes of a twelfth Land. The provisions of this Article concerning the Basic Law will only apply to the extent necessary to prevent a conflict between this law and the Berlin Constitution . . .'. See *Documents on Berlin 1943–1963*, selected and edited by Wolfgang Heidelmeyer and Guenter Hindrichs, (München: R. Oldenbourg Verlag, 1963), p. 121.
3. Quadripartite Agreement, Part II, paragraph B.
4. For details see Eberhard Schulz and Hans Dieter Schulz, *Braucht der Osten die DDR?* Schriftenreihe Aktuelle Aussenpolitik des Forschungsinstituts der Deutschen Gesellschaft für Auswärtige Politik (Opladen: C.W. Leske Verlag, 1968).
5. For this view see Gebhard Schweigler, *National Consciousness in Divided Germany* (London: Sage, 1975). The opposite opinion is held by Peter Christian Ludz, *Die DDR zwischen Ost und West von 1961 bis 1976* (München: Beck-Verlag, 1977). See also Ronald Asmus, 'The GDR and the German Nation: Sole Heir or Socialist Sibling?', *International Affairs*, Summer 1984, pp. 403–18.
6. Figures provided by the Federal Ministry of Inner-German Affairs in its annual *Jahresbericht*.

Berlin, the German question and the future of Europe   133

7. For details see Eberhard Schulz and Peter Danylow, *Bewegung in der deutschen Frage? Die ausländischen Besorgnisse über die Entwicklung in den beiden deutschen Staaten*, Arbeitspapiere zur Internationalen Politik 33, 2nd revised edn (Bonn: Europa Union Verlag, 1985).
8. For a most comprehensive discussion of German–Polish relations see the remarkable joint publication edited by Hans-Adolf Jacobsen, Carl Christoph Schweitzer, Jerzy Sutek and Lech Trzeciakowski, *Bundesrepublik Deutschland– Volksrepublik Polen. Bilanz der Beziehungen — Probleme und Perspektiven ihrer Normalisierung* (Frankfurt: Alfred Metzner Verlag, 1979).
9. Beginning with his Alastair Buchan Memorial Lecture at the International Institute for Strategic Studies in London on 28 October 1977, published in *Survival*, January–February 1978.
10. See Helmuth Plessner, *Die verspätete Nation* (Stuttgart: W. Kohlhammer Verlag, 1959).

5 *Deutschlandpolitik, Ostpolitik* and the Western Alliance: German perspectives on détente

Michael Stürmer

The connections between the 'Eastern policy' (*Ostpolitik*) and the 'policy on Germany' (*Deutschlandpolitik*) of the Federal Republic of Germany, and their links to the Western Alliance, have been the subject of much speculation in the East as well as in the West. This chapter seeks to explain these policies and to assess the prospects for, and limitations on, the Federal Republic's special contribution to the management of conflict in Europe.

The characater and framework of *Deutschlandpolitik*

At the heart of the *Ostpolitik* of the Federal Republic of Germany is inner-German relations and *Deutschlandpolitik*: and central to *Deutschlandpolitik* is the maintenance of the unity of the German nation. At the same time the framework for these policies is provided by the Western Alliance in both its military and its political dimensions. The two formally important dates in *Ostpolitk* and *Deutschlandpolitik* are 1970 and 1972. The treaty between the Federal Republic of Germany and Soviet Union of August 1970 was the equivalent of the 'eastern Locarno' advocated by Churchill in 1953: that is, it recognized the 'current realities' of life in post-war central Europe and prepared the way for a *modus vivendi* between the two states in Germany. Then, in December 1972 the Basic Treaty (*Grundvertrag*) between the Federal Republic and the German Democratic Republic marked a deep *caesura* in the post-war history of the Federal Republic. Relations between the two German states were placed on a new footing of mutual recognition of each other's sovereignty. At the same time, each treaty was accompanied by the 'letter concerning German unity' to the Soviet and East German government respectively. The Federal Republic insisted on its right 'to work for a state of peace in Europe in which the German nation will regain its unity through free self-determination'.

Shortly after the treaty of 1972 a prominent Christian Democratic (CDU) MP, Dr Kurt Birrenbach, chairman of the board of the Thyssen steel company, asked Dr Henry Kissinger, then National Security Adviser to President Nixon, how the United States viewed the future of *Deutschlandpolitik*. Kissinger replied: 'The Federal Republic of Germany does not have the power to pursue its *Ostpolitik* on a purely national basis. Without the military umbrella of the alliance it would be endangered especially over Berlin, but also in its very existence.' According to Kissinger, West German security rested on the support of her allies, above all the United States. The success of *Ostpolitik* depended entirely on the support of the Western Alliance. 'Failing this, the Federal Republic would be unable to motivate the Soviet Union to compromise.' Kissinger's analysis survived his departure from office. It underlines the limits within which *Ostpolitik* and *Deutschlandpolitik* have to operate if they are not to endanger and disrupt the post-war European settlement and, within this framework, the existence of the Federal Republic of Germany.

Chancellor Konrad Adenauer's great achievement between 1949 and 1963 was to anchor West Germany's fate in the West. The achievement of his successors, notably Social Democratic Chancellor Willy Brandt (1969–74), was to open the door to the East. Thereafter *Deutschlandpolitik* was much less dramatic than many outsiders believed. It sought to honour the accords signed in the early 1970s and, when necessary, to remind everybody, inside Germany and outside, of their stipulations. The operative aim of *Deutschlandpolitik* under the Social Democratic–Liberal (SPD–FDP) coalition of Chancellor Helmut Schmidt (1974–82), and then of the new Christian Democratic–Liberal (CDU/CSU–FDP) coalition of Chancellor Helmut Kohl (from 1982), was not reunification on Western conditions or neutralism on Eastern conditions. German unity through free self-determination remains a historical objective, but the agenda of international politics today is different. Like the German Democratic Republic, the Federal Republic forms part of the global balance. In the view of successive governments, the Federal Republic is too large to act as a 'go-between' without upsetting this global balance and destroying the framework of security that it provides. *Ostpolitik* and *Deutschlandpolitik* remain part of the Federal Republic's central European responsibility, essential to its identity and self-esteem. Nevertheless, the form and scope of *Deutschlandpolitik* continue to depend on the Atlantic Alliance and on European integration.

In view of old and new uncertainties — *'les incertitudes allemandes'* of the French —the Kohl–Genscher government found it necessary in its first statement of policy in October 1982 to stress this wider framework. For the first time in recent German history, the term *raison d'état* was introduced — *'Staatsräson der Bundesrepublik Deutschland'*. The intentions were to clarify the relationship of nationhood and state in Germany, to stress the link between German interests and the Western Alliance, and to outline the conditions for inner-German conflict management. In the view of the new government *Deutschlandpolitik* had drifted into a critical zone and needed fresh conceptual and political analysis and explanation. In this process the function of *Deutschlandpolitik* for Berlin had to be clarified and the long-term perspectives and international implications of *Deutschlandpolitik* to be studied. Pragmatism was seen as the basic condition of a practical *Deutschlandpolitik*. At the same time greater conceptual clarity was necessary both inside and outside Germany. In seeking greater clarity the government faced a problem. *Deutschlandpolitik* is not policy for the open political market place, and not the most suitable of policy areas for the acid test of parliamentary debate. Many unspoken assumptions on which it rests ought to remain unspoken. The dilemma of the German situation is that the Federal Republic's Western allies have a right to know what these silent assumptions are; at the same time it would be counterproductive to expose them to too much open debate.

Fundamentally the system of *Deutschlandpolitik* resembles a chessboard. Both sides have a picture of the opportunities, threats and power projections. After nuclear parity and détente and its agonies, the most remarkable new departure in the 1980s was a certain amount of unrest, both psychological and political, within Germany. It originated from forces of neutralism and radical pacifism, associated in particular with the new Green Party which gained representation in the Bundestag for the first time in 1983. They refused to play the post-war game of reasonable Germans and reasonable Europeans.

The answer to the question of where reality ends and illusion begins in *Ostpolitik* and *Deutschlandpolitik* must start from an analysis of the European chessboard as it developed between 1945 and 1948, when the Iron Curtain finally divided the traditional heartland of Europe. Germany became the point of confrontation between two global and antagonistic systems; and German partition was, for the time being, the only viable alternative to the third world war. Since then the German question has had two aspects. The external aspect has been essentially linked to the architecture of the Soviet land empire and the American sea alliance. The internal aspect relates to the question of the moral and political impact that *Ostpolitik* and *Deutschlandpolitik* have had — and continue to have — for the Federal Republic of Germany. This internal aspect of the German question evolved through stages: first, the emphasis on the provisional character of the Federal Republic pending the eventual reunification of Germany, as laid down in the Basic Law of 1949 and reflected in Article 7 of the Basic Treaty of 1972; and second, 'the end of the post-war period' pronounced in 1965 by Chancellor Ludwig Erhard. This second stage implied a transition from *provisorium* to permanence and a quest for identity directed more towards the existing state than towards the divided nation. Global and European détente fostered dreams of convergence, expressed in academic circles, and of the 're-Europeanization' of Europe. On another level it enabled the Germans to find a means of reducing the amount of human misery that resulted from their country's partition. In addition, détente meant that they could play a more participatory and active diplomatic role than had hitherto been accorded to them.

Deutschlandpolitik had both pragmatic and idealistic features. Pragmatism involved a limitation of the human costs of Germany's partition; managing and containing East–West conflict in a narrow but crucial arena; establishing negotiating power by means of a new network of economic, financial and technological relations; and keeping policies towards the GDR in a status of neither external nor internal relations, in fact as a very special relationship. The idealism of *Deutschlandpolitik* found its expression in the hope of keeping open the question of national unity; in leaving possible answers to be posed in a longer historical horizon; and in the search for a European framework for self-determination and a stable order of peace. In *Deutschlandpolitik* pragmatism and idealism were interdependent. Over the last decade a consensus emerged about this kind of *Deutschlandpolitik* and *Ostpolitik* amongst the leaders of the major parties — CDU/CSU, FDP and SPD.

In agreement with the Federal Republic's Western allies, reunification was the leitmotiv of the first post-war decade. With the 'new Eastern policy' (*neue Ostpolitik*) of the early 1970s and the letters concerning German unity of 1970 and 1972, the means — self-determination, freedom and peace — became equal in rank to the final objective of German unity. This change was more than a nuance of principle. It was a new departure, though signs could be found as early as 1958 when Adenauer tried to come to terms with the post-war situation by offering full recognition of Russian territorial gains in Eastern and central Europe in exchange for an 'Austrian' status for the GDR.

Towards the West the German question has always been 'Europeanized', both in theory and in practice. In this way the essential Atlantic and European interests of the Federal Republic were made compatible with the perspective of German nationhood. From 1945 onwards Adenauer emphasized Atlantic security and European integration first, and German unity second. During the initial phase of the Federal Republic, after 1949, *Deutschlandpolitik* was a footnote to *Westpolitik*. By the 1980s it remained still a dependent variable, and necessarily so, as at every stage *Deutschlandpolitik* has been conditioned and determined by changes in the global system. At the same time Germany has been one of the crucial elements in shaping that system. For the Federal Republic *Ostpolitik*, and hence *Deutschlandpolitik*, bind the German past to a radically altered present and shape the terms of its future.

The German Democratic Republic

For a long time the Western policy and *Deutschlandpolitik* of the GDR involved little more than a ritual Socialist Unity Party (SED) commitment to a long-term perspective of a Germany reunited under socialism. There was no independence of the Kremlin. Faced by her rich, efficient and self-assured neighbour in the West, the arrogant statements of the SED power elite reflected an underlying anxiety. In conformity with this long-term perspective the constitution of the GDR was revised in 1974 in order to accentuate the dividing line between the bourgeois nation and the socialist nation, to justify the Berlin Wall of 1961 and to eliminate finally all traces of German nationhood (even the word itself). The GDR was willing and quite happy to pay the price of its own denationalization so that it could reap the fruits of détente and find recognition as 'the second German state'.

The perspective of the SED on *Deutschlandpolitik* changed during the later part of the 1970s. New symbols and signals indicated more self-assurance in dealing with the Federal Republic and more sense of the GDR's autonomy when dealing with German history, the German nation, and Germany. In the East as well as in the West, the term 'identity' crept into the political vocabulary. On the whole, the consequences for *Deutschlandpolitik* were positive. Effective negotiations need partners whose terms of reference are calculable and who themselves operate within a framework of continuity and identity. However, since the late 1970s, *Deutschlandpolitik* was boosted not only by such psychological changes but also, and more importantly, by the Polish crisis and the economic instability of the CMEA countries. Both these developments created enormous problems for the GDR. At the same time they gave more political leeway to East Berlin. The insistence of the GDR regime on its sovereignty is not only directed towards the West. It reflects also long-term aspirations for its relations with the Soviet Union. The cancellation of Erich Honecker's projected visit to Bonn in September 1984 could be read as an indication that East Berlin was weak and had no leeway. However, it could also be interpreted as a sign that the Kremlin was worried about the political ambitions of its most crucial satellite in Eastern Europe, and wanted to set a symbol, thus diminishing the standing of Honecker both among his fellow leaders and in the eyes of the East German population.

Soviet dominance can still be seen very clearly, even if the GDR is no longer run by the Soviet Embassy '*Unter den Linden*' — as one prominent East German leader recently pointed out. Economic and security interests have developed their own momentum. In both these fields the GDR has made full use of *Westpolitik*. There has been a divergence of interests between the GDR and the Kremlin. An element of national communism has surfaced and is more visible in the field of symbolism, monuments and historical concepts than in the *arcana imperii*. In a system where administration and interpretation of history is part of the power game historical signals have more meaning than in the West. The SED is shifting towards a cautious and complex *Deutschlandpolitik* that has little to do with reunification or an immediate desire to swallow the larger German state — notwithstanding long-term objectives. Its *Deutschlandpolitik* represents an attempt at crisis management in both political and economic terms. Correspondingly, the position of the West German government has become more complicated. Neither Bonn nor East Berlin is allowed to forget, even for one moment, that the Kremlin is watching them. Nevertheless, an element of greater calculability and reliability has been added to inner-German relations.

Of course, the SED leadership will not place its own power at risk. It will try instead everything possible to keep well and alive the special relationship with the Federal Republic, so infinitely profitable and absolutely irreplaceable. Long before the Basic Treaty of 1972 West Germany's membership of the European Community in 1957, and even West Germany's integration into the Western military alliance in 1955, had given the East Germans an inconspicuous though vested interest in the status quo. There is, additionally, no alternative to economic cooperation with the West, especially the Federal Republic, as the Soviet Union has indicated, publicly and privately, that there will be no financial umbrella for any of its satellite states in trouble. In fact, more proletarian solidarity is being required from the GDR. The result has been a stubborn insistence by the East Germans that specialization of production and division of labour within CMEA should not go too far. Otherwise the GDR would have little to offer on Western markets. The East German population does not like the aggressive noises coming from the Politburo in Moscow. However, it is not so much respect for public sentiments as a clear idea of international advantage that made the

SED leadership reluctant to join in the propaganda exercise orchestrated by the Kremlin after the breakdown of the Geneva talks on the 'Euromissiles' in 1983. The SED has not neglected its West German agents, partisans and fellow-travellers and will continue to finance them generously. The broad strategy emphasizes, however, cooperation rather than confrontation.

The policy of the Federal Republic is to stabilize a network of interests through a range of agreements. This policy is reciprocated in East Berlin. Both sides will, of course, continue to have different, even mutually exclusive ideas about short-term benefits and long-term objectives. Thus, the questions of principle pronounced by Honecker in 1980 in the East German city of Gera will hang over but not endanger the relationship. The GDR needed them to underline its differences from the Federal Republic and gain more leverage *vis-à-vis* the West. The *modus vivendi* was, however, too comfortable and irreplaceable to be put at risk — and still is.

The equation of *Deutschlandpolitik*

West German *Deutschlandpolitik* has never aimed at changing the antagonistic partnership of the superpowers, either before or after the change of power in Bonn in 1982. Within this antagonism the German question is seen as one element amongst others. The two states in Germany would overrate their proper significance if they sought to use *Deutschlandpolitik* as leverage on important issues beyond their borders. A reasonable and rational state of *Deutschlandpolitik* is, of course, one of the prime conditions for stabilizing the global chessboard. Even more, it is a consequence of such stability. For this reason in particular the Germans tend to find it difficult to part with détente.

Bonn's *Deutschlandpolitik* cannot eliminate or change the antagonism without putting at risk its own support and framework. However, it can contribute, in a most sensitive area, to managing the antagonism reasonably. This dialetical structure of the German question can be utilized to promote stability. As the global antagonism in the centre of Europe implies acute dangers for both sides, there is a common interest in limiting the conflict and keeping it under control, especially in Berlin. This common interest was amply demonstrated in the two great Berlin crises of the post-war period (1948–9 and 1958–62) and, again, when the Quadripartite Agreement on Berlin was signed in September 1971. This ambiguity not only provides the need for *Deutschlandpolitik* but also defines its limitations. A caveat must be pronounced: as *Deutschlandpolitik* is an important part of domestic political consensus in West Germany, and as it cannot function without the cooperation of the Eastern side, it renders any West German government vulnerable to subtle Eastern pressures. However, as yet no government has found a suitable alternative.

Why is *Ostpolitik* important? The answer is that without *Ostpolitik* there can be no *Deutschlandpolitik*. For the West Germans *Ostpolitik* is a matter of their identity, of their continuity, of projecting the image of the West into the East, of preserving a special relationship, and, of course, of keeping alive the equation that secures the viability of Berlin. In the framework of *Deutschlandpolitik* economic issues count for much less than is commonly believed; the motives of conflict management and conflict control count for much more. As Honecker said, *Schadensbegrenzung* (damage limitation) is the name of the game. *Deutschlandpolitik* cannot possibly aim at changing the world order. It has to accept the world as it is and work for piecemeal solutions. A long time will be needed to achieve sufficient changes of quantity in interaction that a change of quality ensues. *Deutschlandpolitik* has to be pragmatic because it is a dependent variable of the global conflict. The operating code of *Deutschlandpolitik* is to bring strengths and weaknesses of both sides into an equation — not to change the nature of this equation, at least not in the short term. It would be a fatal illusion to believe that *Deutschlandpolitik* could, at any time, be simply a matter for the two German states. The view of successive West German governments has been that the search for the neutralization of the two states as an aim of policy would, in all probability, bring instability and incalculability rather than peace to the world. *Deutschlandpolitik* can work hard for small solutions. However, any ambition for global changes, or, even worse, the attempt to mediate between the two main protagonists in the global conflict, would be counterproductive and would isolate the Federal Republic from the Western Alliance. The scope and the substance of *Deutschlandpolitik* can never exceed the fundamental and common interests of the Alliance. If it did, the result would be isolation and an almost complete dependence on the good will — or ill will — of the Soviet Union, the last thing for which any West German government aims.

Deutschlandpolitik remains part of the global antagonism. Its responsibility is the regulation, the minimization and the control of the East–West conflict *in* central Europe because the conflict is, to a large extent, a conflict *about* central Europe and will remain so for the forseeable future. One can ask whether the pragmatism of *Deutschlandpolitik* has not been made possible by the very fact that the ultimate objectives, self-determination or reunification or both, have been set, by silent agreement, in a historical time frame. The same very old and very new German question looms behind all *Deutschlandpolitik*: who controls Germany, and where do the Germans belong? This German question was the key European issue at the Treaty of Westphalia (1648), at the Vienna Congress (1815), at the end of the First World War, when the global system was established for the first time, and at the Potsdam Conference (1945). It has remained one of the crucial problems of the world to this present day.

The German question

The prospects and limits of *Deutschlandpolitik* are determined by the fact that the German question concerns above all the Germans but that it is not their exclusive property. Never in history has it been in their hands alone, least so in divided Germany. The partition of Germany is also the partition of Europe and of the world. At the heart of *Deutschlandpolitik* is the search to reduce the consequences of partition and to secure the freedom of Berlin. However, because *Deutschlandpolitik* is conflict management within the global antagonism, it remains what it has always been, a dependent variable of world politics. If the Germans were to rebel against this condition, as the homeless Right and the far Left suggest, the price would be the security of the Federal Republic, Berlin included. The status of Berlin, the partition of Germany, the integration of the Federal Republic into Western Europe and of the GDR into the Soviet bloc, are interdependent like the elements of a complicated mobile. No element can be put into motion without all others being affected. Nevertheless, the points at which the mobile is fastened are Washington and Moscow, not Bonn and East Berlin.

Deutschlandpolitik remains a critical issue in world politics. The consequences are obvious. First, the relationship with East Berlin can never be substantially better than the relationship with Moscow; every step in *Deutschlandpolitik* needs the approval of the Kremlin. Another consequence is that the Federal Republic cannot at any time throw more weight into the scales of the East than she has in the scales of the West in the form of confidence and influence. Even if half of the education ministers of the West German *Länder* ban history as a school subject, the nature of *Deutschlandpolitik* and the geographical situation of their country does not permit the Germans to forget for one moment that they experienced a total war and a total defeat and that the partition of Germany became inevitable when none of the victorious Allied powers was able to add the whole of the country to its sphere of influence. *Deutschlandpolitik* can succeed only in so far as it asks for the possible, not the desirable.

What is possible must be pursued with energy, tenacity and reason. The limiting factor has always been, and will continue to be, the borderline between the two systems. *Deutschlandpolitik* that aims for more, and ignores the antagonism in which Germany has been, and will continue to be, the top prize, incurs the risk of losing support in the West and of having to hope for fair weather in Moscow.

The early stages of *Deutschlandpolitik*

The German question has always been a central, probably the key problem of Europe. Since 1917 the German question has become a global question and will remain so to the end of history, whether Germany is divided or not. Georges Bidault, Foreign Minister under General de Gaulle, said in 1946: 'Germany has been the decisive factor in forging the alliance, and in forcing it apart.' Hitler had in fact brought about the most unlikely alliance of the twentieth century, that between the United States and the Soviet Union. They were divided by the German question when Germany was no longer a subject of world politics but an assemblage of leftovers of the Third Reich. Between 1945 and 1948 the anti-Hitler coalition fell apart and with it the 'One World' concept of President Roosevelt. The post-war political system of Europe emerged.

Every stage of this development shaped the present situation in Germany and Europe as a constituent element. *Deutschlandpolitik* runs on historical rails. Though it aims to widen these rails, the predicament of Germany is that they must be respected. The actions of Hitler's Reich had formed the wartime coalition, while the German question divided the victors; Germany was occupied, carved up and unable to act. The German question existed, irrespective of the strength and influence of the Germans. The compromises at Potsdam were obsolete before the ink had dried, and the conflict over Germany and in Germany drove a wedge into the coalition. Since then, the more the conflicts over China and her Pacific periphery, and over the Near East and the Eastern Mediterranean, antagonized the United States and the Soviet Union, the more the control of Germany seemed to suggest the answer to the question of who would inherit the earth.

In 1904 the British geographer, Halford Mackinder, wrote that Germany was the great 'Heartland' power of Europe, and that Russia was the 'pivot state'. Russia would be an overwhelming world power if Germany's potential were added to her own, say if Germany were to ally herself with Russia. From 1917 onwards German–Soviet relations have remained the world's major problem, whether it was the alliance of Weimar Germany's Reichswehr and the Red Army in the 1920s, or the Hitler–Stalin non-aggression pact of 1939, or Hitler's attempt to conquer Russia, or the Soviet Union's attempt to project its power westwards into Europe. The same geopolitical and strategic problem continues to confront post-war European diplomacy and to alarm 'the peninsular states' of Western Europe. *Deutschlandpolitik* cannot solve this problem. It can only attempt to control the underlying conflicts and to make its consequences tolerable for the nation most affected, the Germans, and for their neighbours.

When the Allied condominium finally collapsed in 1948, any hope of Germany unity was lost. The Soviet Union had inaugurated a revolution from above in 1945 and prepared for a long time the formation of a communist regime in its zone of occupation. By contrast, the American Marshall Plan of 1947 and the West German currency reform introduced in June 1948 promised a different Europe. At that time German unity could be purchased only at the price of a third world war. The first Berlin crisis was the last. Neither the Germans nor the Western Allies and Stalin would take such a risk. Not even Germany as a whole seemed to be worth this most terrible price. The vast majority of Germans were greatly relieved that they were spared another war; indeed many feared, until the end of the Korean War, that it would come.

The question of Germany's future became one of the leitmotivs of the cold war. He who could determine the answer and engrave his solution into the map of Europe would hold the balance of world power. In its long history the German question never belonged less to the Germans than during those thousand days when allies turned into enemies, from the capitulation of the Wehrmacht in May 1945 to the Soviet blockade of the Western sectors of Berlin in 1948. During this period the political map of contemporary Europe was drawn.

The best prospect for the West Germans seemed to be to accept what had happened, whilst making the reservation that their new state in the West was only a *provisorium* until the day of German unity, and to consolidate the Western German fragment and make it the democratic, prosperous core state for a future unified Germany. The claim of nationhood was based on the ethics of human rights and of national self-determination. For a long time *Deutschlandpolitik* meant waiting for the decline of the Soviet land empire, utilizing the pressure of the cold war to stabilize the West German lifeboat and counting the days until '*die Zone*' ('the one') would ask for permission to come on board. Well into the 1960s the term '*die Zone*' was used to minimize the existence and impact of the GDR.

Double containment

The Federal Republic's success was based on being part of American global containment strategy against the Soviet Union, formulated in the Truman Doctrine of 1947, realized in the following years, and intensified by the Berlin blockade of 1948 and the Korean War of 1950. The West German government of Konrad Adenauer understood that postponement of German unity for a long time was part of the price that had to be paid for security and prosperity in the West. It paid the price with a remarkable degree of realism. Every day the mass exodus from the GDR confirmed its view that the Germany of the Germans was in the West.

However, containment had two faces for the West. On the one hand, it meant the cold war and American troops to protect Western Europe from Soviet ambitions and invasion. On the other hand, the West Europeans were traumatized by Germany. They feared the re-emergence of another Reich, they remembered German–Soviet *rapprochement* with the Rapallo Treaty of 1922 and the ambiguities of the Weimar Republic's foreign policies, and they assumed that national partition and the territorial losses in the East were reason enough for German incalculability. Double containment was the answer. In both cases the West Germans, whether they liked it or not, were accorded a leading role: as *part* of containment against the Soviet Union, and as the *object* of containment within Western Europe.

In the bipolar global system of the early post–war years the German question had found an ambiguous answer. The Basic Law of 1949 embodied the claim of the West German state to be the real and democratic home of the Germans and the guardian of German unity. At the same time the *raison d'état* of the Federal Republic of Germany was founded on the security guarantees by the United States and on integration of the country into the value system, the monetary framework and the economic exchanges of the West. This development was sealed by anti-totalitarian consensus and an evolving agreement among the West Germans that there would and should be no more German *Sonderweg* ('deviation'). The enthusiasm for the West complemented the hope to find reunification in the West and through the West. '*Was tun, wenn der Russe kommt?*': 'What are we to do if the Russians come?' For a long time this question betrayed West German anxieties. General Hans Speidel used these words in an introduction to a long memorandum for Adenauer on

German rearmament. Hitler was the German trauma; Stalin was the German fear. The answer was found, in both cases, in the West.

Though containment and Western integration became part of the German consensus, the process was also very much a product of global forces. The question of European security lay in the hands of the Americans, and in their hands alone, once the French Fourth Republic rejected the proposed European Defence Community in 1954. René Pleven, the French Prime Minister, had anticipated in this 'grand decision' that there would be German soldiers once again. For him the answer was to integrate German forces in a supranational force in order to control them. The same basic principle had inspired the Schuman Plan of 1950 for the European Coal and Steel Community, and in a modified form it governed the first decade of the European Economic Community and EURATOM after 1957. In order to integrate her German neighbour France paid in terms of her economic sovereignty and combined what was economically sensible with the political vision of an integrated Europe. However, what worked well in the economic sphere, at least until the slowdown of the process of integration in the 1970s, never worked in the military sphere. Once the shock of the Korean War had been overcome, and Dien Bien Phu had fallen to the Vietminh, the French National Assembly insisted on salvaging some French sovereignty from the wreckage. The first result was the failure of the European Defence Community; the second was the development of an independent French nuclear deterrent (the *force de frappe*), a kind of ultimate strategic reserve against *'les incertitudes allemandes'*, but also *'les incertitudes américaines'*.

Western European security could not be established and guaranteed on the terms of the West Europeans. It rested on two main factors: that the United States guaranteed the status quo, and that the German question could not be solved and thus reunification would be postponed for a long time. The emerging *pax americana* allowed the Europeans to take a leave of absence from the realities of their precarious situation on the western shores of the Eurasian continent and enabled them to seek their national identities: the British hoping to preserve the stardust of Empire, the French developing their *sanctuaire* within the hexagon, while for a long time the West Germans operated on the assumption that someday, somehow, Western integration would be followed by German unity. The first phase of the pose-war period in Europe was determined by double containment. Integration and interdependence were added in the 1950s.

The weakness of the Soviet empire was underlined by the rebellions in Eastern Europe: in East Germany in 1953 and in Hungary and Poland in 1956. The strength of the Soviet Union was, however, demonstrated by the explosion of its first H-bomb in 1953 and by the launch of the Sputnik and the first test of an intercontinental missile in 1957, thereby breaking the American monopoly. Among the consequences were the second great crisis over Berlin and a profound change in the structure of the bipolar global system, and within it of the German question. The Krushchev ultimatum of 1958, threatening to conclude a separate peace treaty with the GDR and calling for a new status for Berlin as a demilitarized 'free city', was followed by the building, in 1961, of the Berlin Wall despite its four-power status. Was growing Soviet power a chance to end confrontation? Or would the bitterness of the cold war escalate into a hot war? The second Berlin crisis did not provide a conclusive answer. The answer seemed clearer with the Cuban missile crisis of 1962 when the United States confronted the Soviet Union's deployment of medium-range missiles on the offshore island. Here both superpowers learned that there was nothing between themselves and nuclear annihilation other than their common interest in survival. The danger of war and the reality of nuclear parity were the parents of détente. The dual crises of Berlin and Cuba were followed, a year later, by the installation of the 'hot line' between the White House and the Kremlin and the Nuclear Test Ban Treaty that stopped nuclear tests in the atmosphere.

Détente and the New Departure

The Federal Republic of Germany had emerged together with the bipolar global system. If détente became the new formula for global management *à deux*, the German question would have a different role and function. Would the foundations of the post-war European order last, and with them the basis of the Federal Republic? This question was in the background. The foreground was dominated by uncertainties about what détente really meant: for the United States the recognition of nuclear parity and a means to limit global conflict; for de Gaulle's France the promise of more national independence through '*détente, entente, coopération*'; and for the Federal Republic the fear that American guarantees would weaken and the foundations of its political culture would be shaken. The role of *Deutschlandpolitik* had to change. Whilst Bonn feared uncertainty in the East, it feared even more isolation in the West as the last outpost of the cold war. Such a situation would have been bad enough for the Federal Republic; it would have put the position of Berlin at risk.

Under the Christian Democratic Chancellors Erhard (1963–6) and Kurt Kiesinger (1966–9) Bonn discovered that détente promised more freedom of manœuvre. CDU politicians noted with concern that the consequences would be a gain in the international standing of the GDR and a departure from the *Ostpolitik* of Chancellor Adenauer. The Social Democrats saw this price as inevitable. As foreign minister in the Erhard government, Gerhard Schröder pursued a cautious 'policy of movement' in order to achieve 'an opening to the East'. Between 1969 and 1972 the new Social Democratic–Liberal coalition government under Willy Brandt (as Chancellor) and Walter Scheel (as Foreign Minister) pursued détente and *Ostpolitik* as priorities against the background of a precarious Bundestag majority at home. The achievements were a reduction in the pressure of the Soviet Union on the Federal Republic, stabilization of the position of Berlin and new opportunities to project the image of the West into the East. The Allies were informed and consulted, but the scepticism of the Americans was brushed aside. In the West misgivings loomed large that in different circumstances the new *Deutschlandpolitik*, constructed properly within the framework of *Ostpolitik*, could and would gather a momentum of its own, propelled by nationalism and neutralism.

Berlin was the key and the bolt of the German question. The Quadripartite Agreement on Berlin of 1971 had many functions: it anchored the American presence on the European continent with Russian consent; it guaranteed the status quo; it put twenty-five years of conflict between East and West into cold storage; it reminded the Germans of the limits of *Deutschlandpolitik*; it saved Bonn from having fully to recognize the GDR and accept the partition of Germany; and at the same time it opened the way to a new *modus vivendi* with East Berlin. The transit traffic agreement of 1971 and a whole basket of complementary measures were the consequence. The German question was almost buried under a pile of treaty obligations and tacit assumptions. The system of double containment was sealed by the Gordian knot of the various agreements concluded between 1969 and 1972. But was this the end of the German question? In 1972 Kissinger mentioned the possibility that 'one day a German nationalism could emerge and the Federal Government would manoeuvre between East and West'. In Kissinger's view, a latent incompatibility existed between West Germany's national objectives and her ties with the Atlantic and European communities. This fear was only mildly reduced in the following years.

A final goodbye to the German question?

National emotions in *Ostpolitik* were conspicuous by their absence, though they seem to have motivated some of the actors. But what would happen if such emotions were to find a mass following one day? What would happen if German nationalism, together with all the other European nationalisms, were to return to its origins? While the *neue Ostpolitik* cast the German question into a new international setting, many Europeans and Americans asked themselves whether the containment of the German question also meant a final goodbye to German nationalism. From where might new emotional forces come? Where would the German quest for identity end? It was only in the 1970s that these questions began to generate answers and that the more nervous among West Germany's allies began to ask: how Western is West Germany?

In the 1970s four factors were to bring about a new relationship between the German question and German identity. First, there was a shift in the relationship with the United States. The United States gave weak leadership and uncertain signals to the Western Alliance. The founding fathers of the Federal Republic, who had so visibly and successfully identified with American values, were put on the defensive by the Vietnam War and the Watergate episode. In the economic sphere, the long fall of the dollar marked a decline of American economic strength. In the strategic field, the Europeans found extended deterrence no longer convincing and asked for new guarantees in the face of Soviet deployment of a new generation of tactical and intermediate-range nuclear missiles, the SS-20s. New conflicts arose about technology transfer to the East, most notably over the gas pipeline deal with the Soviet Union. After having been, for a long time, the most enthusiastic admirers of America, West Germans began to discover her ugly side.

Second, in the late 1960s Bonn had been very reluctant to jump on the bandwagon of détente and had insisted that NATO's Harmel report of 1967 made military strength the condition of the new *modus vivendi* with the East and included the appropriate words about Germany. In the 1970s and early 1980s it was Bonn that wanted to preserve détente, if not globally, at least regionally. Whilst the United States conducted a post-mortem on détente after Afghanistan and Poland, Bonn insisted that the patient was well and alive. Meanwhile, the CSCE process, and the Helsinki Final Act of 1975, put *Deutschlandpolitik* into a wider European framework. At the same time the government of Chancellor Helmut Schmidt slipped into an ambiguous role: in the Eastern direction the overriding aim was to keep détente alive; in the Western direction the aim was to prevent a decoupling of American security from European security, and especially German security, as a consequence of Soviet deployment of intermediate-range nuclear weapons.

Thirdly, the structure and the mood of European politics were indeed changed in the late 1970s by the Soviet missile deployment. It reminded the Europeans of the grim reality of the nuclear balance and of the fact that the United States, formerly the holder of the balance, had itself become a vulnerable part of it. Whilst European peace movements made their presence felt around American military installations, European governments talked about the dangers of decoupling and insisted — Schmidt in particular — on American deployment of cruise and Pershing missiles. The dual-track decision of NATO in 1979 widened the window of psychological vulnerability of Western Europe, by encouraging Soviet attempts to undermine the Western European security consensus. In the middle of the gravest East–West crisis since Cuba the quest for security became the driving force of a new neutralism with nationalist undertones.

Finally, anti-Americanism, in its many divergent aspects, and neutralism provided the energy fuelling a conflict that in the Federal Republic — in spite of the 5 per cent clause in the electoral law — produced a new political party, the Greens, and drove the Social Democrats into a crisis of identity. No feature was stronger in this double party crisis than a generation gap that threatened to develop into a real generation conflict. Between the founders of the Federal Republic and the ideologists of an alternative lifestyle no interest is shared, no hope finds common ground. They are most divided by the role of United States; what for one side is a lifeline is for the other the hangman's rope. The pragmatism and the silent assumptions of *Deutschlandpolitik* of the last decade found little understanding among the protesting activists who made neutralism their credo. Meanwhile in the West suspicions grew that out of this new German unrest a distinct separation from the West might develop, letting loose forces that could overthrow the postwar settlement of Europe. On the surface all these fears were greatly exaggerated. However, it cannot be overlooked that the German party system has become less calculable, that Germans have been reminded of their bizarre situation at the divided heart of Europe, and that the panic of a small minority of the population was amplified by the very fact that the geostrategic role of Germany has never ceased to have decisive implications for the rest of Europe.

Conclusions

In the mid-1980s *Deutschlandpolitik* faces neither crisis nor collapse. Nevertheless, the new factors that have been outlined in this chapter brought about changes in the frame of reference of *Deutschlandpolitik*. They raised its status and made it more dependent on domestic consensus; they also emphasized to the government the need for Western European integration and for gaining thereby negotiating power *vis-à-vis* the East. More dynamism, wider global implications, and greater dangers were being added to the chess game of *Deutschlandpolitik*.

The focal importance of *Deutschlandpolitik* for the Federal Republic of Germany and the Western Alliance remains unchanged. However, the progress of *Deutschlandpolitik* is still to be measured in millimetres rather than kilometres. The less it aims for a fundamental change in the position of both German states within their respective alliances, the more it can serve to improve and stabilize their relations. Both sides have their historical objectives, and these remain mutually incompatible. Moreover, the West German historical objectives presuppose a fundamentally changed European, and indeed global system. *Deutschlandpolitik* can only work if the historical objectives are left to history. When one surveys the grim border between the two German states, and the ocean of human misery behind it, one realizes that the immediate necessities are sufficient to keep *Deutschlandpolitik* busy for decades. In the view of the West German government, to speak of normalization in a civilized sense, in the meaning of the Helsinki Final Act, is a far-distant dreamland for inner-German relations.

In the final analysis the framework and the very condition of *Deutschlandpolitik* is the Western Alliance. In its mechanics *Deutschlandpolitik* aims at nothing other than overcoming the worst aspects of Germany's partition. In its substance it must try hard to maintain that dialogue of the deaf that is going on between East and West and to fill the equation that is so essential for *Deutschlandpolitik* on both sides with economic and political substance — even if the instrument is a teaspoon rather than a ladle. Nowhere more than in inner-German relations is the truth of Max Weber's observation clearer: policy is the drilling of thick boards and needs staying power and a sense of proportion.

6 Soviet–GDR relations and European détente

Martin McCauley

Andrei Gromyko, addressing the USSR Supreme Soviet in 1975, claimed that one of the results of the Helsinki Final Act was that the German question had ceased to exist.[1] This statement conceded that the Soviet Union had battled unsuccessfully with the problem for three decades. Subsequent events were to prove the Soviet Foreign Minister's assessment much too optimistic. The German problem, from the Soviet point of view, had not been solved and, as we shall see, has still not been solved.

The Soviet Union and the German question in historical perspective

At the Potsdam Conference in July–August 1945 Stalin made the Soviet position on Germany abundantly clear: never again must that country be permitted to become so militarily strong that it could launch another attack on the Soviet Union. The security of the Soviet Union took precedence over German needs and aspirations. The Potsdam Agreement placed responsibility for German security in the hands of the Americans, British and Soviets. It was seen at the time as a prelude to a peace conference that would place Germany again under a German government and permit the occupying powers to withdraw their troops. The Great Powers, of course, would be afforded guarantees that Germany would never again go to war against them.

Had the whole of Germany been occupied by the United States, Britain and France a peace treaty would eventually have emerged. The French would have dragged their feet and insisted on clear guidelines about intervention by the signatory powers when they deemed Germany to be a military threat to their own security. The presence of the Soviets complicated matters and reduced the chances of a peace treaty and a united Germany since Moscow had to be convinced that such a solution would meet its own security needs. The British government was fearful that Soviet influence would cross the River Elbe and was reluctant to see a united Germany until communist influence could be contained.

The Soviet Union espoused two policies towards Germany after 1945. One was aimed at keeping Germany a unit and favoured unification, but the other favoured the evolution of the Soviet zone of occupation into a people's democracy, closely bound to the Soviet Union. The former solution was infinitely superior since the latter opened up a Pandora's box of national, political, economic and military problems. How was the Soviet Union to ensure that its third of Germany became so attractive to Germans across the River Elbe that it was recognized as the model for a future all-German state?

The Soviets vacillated about the future of Germany until 1955 when they came to the conclusion that two German states in one German nation had to be accepted. Konrad Adenauer was invited to Moscow and diplomatic relations with the Federal Republic were established. All this did not prevent West Germany becoming a member of NATO, a bitter blow to the Soviets, and an equal partner in the Western Alliance.

In retrospect it is clear that the Soviets demonstrated little skill in their handling of German affairs. If their strategic goal was clear, a united, socialist Germany closely allied to Moscow, their tactical manœuvring was at times difficult to comprehend. The Soviet response to the currency reform in western Germany and West Berlin in June 1948 was inept. Had Stalin been willing to keep to the broad agreement arrived at with the ambassadors of the occupying powers in Moscow, he would have secured part of his goal of incorporating West Berlin in the Soviet zone. There would have been every likelihood of West Berlin eventually falling into Soviet hands. The Berlin blockade was a diplomatic disaster and led directly to the formation of the Federal Republic and NATO. Another missed opportunity occurred in 1952 when the Soviet Union initiated a debate about a unified, neutral Germany but lacked the resolve to make the concessions that would have brought it about.

After the Berlin blockade the Soviet Union lost the initiative in

German affairs and had to react to events in the Western zones. The founding of the GDR in October 1949 and the incorporation of the National People's Army (NVA) in the Warsaw Pact provide examples of this state of affairs. Indeed so unprepared were the Soviets and East Germans in 1955 that the NVA was not a founding member of the Warsaw Pact. Despite the potential economic and military power of the GDR it could not match that of the Federal Republic. Only a joint effort by Moscow and East Berlin could contain the expanding influence of Bonn.

The GDR's foreign policy

After 1955 there was a division of labour in the German question. The GDR took over the policy of advocating a united Germany and continued to do so until 1968. The Soviets adopted an offensive policy towards West Germany and tried to wean Bonn away from its Washington ties. These ties only cemented the division of Germany, argued the Soviets. A constant goal was the elimination of Berlin's special status. They continued to talk of a 'German peace settlement' until 1964. Indeed Khrushchev, just before his removal, had been envisaging another German initiative. The erection of the Berlin Wall in 1961, and the introduction of conscription in the GDR the following year, had emboldened the Soviet leader to try to interest Bonn in a coming together of East and West Germany.

The advent of the grand coalition in 1966 and then the Brandt–Scheel government in 1969 transformed the situation. Brandt's *Ostpolitik* — recognition of the two German states in one German nation and a desire to effect reconciliation with Poland and Czechoslovakia — alarmed East Berlin. Until 1968 the GDR had posed as the champion of German unity and had advanced proposal after proposal, safe in the knowledge that Bonn would not accept any invitation to enter into negotiations since such a move would have heralded the diplomatic recognition of the East Berlin regime. The GDR immediately changed its constitution. It was no longer a 'socialist state of the German nation' but a 'socialist state of workers and farmers'. It abandoned its policy of working towards a unified German state. Institutions were renamed: the German Academy of

Sciences became the GDR Academy of Sciences and so on. The volte-face in Bonn had shown up the lack of confidence in the legitimacy of the GDR by the ruling communist party (SED). Walter Ulbricht tried desperately to prevent Poland and Czechoslovakia from reaching agreements with Bonn before the Federal Republic had recognized the GDR in international law.

Until 1968 the basis of the GDR's foreign policy had been a close relationship wih the Soviet Union. Indeed one could say that East Berlin's foreign policy was almost exclusively *Deutschlandpolitik*. Only in partnership with the Soviet Union could it hope to force the Federal Republic to recognize it *de jure*. Paradoxically, East Berlin's insecurity in foreign affairs occurred at a time when economically it was successful. The decade from the mid-1960s to the mid-1970s was the golden era of GDR economic development when living standards rose fast. The New Economic System of Planning and Management, founded on the scientific-technical revolution, promised to make the GDR the shop window of socialism. Along with economic change went ideological innovation as Ulbricht and the SED evolved the concept of developed socialism. This newfound self-confidence, however, did not spill over into foreign affairs.

The Soviets, on the other hand, had the confidence to grasp the opportunities the new *Ostpolitik* and détente offered them in their relations with the United States. Not for the first time did a gulf open up between Soviet and GDR interests. The Moscow Treaty, followed by the Quadripartite Agreement on Berlin, contained too many concessions from the GDR point of view. Ulbricht's objections, however, were in vain and only hastened his own removal as leader. The contretemps between Ulbricht and Brezhnev was not about strategy but about tactics: how best to promote Marxist-Leninist socialism in West Germany. Ulbricht plainly overestimated his own power *vis-à-vis* the new Soviet leadership and had the confrontation occurred five years earlier he might have carried the day. However, by 1970 Brezhnev had become *primus inter pares* and was determined to promote détente even if it involved making a few concessions on Germany. Honecker learnt his lesson, and it was not until a decade later that he tried to outmanœuvre Moscow on the issue of Germany.

The Basic Treaty between the two German states in 1972 was a part of the process of détente and a step on the road to the Helsinki Final Act in 1975. The GDR did achieve one of its basic demands in the Basic Treaty, recognition as a sovereign, independent state in international law. A half-way house was reached on official representation, with each state establishing a permanent mission in the other's capital.

During the 1970s the GDR gradually gained in assurance as it was recognized diplomatically by all leading Western states. Membership of the UN and its agencies then followed. This new-found maturity was expressed in many inner-German agreements as the GDR skilfully built up a network of relations with the Federal Republic. A price had to be paid for the benefits which accrued to East Berlin, and it gradually became easier for West Germans to visit the East. To cope with the flood of visitors the GDR attempted to enforce *Abgrenzung* at a personal level but practised *Annäherung* at the state level.

Between 1972 and 1979 there was no fundamental clash between Soviet–West German and East–West German relations. From a Soviet point of view the most important relations are with the United States. If these relations are good then it is not difficult for the allies of the United States to improve their ties with Moscow. The bipolarity of Soviet foreign policy under Gromyko, who can be identified as the key decision-maker in foreign policy from the mid-1970s to the mid-1980s. inevitably meant that if Soviet–American relations turned sour this would adversely affect both Soviet–German and East–West German relations.

Détente was dealt a mortal blow by the Soviet invasion of Afghanistan and President Jimmy Carter's volte-face in his policy towards the Soviet Union. This was accompanied by the NATO decision to deploy Pershing 2 and cruise missiles in Western Europe unless an INF agreement was reached in Geneva. The GDR did all it could to limit the damage to its relationship with the Federal Republic after the Afghan affair, but the events in Poland in 1980 seriously alarmed it.

The GDR raised dramatically the amount of currency Western visitors had to exchange daily, and in Gera Honecker imposed four demands which would have to be met before inner-German relations could improve. The permanent missions had to be raised to embassy level; GDR citizenship had to be recognized; the GDR–FRG frontier had to run through the middle of the River Elbe; and the centre at Salzgitter that monitored civil rights violations in the GDR had to close.[2] These conditions were maximal demands, and to have fulfilled them West Germany would have needed to alter its constitution and thereby fundamentally change its policy towards the GDR. The Basic Treaty would then have been superseded. Oskar Fischer, GDR Foreign Minister, shortly afterwards warned the Federal Republic that if it did not distance itself from the NATO decision it would soon find all it had achieved over the previous ten years in its relations with East Berlin in 'ruins'.[3]

Such a state of affairs did not materialize because the SED leadership, after sober reflection, came to the conclusion that the GDR would lose more than it would gain from a policy of confrontation. As a small state, the GDR is dependent on its foreign trade for two main reasons. One is that, as a resource-poor country, it needs to import a significant proportion of its raw material and energy needs; the other is that it needs to remain competitive in world markets. GDR planners have come to the conclusion that the Soviet Union cannot supply the high technology necessary for the continued viability of East German industry. Since East Berlin exports predominantly finished goods it needs a high value-added content to cover imported raw material and energy inputs. Hence the GDR needs to maintain and expand its trading links with advanced capitalist countries, first and foremost the Federal Republic. In order to entice Bonn into a profitable economic relationship, East Berlin has had to face the hard truth that it needs gradually to normalize relations at government level and ease the way for better contacts at citizen level between the two parts of Germany. This would serve two purposes: to improve the GDR's own economic position and to raise the legitimacy of the SED regime.

Another important reason why the GDR did not wish to follow the Soviet Union in abandoning détente and initiate an era of military-political confrontation with the Federal Republic was that it realized that it could not survive even a limited nuclear exchange. Even a conventional war would reduce it to rubble. The Soviet

Union could plan, and had to plan, to survive both a conventional and a nuclear war, but not the GDR. While General Heinz Hoffmann, GDR Minister of National Defence, continued to echo Soviet pronouncements that the socialist bloc could not be defeated in a nuclear war, Honecker quietly argued that both German states, situated at the heart of Europe, had a special responsibility to ensure that a war never again began on German soil. The SED leadership became convinced that a policy of confrontation in Western Europe would be counterproductive since it would force NATO countries to close ranks with the United States. Europe's fate would then depend on an improvement in Soviet–American relations. East Berlin thought that the goal of military-strategic parity could be achieved by different methods. It believed that a continuation of the dialogue, of negotiations, of finding compromises promised much more. Hence the East Germans favoured a return to peaceful coexistence as quickly as possible.

East Berlin's anxiety at events in Poland was allayed in December 1981 when General Jaruzelski imposed a 'state of war'. The GDR, through its Minister of National Defence, had even advocated Warsaw Pact intervention in Poland in December 1980, but the aged Brezhnev was not willing to take the risk. Indeed the feeble leadership in Moscow must have irritated the East Germans. Yet it did allow the GDR more leeway in defending its own national interests. As the Soviet leader's physical powers waned in Moscow, so his country lost its way in arms negotiations. Soviet initiatives in Geneva became a thing of the past as everyone waited for Brezhnev to die.

East–West German relations were greatly aided by Chancellor Helmut Schmidt's understanding attitude towards the GDR. He was even on an official visit to the GDR when 'the state of war' was proclaimed. This potentially embarrassing situation was quickly overcome by both German leaders agreeing that Poles had every right to solve their own problems in their own way.

The events of 1983–4

The advent of Andropov presaged good Soviet–GDR relations

despite the fact that the East Germans, like the Bulgarians, had honoured Chernenko in anticipation of his becoming the next Soviet leader. Honecker became the first ruling communist party leader to visit Moscow officially in May 1983, and one result of the visit was the removal of Petr Abrasimov, the sharp-tongued and sharp-witted Soviet envoy in East Berlin. Relations between him and Honecker were rumoured to be so bad that the SED leader had refused to see the ambassador because of his cavalier attitude to protocol. Abrasimov had lost several members of his family during the war and was wont to hold the East Germans as responsible for this as West Germans. He was also suspicious of improving East–West German relations and demanded that the Soviets be given more time to consider the implications of these agreements before they were signed. Abrasimov was replaced by Vyacheslav Kochemasov whom Honecker had first met when the former was a Komsomol official and the latter a leading light in the Free German Youth movement (FDJ). One thing was almost certain about the change: Soviet–GDR relations would be smoother than before, at least at the East Berlin end. Also Andropov had replaced an expert in German affairs, Abrasimov, with a beginner in such matters. The arrival of Andropov promised a more subtle approach to East–West relations and the possibility of a compromise on INF deployment, due to start in December 1983.

During his talks with Andropov, Honecker appears to have convinced him that he could be relied upon to protect traditional Soviet and GDR interests in negotiations with West Germany. This led in the summer to a DM 1 billion loan to the GDR by private West German banks. On the face of it this was an astonishing development but even more surprising was the involvement of Franz-Josef Strauss, the CSU leader, in the negotiations leading up to the loan. How was one to explain the volte-face of this previously vehement critic of the GDR? When one of his critics pointed out that it was not the business of West German capitalism to prop up an ailing East German economy, he turned a deaf ear. This episode was enough to sow the seeds of doubt in the least suspicious of Moscow minds.

While in the Soviet capital Honecker had to make at least one concession. He agreed with Andropov that his planned visit to the Federal Republic in 1983 was inopportune since it might give rise to the impression that East Berlin condoned the deployment of the new missiles in West Germany. Moscow continued to put pressure on Bonn during the summer and autumn of 1983, and during Chancellor Helmut Kohl's visit there Andropov spoke of the erection of a 'palisade of missiles' between the two German states should deployment result. Honecker forwarded an open letter to Kohl in which he wrote of a new 'ice age' in relations and appealed 'in the name of the German people' for a halt to INF deployment.

It was becoming clear to the SED leadership during the autumn of 1983 that the INF deployment was certain to go ahead, short of a breakthrough in Geneva. The Kohl government had committed itself, and the Soviet courting of the peace movement in Western Europe had not produced the expected results. The threats of 'punishment' which would attend deployment had not intimidated any NATO government into submission. In addition, Andropov's health deteriorated at a most inopportune time for the Soviet Union. Soviet policy had no dialysis machine to keep it alive, and paralysis again set in. Moscow's alarm at its own ineffectiveness was instanced by the behaviour of its ambassador, Semenov, in Bonn. He hectored Bundestag leaders and sought to blame them 'for the failure of the INF talks'.[4] Bonn protested to the Soviet Prime Minister, Tikhonov, against this attempt to pressurize its MPs and pointed out that the whole episode had been counterproductive.[5].

When the Federal Republic finally decided to deploy the new missiles the only recourse left to the Soviets was to abandon the Geneva talks. They then began to install SS-21, SS-22 and SS-23 missiles in the GDR and Czechoslovakia, an event which Honecker described as evoking no 'jubilation' among the GDR population. Had the GDR had a choice it would not have permitted deployment. The GDR cannot veto Soviet armaments since according to the Soviet–GDR agreement of 1957 the Soviets do not even have to inform the East Germans of troop or material movements. Two other Warsaw Pact states are on record as having said they would not permit deployment of the new Soviet missiles. They are Hungary and Bulgaria. Hungarian utterances in this regard are in line with other comments in Hungarian media about how much independence socialist countries enjoy in their foreign affairs.

In January 1984 the journal *Tarsadalmi Szemle* carried part of a lecture delivered by Matyas Szuros, a secretary of the CC, Hungarian Socialist Workers' Party, responsible for foreign affairs.[6] Szuros placed 'national' ahead of 'international' interests and maintained 'no organized forum exists that could formulate the communist parties' international interests and common strategy'. He went on to claim that the 'historical traditions of relationships and certain current factors make it possible for relations between individual socialist and capitalist countries to develop even though a deterioration in East–West relations and a diminution of contacts is the general trend'. In other words, small and medium states can bridge the gulf between East and West.

Speaking a few days after the decision by the Bundestag to deploy the missiles, Honecker pointed out: 'It cannot be overlooked that the European system of treaties including the Basic Treaty on relations between the GDR and the FRG has suffered serious damage because of this decision'.[7] However he immediately followed this gloomy analysis with the words: 'We are in favour of limiting the damage as far as possible.' This implied that the purely military step of deploying new Soviet missiles in the GDR would constitute the 'punishment' which the Federal Republic could expect for its deployment. The threat of a new ice age in inner-German relations had simply melted away.

The SED leader appealed for a 'coalition of reason' between the two German states founded on a 'community of responsibility' for peace in Europe. 'It is most important that every opportunity be seized so that reason and realism prevail, so that cooperation and not confrontation come to the fore, and that disarmament gets under way and the process of détente is revived'.[8] Honecker made his contribution to better inner-German relations by allowing those East Germans who had sought refuge in West German embassies in Eastern Europe in a desperate attempt to escape to the West to do so. In the same month a process began which was to result in over 36,000 GDR citizens moving legally to the Federal Republic during 1984, over three times the figure of 1983.

When Honecker and Kohl met in Moscow at Andropov's funeral they reiterated the need to maintain peace in Europe and that the very existence of the two German states depended on it. They promised to work together to ensure that the course of international events did not 'get out of control'. It appeared that if the Soviet Union and the United States could not live amicably together, the GDR and the FRG could.

No immediate Soviet response was forthcoming as Moscow was adjusting to yet another aged, ill leader. Instead the orthodox position was enunciated by the Czechoslovak party daily, *Rude Pravo*, on 30 March 1984. It poured scorn on the idea that small states could play a 'special role' in furthering compromise between the superpowers. Fundamental socialist interests must not be 'sacrificed to momentary "national" interests'. An edited version of the *Rude Pravo* article appeared in the Soviet foreign affairs journal *Novoe Vremya* and a hard-line article along the same lines by a Soviet writer appeared soon after. The new Soviet leader, Konstantin Chernenko, entered the argument. He made the Soviet conditions for a resumption of talks in Geneva very clear. They would only recommence when the Americans had restored the situation that had existed before the deployment of the new missiles.[9] However, when Warsaw Pact states met in Budapest in the same month to consider their response to deployment, the communiqué was verbose and imprecise, a clear indication of lack of agreement.

The occasion of the thirty-ninth anniversary of the defeat of Nazi Germany was seized upon by the Soviet media to launch a violent campaign of abuse against the Federal Republic, the like of which had not been seen since the 1960s. There was nothing new about the accusations of 'revanchism and militarism' and of wishing to set aside the results of the Second World War. They had been levelled many times in the past and served a dual function: to intimidate the Federal Republic and to strengthen socialist bloc cohesiveness. Marshal Nikolai Ogarkov, Chief of Staff of the Soviet Armed Forces, went so far as to claim: 'It looks as though the fascists . . . are openly leading matters towards material preparations for a new world war'.[10] Such statements were a striking departure from the Soviet position on West Germany which had presented Bonn in a different light from Washington ever since the early 1970s. Hitherto the more balanced and 'realistic' West German position had been contrasted with the aggressive, 'adventurist' stance of the Americans. Now both were in the same camp, and East Berlin was being reminded that the primary goal of West German policy was the eradication of socialism in the GDR.

East Berlin gave little prominence to the Soviet charges of revanchism and directed its criticisms not at the Kohl government but at the 'ultras' to be found in West German political life. Kurt Hager, speaking for Honecker at a party plenum, declared that the 'offensive peace commitment and the continuation of a political dialogue', supported without reservation by the GDR population, would continue.[11]

Honecker's worries about peace in Europe surfaced in a speech he made at a reception for the Greek Prime Minister, Papandreou, in East Berlin. 'It would be a tragic misjudgement to seek to solve world problems by military means, including the historic contest between capitalism and socialism. Such a course can only lead to disaster'.[12] This statement was the second reference to the catastrophic consequences of a preventive war by a leading SED politician. The first had been in a book published in December 1983 when Kurt Hager had quoted Bismarck in February 1888. He had expressly warned against a preventive war in the 'interests of the European balance of power and our own future'.[13] No Soviet leader had accused the West of getting ready to launch a preventive war. Ogarkov had merely claimed that the West was 'making material preparations for a new world war'. Do these GDR references to a preventive war imply that someone in the Warsaw Pact was advocating such a course?

East Berlin and Bonn agreed that late September 1984 was a possible date for Honecker's visit to the Federal Republic, and intensive negotiations were set in train to draw up the agenda and itinerary. Then on 25 July it was announced that a further credit of DM 950 million was to be made available to the GDR by West German banks. In return the East Germans were to lift various restrictions on travel between the two countries. This turn of events provoked the first full-blooded attack on the course of East–West German relations in *Pravda* on 27 July. The article by Lev Bezymensky, a seasoned writer on German affairs, was headed 'In the Shadow of American Missiles' and was ostensibly an attack on the 'FRG's new and aggressive policies towards the East' but in reality was mainly directed at East Berlin. Bezymensky contradicted

Honecker's current assessment of inner-German relations, quoting past utterances by him which had been critical of Bonn. *Pravda* also cited Honecker in December 1981 when he had told Kohl's predecessor, Helmut Schmidt, that 'good-neighbourly relations cannot flourish in the shadow of new American nuclear missiles'. Relations between the two German states could not be viewed in isolation since they were characterized by a transition 'on the part of aggressive NATO circles to a broad attack on détente and a "crusade" against socialism'. The new loan was seen as a cynical attempt to 'limit the damage' done to inner-German relations, and the West German attempt to create a 'security partnership' was derided. Though both these expressions were cited as West German, they had in fact emanated from Honecker. The second phrase originated in the West German SPD and was then taken up by the SED leader. The Soviets were making it plain to Honecker, through the columns of the official CPSU newspaper, that they were strongly opposed to his interpretation of inner-German relations.

Nevertheless, the GDR leadership did not back down and a *Neues Deutschland* editorial on 1 August 1984, on the occasion of the ninth anniversary of the signing of the Helsinki Final Act, defended its position. This defence was followed by an article in the GDR foreign affairs monthly *Horizont* which maintained that it was 'natural' for differences of opinion to surface among communist parties on such matters and that these could only be resolved by 'comradely discussion'.[14] After all, the international communist movement was nothing more than a 'voluntary community of equal and independent parties'. *Pravda*, in an editorial, counterattacked on 2 August. It saw the new credit as an attempt to 'disturb the stability of the GDR' and condemned the 'Pharisaical logic' of a policy of attempting 'to limit the damage' done by the INF deployment. Again the expression 'limiting the damage' was attributed to Bonn, but it was Honecker who was being criticized. *Neues Deutschland* did not reprint this editorial.

Honecker vigorously defended the SED position on German affairs in an interview with *Neues Deutschland*. He stated that the GDR was striving 'not to expand the damage resulting from missile deployment but rather to limit it'.[15] He went on to say that the 'GDR attached great importance to [the maintainance of a] dialogue with responsible political circles in the FRG'. He was at pains to distinguish between 'ultras' in West Germany, whom he accused of revanchism, and the Kohl government, and only attacked the former. Honecker also reiterated the Gera demands but did not make them a condition for better relations with the Federal Republic. As far as he was concerned the two German states shared a 'community of responsibility' for the promotion of peace in Europe. On 18 August Tass, the official Soviet news agency, carried a report of Honecker's remarks in English and included the Secretary General's remarks on the need for a political dialogue, on the responsibilities that both states shared for the prosecution of peace and the positive role of inner-German relations on the wider international scene. However, on the following day, a Tass version in Russian omitted all mention of the above points and instead concentrated on Honecker's remarks about the alliance between the GDR and the Soviet Union, the rejection of German reunification and his criticisms of American foreign policy. On 20 August *Neues Deutschland* carried a German translation of the Tass report in Russian, thereby making clear to GDR citizens what the Soviets regarded as unseemly for Soviet citizens to learn. *Neues Deutschland* followed this up the following day by reprinting reactions to Honecker's remarks that had appeared in the party organs in Poland, Czechoslovakia and Bulgaria. The GDR's firmest ally remained Hungary. Now everyone could identify those who sided with and those who sided against the GDR in its dispute with Moscow. Honecker then departed for Bucharest to attend the fortieth anniversary celebrations of the overthrow of fascism in Romania. He was the only ruling Communist Party leader in Eastern Europe to accept Ceauşcu's invitation. The Eat German leader was showing solidarity with a statesman with the longest record of confrontations with Moscow. The Soviets could not have been pleased at this extraordinary spectacle.

This phase represented the high water mark of GDR intransigence. Then Honecker backed away from his imminent visit to the Federal Republic. He seized upon two events to effect a strategic retreat. On 21 August Alfred Dregger, a leading CDU politician, voiced the unease felt by some in his party when he stated in an interview with *Die Welt* that the 'future of the Federal Republic does not depend on whether Herr Honecker pays us the honour of a visit'. East Berlin immediately accused Dregger of attempting to sabotage the forthcoming visit of the SED Secretary General. Chancellor Kohl's presence at a rally of expellees in Braunschweig fuelled the flames of suspicion in the GDR. The planned visit was called off shortly afterwards but the East Germans signalled their desire to continue their dialogue with the West Germans and did not favour a serious deterioration in relations.

During the second half of 1984 Moscow conducted a vigorous campaign against the Federal Republic, accusing it of revanchism, militarism and fascism, including all West Germans in its blanket condemnations. The logic that lay behind the accusations — which had little substance in fact — was to create an atmosphere that would permit the Soviet Union to claim that the Federal Republic was 'preparing for war'. The victorious powers in the Second World War have the right to intervene if a former 'enemy state' is 'returning to a policy of attack'. Such a step by the Soviet Union would have contravened the Potsdam Agreement, articles 53 and 107 of the United Nations Charter and article 2 of the Moscow Treaty between the USSR and the Federal Republic. This last clause binds both signatories to seek a peaceful solution to all disputes. Since there are four victorious powers as far as Germany is concerned, all of them would have to agree that one or both German states was preparing for war. However the Soviet Union argued that the United States and the other NATO powers supported and promoted the emergence of aggressive ideas, revanchism and militarism in West Germany. In this way it could have made out a case for Soviet military intervention in West Germany.

The vehemence of the campaign alarmed the GDR and it refused to join in the chorus of abuse against the West German government. Soviet policy was to intimidate the Federal Republic into repudiating the deployment of the INF missiles and needed to sow the possibility of Soviet military intervention in Bonn's mind. The references by Hager and Honecker to preventive war may be relevant in this context. The reasons for Marshal Ogarkov's dismissal as Chief of Staff of the Soviet Armed Forces in September 1984 have never been made public, but the man who would have presented the case against him would have been Marshal Dmitri Ustinov, the Soviet Minister of Defence. It is also of interest that the campaign was at its most intense when Konstantin Chernenko's health was in rapid decline.

Conclusion

If Soviet policy towards the Federal Republic has been one of confrontation since 1983, then the GDR has pursued dialogue and bridge-building. The Honecker visit to the Federal Republic — which remains one of his priorities — has had to be postponed twice. The GDR has continued to expand its international role and to demonstrate its new-found self-confidence. Honecker's visit to Italy was his first to a NATO country, and he was even received by Pope John Paul II in the Vatican. When Laurent Fabius, the French Prime Minister, visited East Berlin in June 1985, he became the first head of government from an Atlantic Alliance country to call there. Sir Geoffrey Howe's arrival was also a first, the first British Foreign Secretary to visit the GDR. These and many other toings and froings demonstrate at last that the GDR has been accepted as an equal on the European stage. Hostile Soviet–American relations and the shadow they cast over Europe have raised the significance of the GDR as a go-between in East–West relations, at least in Europe.

The GDR's attitude to German history, the German nation and its future is indicative of its new self-assertiveness. The final goal is a socialist Germany. But East Berlin would like to detach the whole question of the reunification of Germany from its international milieu and transform it into something that the two German states can decide between themselves. The fusing of the two states is not an immediate priority but can only follow the strengthening of the GDR on the German and European stages. By opening up an all-German perspective the GDR can escape from its dilemma about its own national legitimacy. It would like to become recognized as the German state and the socialist Germany, to whom the future belongs.

The present differences of opinion between East Berlin and Moscow are not strategic but tactical. They concern the methods, techniques and moves which can further the power and prestige of the GDR. East Berlin has come to the conclusion that a policy of peaceful coexistence between East and West Germany is the only viable one because of its economic weakness. However, from Moscow's point of view, the more self-assertive the GDR becomes, the more difficulty the Soviet Union will have in ensuring that GDR foreign policy corresponds to Moscow's interests. The closer East–West German economic relations become, the more difficult it will be to convince the GDR that its economic future rests with further integration in CMEA. The possibility arises that GDR–FRG trade will consist more and more of high-technology goods while the GDR exports to CMEA countries will be less technologically advanced.

The days when the GDR slavishly followed the Soviet Union are over, and the weak Soviet leadership over the years 1979–85 accelerated the process of emancipation. The GDR is now quite capable of defending its own national interests. Its refusal to give full support to Moscow's policy of confrontation with Bonn has blunted that policy. Under Gorbachev there are signs of a more sophisticated approach to Western Europe: and the Soviet Union may again seek peaceful coexistence with the Federal Republic. Such a direction of policy would be warmly welcomed in East Berlin.

Notes

1. *Pravda*, 5 December 1975.
2. *Neues Deutschland*, 14 October 1980.
3. *Neues Deutschland*, 13–14 December 1980.
4. Deutsche Presse-Agentur, 11 November 1983.
5. Deutsche Presse-Agentur, 15–16 November 1983.
6. *Tarsadalmi Szemle*, no. 1, 1984.
7. *Neues Deutschland*, 26–27 November 1983.
8. *Neues Deutschland*, 13 February 1984.
9. *Pravda*, 9 April 1984.
10. *Krasnaya Zvezda*, 9 May 1984.
11. *Neues Deutschland*, 24–25 May, 1984.
12. *Neues Deutschland*, 5 July 1984.
13. Kurt Hager, *Gesetzmässigkeiten unserer Epoche — Triebkräfte und Werte des Sozialismus* (East Berlin: Dietz, 1983), pp. 64–5.
14. *Horizont*, no. 8, 1984.
15. *Neues Deutschland*, 18–19 August 1984.

7 The Soviet Union and European détente

John Erickson

'Admiration, respect and love are the sentiments which will draw towards You [Catherine the Great] not just the hearts of Your own subjects, but of Europe in its entirety.'

These fulsome phrases were set down by way of adulation and congratulation by Prince Repnin to Catherine II in May 1779 on the occasion of the successful Russian arbitration between Prussia and Austria which brought an end to the tiresome and taxing war of the Bavarian succession.[1] Not that Russian power and influence was wholly new to 'Europe in its entirety' (or almost its entirety). Already by 1730, in the words of a Soviet historian, 'European governments were forced to take account of this huge and powerful (in economic, political and military terms) empire and to seek political contacts with her, to conclude alliances with Russia and to conduct all types of talks with her'.[2]

The allure of an 'all-European' approach, enticing Tsarist and Soviet regimes alike, found further expression in Tsar Alexander I's draft of the proposed Holy Alliance in 1815.[3] While emphasizing Russia's leading role in the affairs of the continent, the draft envisaged a new system of international order and peaceful cooperation — 'peaceful coexistence'? — infused with, and enlivened by, a sense of religious commitment, only to be dismissed with the diplomatic snigger that here was nothing but a piece of 'sublime mysticism and nonsense'.

Great though the gulf is between Tsarist Russia and the Soviet bloc, both have evinced a sustained interest in the reorganization of Europe and the construction of a system of continental security, a process combining military weight with political and diplomatic engineering, not to mention a dash of 'sublime mysticism' for good measure. The mystical, however, was never allowed to obtrude upon one very practical and realistic aim, namely, facilitating the absorption of the considerable territorial gains which have been common to both Tsarist and Soviet regimes: a 'reorganized Europe' must perforce not only accommodate such gains but also legitimize them under a newly refurbished system of security. Nor did this transmute itself into an acceptance of the idea of a 'united Europe', much less a 'pan-European' solution, which became an early and very particular Soviet aversion: indeed, the Soviet-inspired 'all-European' blueprint was (and is) expressly designed to forestall the emergence of a 'united Europe' which could itself pose the threat of an inimical combination, a threat much magnified with such a combination under American direction. If 'pan-Europeanism' no longer represents a threat of renewed capitalist intervention directed against the Soviet Union (as Stalin so described it in June 1930),[4] a 'united Europe' linked indissolubly and inextricably with the United States of America represented nothing less than an American military bridgehead on the continental mass. The cultivation of an 'all-European consciousness' might at least dilute this baleful exclusivity.

The creation, at Soviet behest, of an 'all-European security system' has remained a major objective —more than thirty years of effort have gone into it — though fluctuations of style and ambiguities of policy have been unavoidable. The collision between particular objectives and preferred solutions has caused Soviet policies to veer between 'maximalist' and 'minimalist' positions, more often than not impelled in one direction or the other by considerations of the presence of the United States (and the evolution of the superpower relationship). Though President Roosevelt had intimated at the Yalta Conference in 1945 that American troops would be gone from Europe in little more than two years after the defeat of Nazi Germany, this proved to be far from the case. In 1948 that presence was affirmed by the Senate resolution approving American participation in a regional North Atlantic alliance. The thrust of Stalin's policy involved an anti-American drive designed to forestall (or pre-empt) the consolidation of American power and presence, only to produce a countervailing effect by its verbal and political crudity (the Berlin blockade being no exception). Western Europe showed no great inclination to tear itself loose from 'American bondage', the internal contradictions of capitalism were not as acute as Stalin would have them, and the 'US out!' campaign could only recoil on itself when critical questions, not least the German question, and the fact of the American nuclear monopoly could only be resolved by an appeal to a less abrasive relationship.[5]

In the immediate post-Stalin period, the Soviet Union returned with a rush to the idea of a European security system, proposed by Molotov at the Foreign Ministers' meeting in 1954 in the form of a European conference to negotiate the principles of a general 'Treaty of Collective Security in Europe', one effect of which would have been the effective neutralization of Germany. In 1955 Prime Minister Bulganin again returned to the theme of European security at the Geneva Conference, proposing once more a treaty on European security, advocating also disarmament and resolution of the 'German question': the conclusion of a non-aggression pact, embracing the renunciation of force and the peaceful solution of disputes, would be followed by the 'dissolution of the blocs', the East–West alliance systems and the substitution of an all-European security system. Withdrawal of foreign troops from Europe was an absolute prerequisite of this scheme, which took the form of another draft 'all-European treaty on collective security', duly submitted to a meeting of Foreign Ministers towards the end of 1955.

Events under Khruhschev took a somewhat more bizarre turn, with his ill-fated attempt to resolve the 'German question' unilaterally and to impose a 'peace treaty' as part settlement on his own terms. This gave way finally to his emphasis upon a Soviet–American 'superpower compact' (Khrushchev having arrogated to himself the status of military and political equal with the United States). Though the idea of a European security conference seemed to flag, the Rapacki Plan (mooted in its first version in October 1957) kept the notion nominally alive. Primarily the Rapacki Plan, in its first form, proposed international recognition of the Oder–Neisse line, recognition of the German Democratic Republic (GDR) as a sovereign body and the establishment of a nuclear-free zone in central Europe (thus foreclosing the nuclear option to the Federal Republic of Germany).[6]

In a revised form Adam Rapacki reshaped his proposals in 1958 to meet Western reservations which held that 'security' was intimately connected with the Warsaw Pact's superiority in conventional forces. The 'two-stage' Rapacki Plan now envisaged a ban on the production of nuclear weapons in both parts of Germany (FRG and GDR), together with the same ban applied to Poland and Czechoslovakia, plus a 'freeze' on armaments already installed: the second stage envisaged negotiations on reductions in conventional forces coupled with the complete denuclearization of the central European area. 'Gone but not forgotten' might be the verdict on the initial form of the Rapacki Plan, for it had at least a part to play in the revival of the idea of further discussions of European security in 1964.

By this time Soviet policy had already passed through two distinct phases: the first an attempt at a 'Europeanism' which would have shunned the United States and sustained its anti-American bias; the second an abortive and unbalanced form of 'Soviet Atlanticism' with its hint of condominium. It was now to be followed by a return to the 'all-European' approach, which combined the several elements which had gone before, the move towards the encouragement of 'all-European' consciousness being encouraged by President de Gaulle's rebuff to NATO and growing American preoccupation with the war in Vietnam, not to mention the growth of anti-American feeling — a *Europe des patries* seemed to be in the making. Soviet interest in European security revived, together with fresh plans for denuclearized zones, regional cooperation and hints of continental détente, marking under the initial Brezhnev–Kosygin regime a resumption of the Soviet attempt to adjust the balance of power in its own favour, the invigoration of a forward policy in an area of vital political and strategic importance and the attempt to move away from the stalemate of *immobilisme* that had persisted since 1949.

The political demise of Khrushchev coincided more or less with a speedy and obvious revival of interest on the part of the Soviet bloc in 'European security' at large, a movement signalled by the Polish Foreign Minister, speaking at the 19th Session of the UN General Assembly on 14 December 1964. He introduced what was essentially a revised Rapacki Plan, shorn of its second stage and proposing *inter alia* the convening of a 'conference of all European states' to examine the problem of continental security 'in its entirety'. This all-

European convention should, '*of course*', embrace both Soviet and American participation — the role of the United States having previously been a moot point, verging on almost total obscurity, or at best obfuscation.

Losing no time the Political Consultative Committee (PCC) of the Warsaw Pact adopted the Polish resolution in January 1965, issuing its own communiqué which pressed for the 'convening of a conference of European states to discuss measures to insure collective security in Europe'.[7] This document released the flood gates, producing a rush of five documents between 1966–9 which steadily elaborated and embroidered the theme of 'European security', concentrating on the issues of the dissolution of the Pacts (NATO and the Warsaw Pact, though this theme became increasingly muted), the importance to East and West of all-European non-military cooperation, the key role of the German question and the territorial status quo, the interpretation of national sovereignty and the place of an all-European security conference.

The initial PCC statement of January 1965 received further and formal endorsement by Leonid Brezhnev and Andrei Gromyko at the 23rd Congress of the Soviet Communist Party (March–April 1966), only to be followed by the PCC 'declaration' which resulted from the Bucharest meeting in July 1966, a meeting which took place against the backdrop of the French withdrawal from NATO's military organization and growing American preoccupation with Vietnam. This 'Declaration on the Strengthening of Peace and Stability in Europe'[8] made obvious capital out of the situation, stressing the existence of an 'abnormal situation' in Europe, 'hotbeds of tension' which threatened the peace — all attributable to the American presence in Europe, made the more menacing because of American cooperation with 'militarist and revanchist' circles of West Germany and the furtherance of the aggressive policies of NATO. The best recourse, therefore, would be the establishment of a system of European security, one which would involve the broadening of contacts between European states, progress towards military détente, the preservation of the status quo (signifying settlement of the German question), the 'dissolution of the military blocs' (NATO and the Warsaw Pact) and the convening of an all-European security conference.

Evocative though the phraseology was, in effect this was a vague document — no doubt deliberately so. No priorities were expressed, not was there any time-limit proposed for this programme, though one immediate omission — or obfuscation — was that in spite of the proviso that 'all interested states' could be parties to the 'Declaration' (and presumably participants in any conference), the United States was, in effect, pushed on to the sidelines, if not actually excluded. A cardinal point revolved round the matter of the status quo: in effect, preservation amounted to an acceptance of the two German states, recognition of existing frontiers (including the Oder–Neisse line), the equal participation of both Germanies in European cooperation and their mutual renunciation of nuclear weapons (shades of 1945!). What was conspicuously lacking, however, was any reference to the manner in which this status quo was to be consolidated, in particular, the requisite military and political structures.

Not surprisingly, the main thrust of the arguments relating to 'European security' reverted to the notion that threats to peace arose from the differences between the 'Atlanticists' and the 'Europeanists', the former tied hand and foot to the United States and thus not only endangering peace but hindering European cooperation. 'Continental cooperation' was increasingly coming to mean economic cooperation, which was projected as a means of rescuing Europe from the twin dangers of 'American imperialism' and West German 'revanchism'.

A further step in the elaboration of the campaign for an all-European security conference came with the statement issued in the wake of the conference of European Communist and Workers Parties, held in Karlovy Vary in April 1967. Already the Soviet bloc was beginning to trip over its own feet, since Romania had already gone its own way and established full diplomatic relations with the Federal German Republic, much to the undisguised fury of other Pact members, though Romania was not alone in turning its back on the Karlovy Vary meeting — Yugoslavia was also conspicuously absent. The conference document — 'For Peace and Security in Europe' —unleashed a condemnation of American, West German and NATO policies which was fiercer than the Bucharest Declaration and went on to enlarge on the Bucharest platform: the German question now occupied the centre of the stage, with added emphasis on full recognition for the German Democratic Republic, complemented (or supplemented) by arrangements for denuclearized zones and steps towards greater regional cooperation. The idea of an all-European security conference still came to the fore, but there was also a suggestion to convene a conference of representatives from all European parliaments, though this paled into insignificance compared with the call for a 'popular front' approach, the mobilization of 'progressive forces' in Europe to bring about the abolition of NATO.

For two years — two troubled years, which boded ill for Soviet policy — the siren songs from the East ceased. Obstacles already existed which inhibited Soviet execution of its grand European design — the American presence in Europe, the existence of NATO, integration pursued by the EEC and, not least, the misgivings on the part of the Soviet Union's own allies about demands *vis-à-vis* the German question and the issue of the status quo, to which were added the contentious aspects of the doctrine of 'limited sovereignty'.[9] The Czechoslovakia crisis of 1968, the ill-fated 'Prague Spring', threw a garish, not to say cruel light on that question, regulated as it was by Soviet military intervention, *pour encourager les autres*.[10] Yet within months of that stark event the dialogue (or the monologue) was resumed with the 'Appeal by the Warsaw Pact Member States to All European countries' issued from Budapest on 17 March 1969.

Though still maintaining a somewhat pessimistic tone over the state of Europe, the Budapest statement toned down direct attacks on the United States and West Germany, referring only to 'certain forces' which were held responsible for the divisions on the European continent. The statement went on to affirm the Bucharest Declaration, but emphasized the theme of wider cooperation (political, economic and cultural), the need to accept the status quo (with special reference to the German question) and the calling of a European security conference.[11] Participation on the part of the United States (and Canada) did not figure in this latest announcement: the hint dropped in the Polish document of 1964 was not taken up, the ambiguity of the Bucharest statement was not pursued and this key point obscured for the moment by reference to a 'European' emphasis. In fact the inconsistency and the implausibility of this stance was about to suffer a sea-change, as Herr Brandt's *Ostpolitik* coincided (or coalesced) with Mr Brezhnev's version of *Westpolitik*.

Bilateralism asserted itself through the *Ostpolitik* initiatives which finally brought agreement between West Germany, Poland and the Soviet Union, with the Poles and the Romanians in the van of this process. Multilateralism also entered the scene with the negotiations leading to the Quadripartite Agreement on Berlin, a process which inevitably involved the United States with the Soviet Union, as well as Great Britain and France.[12] Nor could Mr Brezhnev ignore the crisis on the Soviet Union's Far Eastern borders bringing about the Soviet–Chinese clash on the Ussuri, a portent which could conceivably encourage a form of Sino-American compact or even cooperation. The imperative of American participation was also sustained by growing Soviet interest in and concern with the import of advanced technology, though on a wider front the question of 'European security' had become more fully engaged with NATO's own response, set out in the declaration which resulted from the NATO Council meeting in Brussels in December 1969. The NATO view emphasized that any conference must be preceded by agreement on the German question (and the problem of Berlin), and the issue of the reduction of conventional forces — so glossed over in the Rapacki plan(s) — should be taken up, even though France dissented at this stage.[13]

Already the Western position was moving visibly towards emphasis on freer movement of peoples, the notification of military manœuvres and the protection of the human environment as essential ingredients of any discussion of 'security and cooperation', items which were to exercise a major influence on what eventually evolved as CSCE. Moscow could also take note of the change in the situation induced by Mr Gomulka's initiative in approaching Bonn on the question of the Oder–Neisse line, while the German elections had produced a coalition government disposed to give *de facto* recognition to the GDR and to sign the Nuclear Non-Proliferation Treaty as a sign of good faith and benign intent. At the end of October 1969 the Soviet bloc formulated its response through the meeting of the Foreign Ministers of the Warsaw Pact in Prague, resulting in a brief 'declaration' which recorded satisfaction that proposals for an all-European security conference had met with a 'positive reception' and proposed that an actual conference might be convened in Helsinki in the first half of 1970. While not advancing an agenda as such, the document suggested security at large and the renunciation of force between nations as a theme, together with a programme to extend and expand cooperation among European nations.

The world had not long to wait for further elaboration of this somewhat flimsy document. At the beginning of December 1969 a Pact conference produced yet another communiqué which addressed the German question more directly, acknowledging that progress had been made in relations with Bonn though warning of the dangers of revanchism and neo-Nazism in West Germany The GDR's claims for full recognition were publicly supported though not set out as a precondition for further contacts. In effect, Moscow was disposed to countenance, if not actually to sanction, further bilateral arrangements with Bonn. As for disarmament, only an end to the arms race and general and complete disarmament (GCD), also embracing nuclear disarmament, could bring peace and stability.[14]

The *pronunciamentos* of 1969 certainly marked a change in approach, if not an abandonment of long-range objectives, on the part of the Soviet bloc. The immediate tactical aim now was to get a conference off the ground and to set European negotiations in train, which accounted for a cessation of the abrasive and vituperative attacks on 'American imperialism', 'West German revanchism' and NATO's iniquities, as well as moving from some vague 'grand design' towards particular problems.

At the beginning of 1970 the Soviet Union abandoned its opposition to American participation in the proposed European security conference, signalled by Zamyatin's statement on 13 January 1970, which linked the 'all-European' character of the forthcoming conference with the prospect of American participation. This was not simply a cosmetic change; it indicated revised thinking about any 'all-European security system' and the implications of Brezhnev's détente strategy at large. The days of 'rush tactics' were over,[15] the attempt to split Western Europe, isolate West Germany and shut out America from European affairs displaced in favour of a form of political *ju-jitsu* which was to engage the United States in this 'Europeanization' process in a 'constructive way'. This process could lead to reducing American influence, drawing down American military power in Europe yet without running the risk of producing a power vacuum. Indeed, the separation of the United States from Western Europe would not serve Soviet policy purposes, even if it were a realistic prospect (which it was not, nor is it now).

By the end of 1969 and the beginning of 1970 the focus had begun to narrow on the actual convening of a conference, as opposed to the 'broad-brush' approach. Enthusiasm for the dissolution of both NATO and the Warsaw Pact had waned in very marked fashion, though this did not preclude the hope of NATO's self-liquidation. However, the disappearance of NATO could only be viewed as a distant prospect. In spite of verbiage, there was a pronounced reluctance to spell out the *military* aspects of a European security system (much to the discomfiture of Romania, which looked in vain for military preconditions). Gradually the emphasis was shifting from 'security' as such to 'cooperation', non-military and economic/cultural, first outlined in the Bucharest programme. Other shifts were more subtle. The turn to 'economic cooperation' did not mean a Europe of economic blocs — on the contrary, Europe without such blocs would pave the way to its further security, while 'all-European cooperation', so conceived, would afford protection against American economic imperialism and West German capitalism.

The doctrine of 'limited sovereignty' also received a new twist with respect to the bilateral agreements pursued by Eastern European states with capitalist countries, agreements which must be coordinated with 'the interests of socialist development'. As for neutral states, theirs could and should be a positive role, specifically in encouraging regional cooperation. However, the attempt to develop a 'small state theory' was pounced on, any special 'mission' for small nations was denounced and the place of class policies and hence fundamental differences heavily emphasized. As for neutrality and neutralism, what might be applicable to and desirable in NATO countries was expressly excluded for the socialist camp.[16] In all, this revised approach looked forward to a process which would involve very broad agreements, virtually unprecedented in scope, to a form of Western commitment to expanding East–West trade and to engaging *both* Western Europe and the United States in an all-embracing approach to the conference, rather than playing the game of exploiting 'capitalist contradictions'.

While the Pact members skirted round the problem of the 'dissolution of the military blocs' and handled questions of 'partial measures towards military détente' very gingerly, non-military cooperation became a far more dominant theme — not so much a Europe bereft of its military blocs but rather a Europe united economically, a Europe less vulnerable to American exploitation and so organized as to provide the 'material base' for European security. The campaign for a Europe without 'economic blocs' was also a means of inveighing against Western European integration, where the Common Market was seen as the economic arm of NATO and where 'bloc integration' could only serve the interests of 'American imperialism' in yet another guise seeking yet another form of domination. Though, by way of awkward paradox, the very drumming on the theme of doing away with 'bloc integration' seemed to reinforce the urge among several Eastern European states to pursue, albeit prudently, their own contacts with the Western bloc.

While the Soviet programme lumbered along, temporarily halted in its tracks thanks to the invasion of Czechoslovakia, a certain note of urgency was injected by the Prague meeting in October 1969 which did, after all, direct attention to an actual conference, made the more feasible since the Finnish government had intimated that it would be willing to organize and house a conference on European security. That intimation went to the European governments, as well as to the American and Canadian governments, though Western European endorsements were hardly effusive in the first instance. The Austrian government, for example, accepted 'the principle' of such a conference but entertained considerable reservations about the absence of American participation, an attitude (by no means confined to the Austrians) which caused Moscow towards the end of 1969 to recognize that there would be no precipitate rush to a conference.

Although Western obstruction inevitably came under attack for this state of affairs and Western attempts to bring cogency to a possible agenda denounced as nothing short of sabotage, the vagaries coupled with the inconsistencies of Warsaw Pact statements themselves contributed to the dragging pace. In a sense, the idea of an 'all-European conference' on security had become trapped in its own harness, for manifestly no single conference could possibly deal with the complexities of a treaty of collective security. Nor did the verbal (and textual) manipulation about 'preconditions' do much to clarify the situation. Here we come back to the problem of the status quo, agreement on which should be a condition of European peace and security but not a precondition of any conference. It required a diplomatic whirligig, or the semblance of it, to enliven a faltering campaign, which the Moscow meeting in December 1969 could not disguise. The Hungarian Foreign Minister, Janos Peter, had already admitted that no speedy assembly was feasible, paving the way for Zamyatin's statement in January 1970 which cut through some of the ambiguities, notably the question of American participation, though the 'all-European character' would be preserved by moving beyond the confines of a NATO–Warsaw Pact context. Promising further consultation, which could well involve the proposed agenda, Zamyatin retreated from the Prague 'timetable', though not without a tart observation on those within NATO who were throwing a variety of spanners into the conference works.

NATO continued to figure prominently in the Soviet campaign to revitalize the move towards a conference, coming under attack for obstructing progress towards an all-European conference by clinging to the notion of indissoluble military blocs, the 'Atlanticists' in particular for attempting to shut out the neutral states, while a further delaying tactic, indeed a means of undermining the whole idea, involved advancing issues which by their very complexity precluded agreement at this stage. Meanwhile the peripatetic Janos Peter pursued his own consultative paths, intimating that a more receptive attitude on the part of NATO could mean a meeting in the not too distant future, though the question of the agenda and actual procedure had yet to be settled.[17] In fact, for all practical purposes both had yet to be defined.

From the bundle of inconsistencies one consistency at least emerged, namely, insistence on the consolidation of the status quo which revolved in the first instance round the 'German question'. This latter issue was 'de-coupled' from the conference as such but included as an essential element in any overall consideration of European security. On the other hand, formal recognition of the GDR was a prerequisite of that long-standing proposal for an all-

European agreement on the renunciation of the use of force. The main thrust, however, was directed at emphasizing that the resolution of the German question — principally recognition of the GDR and of the Oder–Neisse line — was fundamental to European security at large and was not linked directly with any conference on security (though this did not preclude discussion of this question at any forthcoming conference).[18] Put succinctly (which was rarely the case), the 'legitimate claims' of the Warsaw Pact states were to be seen as one of many 'preconditions' of European security at large, but these were not to be construed as 'preconditions' pertaining to the conference itself, which would and should of its own workings generate 'preconditions' relevant to improved security for Europe. That is known as having one's cake and eating it.

However, once the genie of bilateralism *vis-à-vis* relations with Bonn had been uncorked, Ulbricht's difficulties proliferated, a situation which could not be eased by proposing the resolution of the 'German question' through the instrumentality of an all-European conference with both German states participating *on equal terms*. The Moscow summit (1969) obliged Ulbricht to come to terms with bilateralism, though he drove something of a hard bargain, requiring firm bloc support for his demand not merely for recognition but for the establishment of relations with Bonn 'based on the principles of international law' — completely *equal* treatment under international law. As for the proposed security conference, it should be convened without undue delay and involve the *equal* participation of the GDR.

While guarding their precious and somewhat precarious bilateral contacts with Bonn, the Warsaw Pact states lent varied aid to Ulbricht in his campaign for full recognition of the GDR. In most respects, the Warsaw Pact states held to the Soviet configuration of the campaign for a European security conference — with the marked and highly visible exception of Romania, which had been the first to break ranks in making contact with Bonn. The stamp of individuality, not to say independence, was amply demonstrated by the Romanian refusal to attend the Karlovy Vary assembly, insisting (together with the Yugoslavs) that European security arrangements were properly the concern of governments rather than the business of a meeting of communist parties. That same obduracy also enabled the Romanians to slip the anti-Chinese net which was in the making.

Not that this encompassed the range of Romanian dissent, which led increasingly to promoting what was virtually an 'alternative future' with respect to a European security system, with emphasis on the *military* measures which would induce real security. Romania did not (and does not) regard the idea of the 'dissolution of the military blocs' as a mere ritualistic expression but as a significant measure of military détente, made more necessary by the Soviet invasion of Czechoslovakia. That event further stiffened Romanian resolve (or intransigence), rejecting the notion of limited sovereignty in the guise of the 'Brezhnev doctrine', in contrary fashion affirming and reinforcing the principle of inviolate national sovereignty, seeking regulation upon the use of force (complete with guarantees), stipulating the removal of foreign bases and the withdrawal of military forces from countries other than their own. For the Romanians, more than the status quo was at stake and they were evidently not prepared to subscribe to the phraseology of a Europe free of blocs as the Soviet bloc steadily closed its ranks and consolidated its political hold and military capabilities. There was, as might be expected, much more to be heard from the Romanians and, in the cause of the small nations, not from them alone.[19]

Slowly the Soviet attitude of political and ideological confrontation towards West Germany eased, a change reflected in the 1970 treaty and accelerated by the deft displacement of Ulbricht in 1971, taking his obsessive approach to legitimacy and recognition of the GDR with him. The bilateralism that brought about the agreement between the Soviet Union and the Federal Republic, together with the agreement between the Federal Republic and Poland, paid off, complemented as they were by the Quadripartite Agreement on Berlin in 1971 (with its final protocol signed in June 1972). Agreements were much in the air and with them a sense of compromise over *Ostpolitik* (or the converse, the Soviet *Westpolitik*), all of which could only encourage Mr Brezhnev, indeed impel him or propel him to a radically revised outlook, to a virtual fervour of reconciliation even to the point of keeping open the notion of eventual reunification of the two Germanies. Not that this disposed of the underlying ambivalence in Soviet policy and attitudes — the doubts and the misgivings over which component, West Germany or the United States, posed the greatest long-term danger. Yet the immediate agreement did at least minimize the danger of West Germany becoming a nuclear power. The Soviet Union could put a brake on 'revanchism' and settle the problem of the recognition of the GDR for all practical purposes. Above all, for all the risks, these developments could suggest a pattern, or a style for the burgeoning Soviet–American détente. But détente with Bonn was a stunning start, demonstrating Moscow's preference for a 'German-led' détente with NATO rather than the political mirage of de Gaulle's Europe free of dependence on the United States — an improbable vista, far beyond political reality.[20]

Soviet opinion holds to the view that the Moscow Treaty and the Quadripartite Agreement 'did much to pave the way for the Conference on Security and Cooperation in Europe and the Helsinki Final Act'. Preparatory talks for the conference finally opened in Helsinki on 22 November 1972, launching seven months of work on the part of thirty-five nations before the CSCE proper convened on 3 July 1973. The preliminary wrangling did ultimately produce an agenda, divided into three basic components (the famous 'Baskets'): (a) questions relating to security in Europe (including principles guiding relations between states and the document on confidence building measures, plus 'certain aspects' of security and disarmament); (b) cooperation in economics, science, technology and the environment; and (c) cooperation in humanitarian and other fields. A fourth section covered meetings which would review the whole CSCE process, with the entire procedural aspect assembled into the 'Blue Book' with its 96 items. Western ideas and NATO opinion had already been set out in the declaration of the NATO Council (December 1969), which required that any 'agenda' should incorporate items dealing with the freer movement of peoples, ideas and information between East and West, prior notification of military manœuvres and protection of the environment.

The trade was implicit. For acceptance or admission of its security requirements, minimally *de facto* acceptance of the status quo — the territorial status quo in Eastern Europe — the Soviet Union perforce committed itself, in principle at least, to undertakings on human rights under the rubric of 'cooperation'. Though not immediately apparent, the entanglement increased with time and became the more complicated as East–West tensions developed once more towards the end of the decade. Disagreements, however, surfaced at once, with the Soviet Union having to countenance a Romanian proposal embodying the principle of the non-use of force and a Swiss amendment concerned with the peaceful settlement of disputes, none of which was to Soviet liking, not to mention the acrimony over basic human rights and fundamental freedoms. In the event, the Soviet Union was obliged to accept the Romanian proposal and the principle of human rights in exchange for *de facto* recognition of the revised Polish frontiers and the status quo in Germany, though that could be registered as a very considerable gain.

The military aspect of security, the approach to confidence-building measures (CBMs), inevitably produced its own tensions, with the Warsaw Pact opposing at each turn prior notification of military manœuvres and attendance of observers. The Pact moved only grudgingly, insisting on the voluntary fulfilment of the proposed obligations and yielding finally at a point when it was clear that the Conference could well founder without an agreement on the military aspects.[21]

As for the numbers game, by way of compromise (though somewhat muddled at that), the figure of 25,000 men was fixed as the indicator for notification of manœuvres, a 'quick fix' which did not, however, resolve the problem of what geographical space for CBMs would be applicable: the Western demand for 600 km (with Moscow offering only 100 km of its territory) led to the adjustment of a 250 km slice of territory within the Soviet Union and Turkey. The upshot, after two full years of involved negotiation, was a five-point agreement on CBMs, including notification of manœuvres (twenty-one days' notice for those involving more than 25,000 men), voluntary notification of smaller exercises, bilateral and voluntary exchange of observers plus exchanges by military delegations.

Basket Three, on cooperation in humanitarian and other fields — 'human rights' — duly inflamed feelings and ignited passions, neither easily subdued or extinguished, though the phase of negotiation pursued in Geneva led to the formulation and conclusion of the 'Final Act', signed in Helsinki on 1 August 1975, acclaimed then (and later, on its tenth anniversary) by the Soviet Union, affirming as it did the principle of sovereign equality, refraining from the use of force, the inviolability (not 'immutability') of all European frontiers, respect for territorial integrity, the resolution of disputes by peaceful means, non-intervention in the internal affairs of other states and respect for human rights.[22]

Soviet views on the nature or the validity of the 'Final Act' have diverged considerably from those held in the West, principally in the matter of interpreting the 'Final Act' as an 'international legal norm', incorporating decisions of a 'differentiated legal character', with the Declaration on Principles embodying 'norms' which are 'absolutely binding' in nature under international law. Conversely, Western opinion was not inclined to accept the 'Final Act' as a treaty as such, nor did it signify *de jure* regulation of the 'German question'. The division of Europe still stood, lamented on all sides, though the Soviet stance seemed to preserve the option of resolving it on unilateral military-political terms.

The euphoria soon faded, to give way to a situation of growing tension and discord verging on outright acrimony. It is, perhaps, fair to regard the 'Final Act' as a 'diplomatic equilibrium' or a fine balance in its own right. Soviet reluctance to accept general principles governing inter-state relations and the improvement of human contacts (human rights) was counter-balanced by the insistence on sovereignty and non-interference in internal affairs, with Western Europeans also approving the endorsement of sovereignty and the recognition of human rights. Even the small nations could breathe a little more easily, or so it seemed, admitted as they were to what appeared to be a reconstructed 'concert of Europe'. But the façade crumbled all too soon, revealing all the deep divisions between East and West.

The cloud gathered with the growing suspicion over Soviet intentions, bringing Brezhnev's détente strategy into question, if not into a certain disrepute, begging the question as to whether here was or was not some convenient tactical compromise. Indeed, the whole notion of *razryadka*, 'relaxation of tension', became suspect and increasingly so as Soviet support for 'progressive forces' in Europe, all with the object of inducing political change, did not relate to any corresponding move or movement in Eastern Europe. This stance had been spelled out quite brusquely by Boris Ponomarev in July 1975 when he insisted that 'in conditions of détente, the front lines of ideological conflict do not become silent. On the contrary, they become *deeper and wider*.' Soviet policy did not desist from support for national liberation struggles in the Third World, a distant but disturbing phenomenon though not to be compared with the misgivings brought on by the steady Soviet military build-up in both strategic and theatre weapons, nuclear and conventional alike.

As the short-lived Soviet–American détente began to erode, or fray at the edges, American impatience with the tardiness of change in the Eastern bloc grew apace, all unheeding of the Soviet requirement to 'hold the line' with respect to these new-found openings to the West. The clamour over human rights grew, much to the discomfiture of the Soviet leadership which had not perhaps foreseen the full implications of the 'Final Act'. Even the prospect of improved economic interchange proved to be a disappointment in a relatively short time. It was amidst these disturbing portents that the review conference met in October 1977 in Belgrade, the first follow-up meeting after the signing of the 'Final Act'.[23]

Western insistence upon a review conference and the review process seems to have come as something of a surprise to the Soviet bloc, which adopted an attitude of what has been called 'defensive disengagement'. That interest in the whole CSCE process had not withered on the vine was amply demonstrated by the 100 proposals which were put forward, but the balance that had been achieved at Helsinki was abruptly and visibly fragmented. In an attempt to outflank the growing volume of criticism over human rights, for the principle of 'non-interference' had not proved to be a barrier against such criticism of the human rights situation in the Eastern bloc, Soviet efforts were directed towards reviving and revising issues of security and sovereignty under the formula of the 'consolidation of military détente in Europe'. Rather than repudiate the whole Helsinki process, which would have prejudiced political (if not legal) recognition of the post-war borders, Soviet CSCE strategy appeared to veer towards making the security issue paramount and thus 'splitting off' the component dealing with human rights and cooperation in the humanitarian field. As if to emphasize this approach, Western protests produced no visible change in the policies of the Eastern bloc and, if anything, made the predicament of proponents of human rights in the East even more uncomfortable and increasingly dangerous.

The final Belgrade communiqué was bereft of references to human rights, though the decision to proceed with a further review conference signalled that détente, even limited détente, was not entirely dead. However, the battle lines certainly hardened at Madrid, the scene of a dour confrontation. Between Belgrade in 1977 and Madrid towards the end of 1980 the CSCE thread, if it can be called that, was maintained by three meetings of experts — the Montreux meeting on the peaceful settlement of disputes, the discussion in Malta on Mediterranean questions and latterly the Hamburg conference on scientific cooperation held in February 1980 (a meeting which referred once again to the importance of human rights and freedom as a prerequisite for this and other forms of cooperation).[24]

The Soviet invasion of Afghanistan and the growing crisis in Poland did not promise the most auspicious circumstances for the Madrid review conference, whose preparatory meeting opened in September 1980. Once again, the agenda and the rules of procedure — all fashioned in *ad hoc* style — furnished an immediate battleground. There was no hope that the Belgrade 'Yellow Book', establishing a procedure, would meet Soviet requirements on this occasion, anxious as it was to limit to the bare minimum any review of the full implementation of the 'Final Act'. In what could have passed for the theatre of the absurd, the deadlock in the preparatory meeting was finally broken, and the review conference established its procedure in the 'Violet Book', separating the conference into two phases. The West could claim that it had won time for a review of the implementation of the 'Final Act', the Soviet Union could look upon a tactical gain in reducing the time available for this and also the prospect of steering the meetings steadily in the direction of 'security' *tout court*, military détente in Europe, with the emphasis on securing approval for a conference on disarmament.[25]

That, however, was not the sole Soviet stake in Madrid. There was Brezhnev's own prestige, much of it invested in the CSCE process and his designation as 'the main architect of détente'. He was unlikely to pull his own house down about his ears. There was also a new American administration to be tried out for size and the increasingly complicated situation engendered by NATO's 'dual-track' decision and the future of intermediate-range nuclear forces. Nor had all hope of further economic cooperation and technology transfer entirely faded. The price was a battering over human rights and an insistence on a form of 'balance', namely, no post-Madrid meeting on military security without concessions on human rights.

As agreement hung in the balance, literally and figuratively, the question of the disarmament conference was beset with difficulties, not entirely eased by the variety and vagaries of the several proposals — Polish, French, Romanian, Yugoslav and Swedish. Nevertheless, there was a certain common ground in envisaging two phases, the first covering CBMs and the second actual disarmament. The French proposal was the most expansive, prescribing the area to be covered by CBMs, nothing less than 'from the Atlantic to the Urals'; the Polish proposal left the question open to the deliberations of an actual conference. Additionally, Romania and Austria tabled proposals dealing with CBMs, adding great detail to the original Helsinki proposals. The Soviet attitude was studiously ambiguous; though accepting the notion of 'the Atlantic to the Urals', the point was driven home by including the North Atlantic and North America in the zone to be covered by CBMs. Whilst Soviet insistence on that latter point almost undid what meagre progress had been made, the Concluding Document at Madrid did include a mandate for a Conference on Confidence and Security Building Measures and Disarmament: this would meet some of the implications of Basket One in CSCE. 'Balance' of a kind was preserved by wrestling Soviet agreement to a meeting in Ottawa on human rights and a further review conference in 1986.

Much to the surprise of a number of observers, taking account of the sustained barrage over the violation of human rights and the Western insistence on 'balance' with respect to Baskets One and Three, the Soviet Union did not turn its back on the 'Helsinki process', even if obliged to remain on the defensive and turn to damage limitation (as indeed has been the case at the recent Human Rights Conference in Ottawa, even though the clashes took place behind closed doors).

Once again a certain price had to be paid for more tangible gains pursued at the Stockholm Conference. Here real prizes were in the offing, in particular, pressing the case once again for a NATO–Warsaw Pact treaty on 'no first use' (for nuclear and conventional forces). This proposal was construed by Western observers as a step to weakening the Western alliance and even more pertinently encouraging the neutralization of West Germany, all without impinging on the military capability of the Warsaw Pact. Already the Soviet position had been adumbrated in the Political Declaration of the Warsaw Pact, issued in Prague on 5 January 1983.[27]

Of the six Soviet proposals, the first two embodied key objectives — an obligation on the part of states possessing nuclear weapons not to be the first to use such weapons and a treaty on the non-use of force; the remainder of the proposals covered the freezing and reduction of military budgets, the elimination of chemical weapons from Europe, support for nuclear-free zones in Europe and improvements to the CBMs already projected at Helsinki. The Western response was to insist that CBMs should be both militarily significant and verifiable (as well as binding), including ground and air inspections supplemented by non-interference with 'national technical means'. Notification of manœuvres was a case in point, where the Warsaw Pact exercise Soyuz-81, held in March 1981 as the Polish crisis seemed on the point of boiling over, was dismissed as a 'command and staff' exercise, routine in nature though involving motorized units, armour, artillery, tactical air, helicopter and amphibious exercises. Zapad-81, held in September, included the elements of some eight divisions exercising in an area covering the Baltic, the Baltic Military District and the Belorussian Military District, duly 'notified' but without furnishing any detail on the designation of the exercise or the numbers involved.[28]

From the Soviet point of view the 'balance sheet' of the CSCE process is demonstrably mixed, though successful enough if it is seen as but one component of a programme or policy to settle the European military-political problem on Soviet terms. The gain on the issue of the territorial status quo is balanced by the failure, so far, to win full legitimization of the shape of post-war Europe or an actual endorsement of Soviet military and political hegemony over Eastern Europe — witness European reaction to the Polish crisis and the calls for a 'revision' of the Yalta provisions. Nor, so far, has the attempt to transform the European political system from within registered substantial gain. On the contrary, a swing to the Right in public opinion has counteracted these efforts, and Soviet sources now speak of 'social revanchism' in West Germany, an old threat in a new guise now rearing its head. Finally, the aim of complicating, even neutralizing NATO's 'flexible response' has not been fully realized.

There can be no drawing back on the part of the Soviet Union. It has pursued its aim of remodelling 'Europe in its entirety' with persistence and a gritty continuity, whether pursuing short- to medium-term interests in European 'security' and the search for greater confidence (which, to be significant, must be a product of real security) or the long-range quest for a solution largely configured after Soviet requirements. The two cannot be entirely separated. Though the road may well be littered with tactical compromises and enforced retreats, the 'Helsinki process' does not seem to have exhausted its possibilities or its promise for Soviet policies in search of an 'all-European' solution. This solution appears to embrace a Europe of medium and small powers, loosely grouped, without any major integration process and with its defence link with the United States eroded, a Europe of unchallenged (but not immutable) territorial frontiers, a Europe where defence establishments and expenditures are at a minimum level, a Europe without any military force deployed beyond its own frontiers, a Europe committed to bilateral agreements with the Soviet Union and sharing the same fundamental outlook on 'security', and a Europe where détente flourishes on the basis of state-to-state relations but without application to the internal affairs of the 'socialist camp'. That is an 'all European' solution *par excellence*.

Notes

1. See Christopher Duffy, *Russia's Military Way to the West: Origins and Nature of Russian Military Power 1700–1800*, Routledge & Kegan Paul, London, 1985 edn., p. 185, for quotation and text.

2. See G. A. Nekrasov, *Rol' Rossii v evropeiskoi mezhdunarodnoi politike 1725–1739 35*, Moscow, Nauka, 1976 (English summary, pp. 312–13).
3. For drafts, see *Vneshnyaya politika Rossii XIX i nachala XX veka*, no. 1, vol. VIII, Moscow, Politizdat, 1972, Doc. No. 225 ('Proekt Akta o Svyashchennom soyuze . . .), p. 502 and Doc. No. 231 ('Akt o Svyashchennom soyuze . . .), p. 516: see also Henry A. Kissinger, *A World Restored*, Boston, Houghton Mifflin, 1957, pp. 184–90.
4. See Elliot R. Goodman, *The Soviet Design for a World State*, New York, Columbia University Press, 1957, pp. 380–2 (and footnote 31 to p. 382).
5. Hannes Adomeit, *Soviet Risk-Taking and Crisis Behavior: A Theoretical and Empirical Analysis*, Allen & Unwin, London, 1982, pp. 67–182: see also Hannes Adomeit, 'Capitalist Contradictions and Soviet Policy', *Problems of Communism*, May–June 1984, pp. 1–8.
6. See *The Rapacki Plan: Documents*, Warsaw, Dept. of Information for Abroad of the Polish Press, 1961; also *Plan Rapackiego: Dokumenty i materialy opracowali Wojciech Nagorski-Mieczyslaw Tomala*, Ksiazka i Wiedza, 1959, 179 pp. (Pub: Polski Instytut Spraw Miedzynarodowych), on disengagement in Europe; also *Bibliografie k problémům evropské bezpečnosti*, Praha, Ustav mezinárodnich vztahů, 1971, svazek 30, 71 pp.: Polish section, pp. 51–64.
7. *Pravda*, 22 January, 1965.
8. *Pravda*, 9 July 1966.
9. Known familiarly as the 'Brezhnev doctrine', it was first and formally enunciated in *Pravda*, 26 September 1968 under the rubric of 'Sovereignty and the International Obligation of Socialist Countries' (though the existence of such a doctrine, the 'Brezhnev doctrine' has been strenuously denied by Soviet authorities); for a recent and extensive discussion of the background, see Joseph L. Noges and Robert H. Donaldson, *Soviet Foreign Policy Since World War II*, Oxford, Pergamon Press, 1985 (2nd edn,), pp. 204 ff. under ch. 7, 'The Socialist System Becomes Polycentric'.
10. For reference, Robin Alison Remington, edn., *Winter in Prague: Documents on Czechoslovak Communism in Crisis*, Cambridge, MIT Press, 1969, *passim*; Robert Littell, ed., *The Czech Black Book* (Orig. *Sedm Pražskych Dnů*: 21–27. srpen 1968, Prague), New York, Praeger/Avon Books, 1969; Journalist M., *A Year is Eight Months: Czechoslovakia 1968*, (intro. Tad Szulc), New York, Anchor Books, 1971: V. V. Kusin, ed., *The Czechoslovak Reform Movement 1968*, London, IRD, 1973. For the counter-point (or the counter-blast), in addition to the Soviet *White Book*, see Miloš Marko, *Čierne na bielom*, Bratislava, Nakl. Pravda, 1971; and *Zprávy v boji proti kontrarevoluci*, Praha, Nakl. Svoboda, 1971 (collected essays/articles).
11. *Pravda*, 18 March 1969.
12. See the documentary collection, *Die Entwicklung der Beziehungen zwischen der Bundesrepublik Deutschland und der Deutschen Demokratischen Republik 1969– 1976: Bericht and Dokumentation*, Bundesministerium für innerdeutsche Beziehungen, 1977, here pp. 112–17; also R. F. Alekseyev, *SSSR–FRG: proshloe i nastoyashchee. Sovetsko-zapadnogermanskie otnosheniya 1955–1980 gg*,

Moscow, Politizdat, 1980 (here Ch. 3) and V. I. Milyukova, *Otnosheniya SSSR–FRG i problemy evropeiskoi bezopasnosti*, Moscow, Nauka, 1983, *passim*.

13. See Colonel John G. Keliher, *The Negotiations on Mutual and Balanced Force Reductions*, New York, Pergamon Press; for the subsequent phase, see Prof. Wojciech Multan, ed., *Rokowania wiedeńskie w sprawie wzajemnej redukcji silt zbrojnych i zbrojeń w Europie Środkowiej: Wybór dokumentów 1973–1978*, Warsaw, Polski Instytut Spraw Miezdynarodowych, 1980. See also the survey in *Evropeiskaya bezopasnost' i sotrudnichestvo: predposylki, problemy, perspektivy*, Moscow, Nauka, 1976, Ch. 6 (Yu. A. Kostko), 'Voprosy voennoi razryadki v Evrope', pp. 124–52, also *Problemy voennoi razryadki* (collective authorship), Moscow, Nauka, 1981, Ch. 7, p. 210–33 for further comment.
14. TASS, 4 December 1969; also *Organizatsiya Varshavskogo dogovora: Dokumenty i materialy*, Moscow, Politizdat, 1980, Doc. No. 31, pp. 118–20.
15. On the abandonment of 'rush tactics', see an excellent study which has by no means lost its relevance though compiled before the actual convening of the CSCE, Charles Andras, *'European Security' and the Security of Europe (The Warsaw Pact Campaign for a European Conference)*, RFE (Munich), n.d., 55 pp., here p. 52; also background in Adam Ulam, 'Europe in Soviet Eyes', *Problems of Communism*, May–June 1983, pp. 22–30.
16. For a review of the several positions and relevant press citations, see Charles Andras, op. cit., under IV(D), 'National Sovereignty and the Future of Small Nations', pp. 31–4; also Harto Hakovirta, 'The Soviet Union and the Varieties of Neutrality in Western Europe', *World Politics*, vol. 35, July 1983, pp. 563–83.
17. Charles Andras, op cit., under IV(E), 'The All-European Security Conference', pp. 34–40.
18. There are voluminous commentaries and analyses of these questions — the 'German question' and the status quo — but I might direct attention to two rather singular works, Józef Kokot, *Od Poczdamu do Helsinek: Koniec okresu powojennego w Europie*, Instytut Śląski w Opolu, 1974, a politico-juridical study; also A. A. Roshchin, *Poslevoennoe uregulirovanie v Evrope*, Moscow, Mysl, 1984, esp. Ch. 9 (and documentary supplement); also V. I. Milyukova, *Otnosheniya SSSR–FRG*,. op. cit., Ch. 2; also a recent pamphlet publication, Vadim Nekrasov, *The Roots of European Security: 40 Years after the Yalta and Potsdam Conferences (1945)*, Moscow, Novosti PA, 1984.
19. For a succinct and pertinent summary of the Romanian position, Alex Alexiev, 'Romania and the Warsaw Pact: the Defense Policy of a Reluctant Ally', *Journal of Strategic Studies*, Vol. 4, No. 1, March 1981, pp. 5–18.
20. Discussed at some length in Jonathan Steele, *The Limits of Soviet Power: The Kremlin's Foreign Policy — Brezhnev to Chernenko*, Harmondsworth, Penguin Books, revised ed. 1985, here Ch. 5, pp. 71–4.
21. CBMs: Johan Holst and Karen A. Melander, 'European Security and Confidence-Building Measures', *Survival*, Vol. 19, 1975; Col. Jonathan Alford, *Confidence-Building Measures in Europe: The Military Aspects*, Adelphi

Papers, No. 149; *Confidence-Building Measures in Europe*, New York, Institute for East–West Security Studies, 1983. On the Soviet concept of 'military détente', for background, see N. Yuryev, 'Confidence-Building Measures and Security in Europe', *International Affairs* (Moscow), January, 1984, pp. 23–8.

22. See 'For Peace and Security in Europe' (Tenth Anniversary of the Conference on Security and Cooperation in Europe): Exchange of Opinion, *International Affairs* (Moscow), September, 1985, pp. 70–81, esp. Prof. I. Orlik, pp. 79–81; V. Lomeiko, 'Peace, Security and Cooperation for Europe', *International Affairs* (Moscow), October 1985, pp. 17–22: on the 5th anniversary, K. Chernenko, 'Trust and Cooperation Among Peoples . . .', *International Affairs* (Moscow), September 1980, pp. 3–11: 'Security and Cooperation in Europe: Achievements and Prospects', *International Affairs* (Moscow), October, 1979, pp. 3–10: also 'Soviet Efforts to Ensure European Security', *International Affairs* (Moscow), August 1985, pp. 3–12. For further statements and documents, see *Po puti, prilozhennomu v Khel'sinki: Dokumenty i materialy*, Moscow, Politizdat, 1980, p. 511. 'Recommended reading' is to be found in *Vneshnyaya politika SSSR—voploshchenie leninskikh idei bor'by za mir*, Moscow, Kniga, 1981, pp. 51–2.

23. See 'the Background to Madrid' in H. Gordon Skilling, 'CSCE in Madrid'. *Problems of Communism*, July–August, 1981, pp. 1–2; also *Ot Khel'sinki do Belgrada: Sovetski i Soyuz i osushchestvlenie Zaklyuchitel'nogo akta obshcheevropeiskogo soveshchaniya: Dokumenty i materialy*, Moscow, Politizdat, 1977 (statements and documents); also *The Belgrade Followup Meeting to the Conference on Security and Cooperation in Europe: A Report and Appraisal*, Washington, US House of Representatives, May 1978.

24. H. Gordon Skilling, op. cit., pp. 2–3.

25. For a detailed discussion and analysis, H. Gordon Skilling, ibid., pp. 3–16; also Ambassador Max Kampelman, 'Negotiating with the Soviets in Madrid', *World Affairs*, Vol. 144, pp. 440–6.

26. Note 'The USSR and the West Clash at Ottawa' and 'Ottawa Conference Ending Review Phase', *Radio Liberty Research Bulletin*, 22 May 1985 and 5 June 1985 respectively.

27. On the Soviet/Warsaw Pact position, N. Yurev, 'Confidence-Building Measures and Security in Europe', *International Affairs* (Moscow), pp. 24–8.

28. For details of Soviet/Warsaw Pact exercises and 'post-Helsinki Exercise Politics', see Jeffrey Simon, *Warsaw Pact Forces: Problems of Command and Control*, Boulder, Co., Westview Press, 1985, pp. 139–84 and pp. 186–97; also Roland Eggleston, 'Why NATO Wants Compulsory Notification of Maneuvers', *RL Research Bulletin*, 6 March 1985. Conjecture has it that the outcome at Stockholm could well be a compromise: for the Warsaw Pact a form of re-affirmation of the non-use of force; for NATO improved notification of military manœuvres and obligatory attendance of foreign observers at manœuvres, designed to decrease the danger of surprise attack;

for the neutrals and non-aligned (NNA) a ceiling on troop strengths for certain types of military exercises. See also 'The Need for Progress at the Stockholm Conference', *International Affairs* (Moscow), November, 1985, pp. 76–80.
29. For a very recent Soviet view of problems and prospects, see Yu. Karelov, 'USSR–Western Europe: Guidelines of Cooperation', *International Affairs* (Moscow), November, 1985, pp. 23–8 and contd. p. 75.

8 National independence and Atlanticism: the dialectic of French policies

Philip Cerny and Jolyon Howorth

Since the 1940s there has been a remarkable consensus on the broad aspirations of foreign and defence policy in France. From de Gaulle's speeches during the Second World War to the policies of the Mitterrand presidency there have been three broad strategic dimensions that together form a vision of France's proper role in the world. They have proved problematic in their application to specific circumstances. Nevertheless, their interaction over time provides the key to analysing the path of French foreign and defence policy, and to understanding its overriding objective: to use French power and influence, independently established, to further the development of détente in Europe. Détente was not simply to be imposed by the superpowers on other nations on the basis of a bipolar logic; it was to be centred on constructive nationalism and the freeing of nation-states to pursue their national interests within a wider international consensus.[1]

The first of the three strategic principles has been the desire for a Europe-wide settlement of frontiers and national disputes. Stated most dogmatically in President de Gaulle's call for a 'Europe from the Atlantic to the Urals', its more practical side has been seen in a range of proposals for European cooperation. The range extends from wartime proposals for broad political and economic cooperation in central Europe based on nation-states (which eventually ran foul of both the Soviet Union and the United States); through the supranational European Community-building of the 1950s and a variety of other schemes for reorganizing the North Atlantic Alliance, setting up European political cooperation, calling (from a very early date) for Helsinki-type negotiations, creating flexible and pragmatic organizations in such fields as space and technology (e.g.,

Ariane and the recent Eureka negotiations); to the attempt to establish direct links on an independent basis between France and the Soviet Union (as well as the Eastern European states), from the Franco-Soviet Friendship Treaty of 1944 through de Gaulle's visit to the Soviet Union in 1966 to Giscard's Warsaw meeting with Brezhnev in 1980. The desire to create a Europe-wide settlement has been seen not only by French leaders, but also by French public opinion, as being an objective which was both of primary necessity — as a key to solving outstanding problems of a more global nature — and something beyond the power of the superpowers to do for themselves. For, in the French view, the superpowers have been imprisoned by their bipolar logic with its imperative of the centralization of decision-making in the hands of the 'senior partner' of each bloc. They are therefore incapable of seeing that only a European settlement that *diffuses* rather than centralizes power will be able to lay a firm foundation for a viable and self-sustaining post-cold war international system. De Gaulle, for example, saw détente as only the first stage — the thaw — in a process that would lead to greater mutual understanding and ultimately to Europe-wide economic and political cooperation — détente, entente, cooperation (sometimes the word 'disarmament' was substituted for 'cooperation' as the third element in the triptych).

In aiming for such a far-reaching European settlement, in hoping at least partially to dismantle the Iron Curtain itself, French leaders of all parties have defined a special and distinct role for themselves and for French policy. In their view Germany cannot play this role. With its national identity too closely associated with aggressive authoritarianism, twice defeated, now divided, Germany has been seen to lack credibility both internally and externally for such a leading role. As Churchill told de Gaulle during the war, if Britain were faced with a choice between the continent of Europe and *le grand large* ('the open sea', i.e. America and the Empire), she would always choose the latter. It fell, therefore, to France to put Europe first — whether the 'United States of Europe' of Jean Monnet, the *Europe des États* (from the Atlantic to the Urals?) of de Gaulle, or the two-tier 'variable-speed' Europe implicit in de Gaulle's offer of 'association' to Britain in 1967, the abortive feelers of the 'Soames Affair', or the wide range of proposals and pragmatic adjustments characteristic of the European Community of the 1970s and 1980s (like the European Monetary System and Eureka). Of course, in associating in this way the French national interest and the wider global interest with their own version of the 'European interest', French leaders have been as guilty as any of self-deception and special pleading. None the less, the notion of a European settlement, linked with a Europe-centred détente process, has been crucial to the way in which foreign policy objectives have been perceived at both elite and mass levels in France since the Second world War, and is as vital today as ever.

The second of the three principles, and the one which at first seems to clash most directly with the first, is that of Atlantic solidarity. With Europe and the world divided into antagonistic blocs it became necessary for French policy-makers to put their aim of a Europe-wide settlement on the back burner after the failure of the Allied powers to agree on an occupation policy in Germany and the ringing down of the Iron Curtain in 1946–8. In such a context, France, with its liberal-democratic traditions, solidly rooted in 'Western civilization', culture and (though more unevenly) industrial society, quickly put aside the consensual euphoria of the liberation period to throw in its lot with the United States and Britain. As Alfred Grosser has emphasized, the main international cleavages of the post-war decade were ones that paralleled political conflicts within France itself. With the French Communist Party (PCF) laying claim to the revolutionary tradition of 1789 and 1871, the cold war meant its 'ghettoization' and the displacement of the centre of gravity of French politics towards the Right. Furthermore, with the French Empire (now the Union) as an essential element in the political, social and economic development of metropolitan France, French society was painfully imbricated in the dismantling of its colonial heritage, on both the Right and the Left.[2] In both cases, the problems that faced French politicians drew state and society into the Western orbit, even though this process led to a domestic cold war and virtual civil war between different groups of French people (mainly over Algeria).

France's first priority in the mid-1940s had been to prevent the revival of Germany. However, once the United States and Britain had decided on the necessity of reviving western Germany for cold war reasons in 1946–7, France had no choice — because of geography, majority ideological sentiment, politics, and the emerging post-war economic settlement in the West — but to join in the process. Though French public opinion was characterized by a strong neutralist current that reflected the liberation consensus and the European orientation described earlier, it was divided into a minority of strong neutralists and also PCF supporters, on the one hand, and, on the other, a majority for whom, in a divided world where one *had* to choose, a pro-American stance was imperative. On the Right, even de Gaulle's fundamental adherence to Alliance solidarity, as evidenced in the Cuban missile crisis of 1962, was unwavering despite his strong reservations on structure and process. On the Left, the Socialist Party (SFIO), traditional enemies of the Bolsheviks, who betrayed them in 1920 and called them 'social fascists' in the early 1930s, was a pillar of Atlanticism after 1947. And beyond the cold war (though intertwined with it too), the painful disentanglement from Empire put France into a category with Britain and Portugal, a Western power facing the barrel of Mao's gun. Meanwhile a new structure of relations between industrial countries and between them and the emerging 'Third World', the post-war capitalist world economy growing under the American security umbrella, attached France firmly to her Atlantic allies. Even the abrupt withdrawal of France from the NATO military organization in 1966 proved to be a symbolic act; Atlantic solidarity was little disturbed in practical terms. Indeed the threads were woven more closely together again from the mid-1970s as both France and the United States extended the concept of 'deterrence' to tactical nuclear combat.

It will be obvious that the uneasy coexistence of these two principles has meant that French foreign and defence policy has been something of a balancing act between the desire for a Europe-wide settlement and the acceptance of the need for Atlantic solidarity. One aim has not taken clear or lasting precedence over the other. Some of the most important episodes in the post-war history of French policy have involved attempts to reconcile these two principles in ways that have exacerbated tensions rather than alleviated them — the conflict over the European Defence Community project in 1952–4, de Gaulle's NATO memorandum in

1958, or attempts to create closer military cooperation directly with West Germany (most recently in July 1985).

In the absence of any easy formula for reconciling these two potentially contradictory principles we can perhaps best appreciate the importance of the third principle — French independence. For elite and mass public alike, the notion of French independence has not been an absolute one. It has involved an attempt to draw and to maintain a bottom line of decision-making autonomy in crucial circumstances in order to avoid having major decisions forced upon France by the unilateral actions of her allies. The principle of independence has a number of implications at different levels and in different spheres of world politics. It means that French policy-makers wish to ensure that they are closely consulted before major decisions are made. De Gaulle's support for the United States' position in the October 1962 Cuban missile crisis did not diminish his anger that France was not consulted prior to the decision to put American forces in Europe on 'red alert'. It means that in certain areas of the world, such as Africa or the Middle East, where France has its own interests, or where its perception of the common Western interest is different from that of the United States, French leaders will pursue their own conception rather than adopt the American. In this sense the French see themselves in a fundamentally different position from the West Germans, who are beholden to the Americans for their very existence as a state, or from the British, who are thought to be spontaneously closer to the United States because of a community of language and history. Thus French leaders believe that France can be more constructively independent in finding a middle way, more in sympathy with the indigenous peoples in the Middle East, than can the Americans, who are wedded to a visceral anti-communism that sees the Soviet Union behind every Arab nationalist or Palestinian guerrilla. De Gaulle's call for the neutralization of Indo-China in 1965, Giscard's futile attempt at arbitration over Afghanistan in 1980, and even Mitterrand's support for Nicaragua and for negotiations with El Salvadorean guerrillas in 1981–2 come into this category.

Of course, the most important arena for the exercise of French independence is seen to be the encouragement of détente in Europe. *Détente* is a French word, and French leaders are rather possessive about the very concept of détente itself. De Gaulle used the word extensively before it came into fashion in the United States, and it is widely acknowledged that de Gaulle's approach had a marked influence in the course of the 1960s on both Henry Kissinger and his future patron, former American Vice-President Richard Nixon, who made clear his admiration for the General. It was no accident that the heyday of détente at the superpower level occurred under Nixon, elected President in 1968, and his National Security Adviser and later Secretary of State Kissinger in 1970–4. Although French leaders were wary of a détente process worked out at the level of the superpowers — what they called 'Soviet–American condominium' — President Pompidou and others were pleased by the spreading of the Gaullist lesson and by the ostensible success of their particular balancing act. The consummation of this process was the Conference on Security and Cooperation in Europe and the Helsinki Final Act of 1975. It reflected French appeals for such a conference throughout the 1960s when other Western allies were hostile to the idea. It represented also a characteristically Gaullist balancing of objectives — the recognition of the inviolability of post-war frontiers in Europe (a major Gaullist theme in French relations with the Eastern European states), a call for more trade and economic cooperation, and a concomitant internal liberalization within the physically more secure (and thus hopefully less paranoid) Soviet sphere of influence. The partial failure of Helsinki over the past decade has caused more recent French leaders to alter the focus of their balancing act: partly by closer military links with the United States, and partly by the French Left and parts of the French Right rediscovering Soviet 'totalitarianism'. Nevertheless, they continue to see the détente process of the 1970s as a move in the right direction, and as an opportunity lost because of unpredictable circumstances: the swings of American policy between an overoptimistic view of détente, a naive human rights policy and an equally naive anti-communism; the perfidity of the Soviet Union; or some combination of these factors.

The most significant dimension of the principle of French independence, is its own bottom line — the independent nuclear deterrent. It is by now regarded, in an almost fully consensual manner, as the minimal guarantee of a capacity for autonomous action. Like all nuclear arsenals, it is terrifying in the scope of the potential destruction that it could cause. And like all nuclear arsenals, its reality lies paradoxically in its symbolic value, in the fact that its most important imperative is that it never be used. Upon it is seen to rest the capacity of France — otherwise a largish but essentially middle-ranking power — to choose its own balancing act, to pursue objectives like European cooperation, Third World links or détente in its own way at least part of the time. Thus atomic research was promoted despite American and British hostility during and after the Second World War; nuclear weapons development was pursued, partly clandestinely, by various coalitions under the Fourth Republic; de Gaulle made the Strategic Nuclear Force (FNS) the centrepiece of his defence and foreign policy; a larger nuclear repertoire was developed under Presidents Pompidou, Giscard d'Estaing and Mitterrand; the French Left (including the communists) came to accept the central role of the nuclear force in the 1970s; and public opinion was far less opposed to an independent nuclear force than in most of the rest of Western Europe. The FNS has, in other words, been institutionalized in both state and society in France.

Its existence is not widely challenged. The traditional communist-dominated peace organization, the *mouvement de la paix*, accepts the need for a French arsenal while the superpowers still have theirs, and other anti-nuclear weapons movements have small followings and little impact.[3] It is widely accepted that the FNS ought not to be included in the current Geneva arms negotiations along with those of the superpowers, as the FNS is believed to be a way of keeping the superpowers from becoming too reckless with each other (the 'trigger' theory).[4] The conception of the FNS and its future development are, nevertheless, central to public debate. In particular, the relationship of the FNS to conventional forces, and the role of each especially in a period of greater stringency in defence spending, is frequently debated, although conventional forces have been the harder hit by limited funds in the economic austerity of the 1980s. Even more importantly, however, the mix of weaponry evokes controversy as the FNS evolves. The form and structure of the FNS are directly related to its role in maintaining French independence and, in turn, in permitting France to play its balancing act between, on the one hand, the more Europe-centred independence associated with de Gaulle's presidency and, on the other, the call for modernization and effectiveness, which is often linked with a perceived need for greater coordination between France and her Atlantic allies on strategy, tactics, stationing of troops, the development of new types of weapons, procurement, etc. Thus the very maintenance of an independent deterrent raises a range of questions that go to the heart of the French notions of independence and détente, and of the problematic relationship between the two.

Accordingly, French foreign policy has three main themes. Firstly, after French defence policy and its nuclear core had taken its current shape in the 1960s, it played a central role in the French approach to foreign policy and to détente in particular. In giving symbolic credibility to France's principle of independence, it enabled the balancing act of Gaullism and Atlanticism, so explosive under the Fourth Republic (witness the saga of the EDC), to be stabilized in a form that continues to underpin France's approach to détente and allows France to play a key role in East–West relations in Europe. Secondly, through its importance to the state, to economic development, and to domestic politics, the independent deterrent is a key factor in maintaining the continuity of the French role in the world. Thirdly, though the continuing dialectic of Gaullism and Atlanticism, centred on defence policy and the nuclear deterrent, has still characterized French policy in the 1980s, a partial swing towards Atlanticism in the Mitterrand presidency raises new questions about the sort of role that France is capable of playing in the mid-1980s, particularly as a new and younger Soviet leadership reappraises its country's position in the 'second cold war'.[5]

France and NATO: the conflicts of the 1950s and 1960s

The 'diplomatic autonomy' conferred by the possession of nuclear weapons had wide ramifications, mainly on the Atlantic Alliance and its military arm.[6] Through the early and mid-1960s, France and the United States seemed on a collision course. Even under the Eisenhower administration, the French determination to acquire a nuclear capability had led to clashes. American policy under the Kennedy administration moved towards a new strategic doctrine of 'flexible response', involving a build-up at all levels, nuclear and conventional, to meet a wider variety of threats at any point on the globe — from the new Soviet capability in intercontinental missile technology of the late 1950s to national liberation movements in Latin America and South-East Asia. On the strategic nuclear level, it involved the replacement of the 'countercity' strategy of massive retaliation (a strategy adopted by the French to compensate for the small size of the FNS) with the more complex 'counterforce' strategy, which involved targeting nuclear missiles on the enemy's own nuclear forces and brought into the equation the ever more crucial concept of a 'second-strike' capability. This complex and expensive American doctrine went against the emerging French strategy on a number of points: the level of the nuclear threshold, which was low in both the massive retaliation and French doctrines in order to deter conventional as well as nuclear attack but higher in 'flexible response'; consequently greater emphasis by the United States on the role of the European conventional 'shield', just as France was preparing to run down its colonial army; the targeting of weapons, which for the French, with a small force, meant wreaking the greatest potential social, economic and political (rather than merely military) damage through the countercity strategy, in order to deter a large force with a small force; the interlocking of American NATO forces with the United States' world-wide strategy at a time when de Gaulle had been calling for greater French participation in such a strategy (through the September 1958 memorandum) but had been turned down; and, to make flexible response militarily credible, American pressure for a greater integration of the Allied command structure in order to coordinate and fine-tune Western reaction in various set-piece 'scenarios' popular among nuclear strategists just at the point when de Gaulle's entire policy was coming to revolve around the national basis of defence and the need to *reduce* the level of military integration.[7] The specific clashes between France and the United States on technology transfer, commitment of specific forces to NATO, cooperation in NATO military exercises, and the eventual withdrawal of French forces from NATO and ejection of American forces from France in 1966, flowed from the conflict between these fundamentally opposing perspectives. De Gaulle's resolve was hardened by the October 1962 Cuban missile crisis, when American forces (and thus the key elements of the integrated NATO command structure) in Europe were put on full alert without consultation of the Allies because of a crisis outside formal NATO jurisdiction — despite his political support for the American stance in the Cuban situation *per se* and his swift offer of full cooperation. The ultimate issue of French freedom, under the terms of the 1949 North Atlantic Treaty, to disagree with an American definition of *casus belli*, became the core of the dispute, only to be resolved by the French measures in 1966.

French freedom to determine its own definition of, and reaction to, external threat involved also differences with the United States on the broad direction in which the international system was, and should be, moving. De Gaulle's critique of bloc politics was the core of an approach in which progress towards the relaxation of cold war tensions — détente — could come about only through the loosening of the two blocs themselves and the development of more, not less, freedom of action on the part of the non-superpowers on both sides, with tissues of cross-cutting bilateral relations at 'lower' levels restraining the superpowers themselves from both aggressive behaviour in inter-bloc relations and hegemonic behaviour in the intra-bloc relations. It involved a Europe 'from the Atlantic to the Urals' — stronger ties of Western European countries not only with the Soviet Union but also with the nations of Eastern Europe — and closer relations too with the Third World and China. Yet this approach to East-West relations was not a renunciation of primary alliances as such. It recognised that in a complex world different types of cross-cutting ties — diplomatic, strategic, political, economic and cultural — had a dynamic of their own and could not be forced into the rigid framework of alliance integration. It agreed that such overlapping ties, rather than increasing the possibilities of conflict, as the Americans believed, would in the long run reduce those possibilities by strengthening the sense of cooperation and political responsibility of individual nation-states with closer proximity to the needs and interests of their own peoples. Such a system would thus express a deeper legitimacy, linked with the legitimacy of states themselves, more closely bound up with their own societies, and consequently a greater stability, as well as a greater openness to the aspirations of Eastern European and Third World countries. De Gaulle's conception of East–West relations reflected, on the international level, the principles which de Gaulle proclaimed for the French themselves in the Fifth Republic. These rather abstract, symbolic aspirations were, in fact, firmly embedded in an understanding of the need for alliances and of the limits of independence in the real world. None the less, they found a widespread resonance not only internationally but also in French domestic politics. Nuclear weapons in France have since the 1950s represented a common ground for political forces that disagreed sharply in other issue-areas. In his search for political stability, economic modernization and French independence in international affairs, General de Gaulle was able to exploit this advantage, turning the bomb into a core symbol of the change implied by the Fifth Republic. Thus it had a significance which went far beyond the military impact of the FNS itself to the whole fabric of French politics, the position of France in the world, and the future of détente.

The Mitterrand presidency: the politics of nuclear diplomacy

When Mitterrand was elected the first socialist President of the Fifth Republic in 1981, the INF issue was the most complex and salient issue in France's external relations. Two interrelated secondary issues rendered it even more so: first, Mitterrand's stated intention of 'renegotiating' certain aspects of the Atlantic Alliance; and second, his decision to appoint four communists to his government. Vice-President Bush, visiting Paris immediately after this latter decision, ominously warned that relations between France and her Alliance partners could be seriously affected by the appointment of communist ministers. Mitterrand's margin of manoeuvre was tightly circumscribed. Retreat into a defence strategy based solely on France was as politically hazardous as was complete reintegration of NATO. He could not afford to alienate the Americans for two reasons: France still depended on American satellite and other technology for her own defence systems: and American potential for economic sabotage of the French socialist experiment was considerable. All these considerations no doubt help to explain the President's decision, in July 1981, to offer enthusiastic support for the deployment of Pershing 2 and cruise missiles. Mitterrand's enthusiatic support for the NATO 'dual-track' decision was based more on a diplomatic gamble than on strategic principle. Irrespective of the eventual outcome of the Euromissile crisis, the risks for France in open support for NATO were considerable. First, there was the risk of blurring the distinction between superpower nuclear forces and the French strategic system. Second, there was the danger of prejudicing France's hopes of acting as an 'honest broker' between the United States and the Soviet Union with a view to bringing them to the negotiating table (the principal stated aim of socialist diplomacy). Finally, such a stance was likely to be very destructive of the political bases of the government's internal support. On the other hand, Mitterrand felt there was much to be gained from demonstrations of Franco-Atlantic solidarity. The sympathy of Ronald Reagan and Helmut Schmidt was essential for the defence of the franc which was already under intense pressure on the money markets. It was also necessary to 'buy' a certain amount of domestic 'peace' from the French Right. Finally, Mitterrand clearly believed that 'nuclear diplomacy' works and that the Soviet Union would eventually concede to a united Western front what it would not have yielded to a less resolute negotiating partner.

Actively playing the game of nuclear diplomacy was not seen by Mitterrand simply as a way of entering into the debate between the superpowers. It had an important bilateral dimension. The aim was to show both superpowers that France remains mistress of her own destiny. Thus, while the Foreign Minister, Claude Cheysson, insisted on France's desire to improve relations with the Soviet Union at every level, the President continued to refuse to meet the Soviet leaders as long as they maintained troops in Afghanistan. Yet, at the same time, France vigorously resisted American attempts to impose commercial sanctions on the Communist bloc and, after the imposition of martial law in Poland, successfully killed off American attempts to prevent European states from signing gas pipeline contracts with the Soviet Union. Similarly, although Mitterrand has been vociferous in his support for Reagan's nuclear diplomacy, he has been outspokenly opposed to American foreign policy on almost every other issue: Central America, Africa, and international economic policy.

The main bilateral thrust of Mitterrand's nuclear diplomacy has come in the field of Franco-American relations. It was in the context of his much publicized desire to 'renegotiate' aspects of the Atlantic Alliance that he made his dramatic flying visit to Washington on 12 March 1982. The object of the exercise, it was argued by many, was for Mitterrand to consecrate his position as 'spokesperson for Europe' which he felt France's nuclear arsenal gave him the right to claim. Mitterrand seems to have raised four basic points. The first was that the Alliance had to be seen as a comprehensive unit in which mutual duties and responsibilities, diplomatic, political and economic as well as military, needed to be carefully weighed. The second point was that, at the European end, the most vital task was to ensure that Germany be recemented to the Western bloc and prevented from sliding towards 'neutralism'. In order to achieve this, Mitterrand discussed with Reagan the prospect of much closer military collaboration between the two continental European powers. His third aim was to persuade the American President that, while nuclear diplomacy was a necessary game to be played, it had to be played sincerely and intelligently. He argued that it was vital not to provoke the Russians, not to bury détente altogether, and not to scuttle the Europeans' chance of establishing a viable *modus vivendi* with their Eastern neighbours. Finally, he wished to reassert France's absolute refusal to consider participating in the INF talks in Geneva. In this way, while offering France's enthusiastic support for one aspect of American nuclear diplomacy, Mitterrand was able to suggest to the Americans that he was by no means a slave to the Pentagon. The same trip had the collateral effect of reminding the Russians, in case they should imagine that the gas pipeline contracts signalled a 'weakening' of Western resolve, that Washington was only three hours away on Concorde.

Not surprisingly, 1983, the year of Pershing 2 and cruise, produced an intensification of France's participation in the game of nuclear diplomacy. This was the result of a variety of new developments. The new Soviet leader, Yuri Andropov, reacting to the unquestioning support for NATO that was forthcoming from France under Mitterrand, proposed that a solution to the stalled INF talks in Geneva would be for the Soviet Union to reduce its intermediate-range nuclear missiles to the level of the combined French and British totals in exchange for non-deployment of cruise and Pershing 2. Mitterrand's 'independence bluff' had been called.

President Mitterrand was not to be deterred. On 20 January 1983 he addressed a specially convened session of the German Bundestag and urged the German people to welcome INF on to their soil as the only way of establishing a nuclear balance in Europe. To enthusiastic applause from Christian Democratic benches, and mortified silence from his fellow socialists of the SPD (including his personal friend, Willy Brandt), Mitterrand put the entire weight of his authority behind the NATO 'dual-track' decision which was, to some extent, at the heart of the forthcoming German election campaign. The right-wing Bavarian leader Franz-Josef Strauss later estimated that Mitterrand's speech had been worth an extra 3 per cent of the votes for the right-wing candidates.[8] Mitterrand feared that an SPD victory at the German polls would break the ongoing dynamic of nuclear diplomacy. There is an element of self-fulfilling prophecy in nuclear diplomacy that involves the players in getting more and more deeply involved the longer they play. The Williamsburg summit brought this lesson home to the French President in no uncertain terms.

In May 1983 Mitterrand allowed himself to be maneouvred by Mrs Thatcher and President Reagan into signing a joint communiqué on the security of the Western World. The anomaly of the Williamsburg communiqué derived not only from the fact that this was the first time an economic summit had given rise to a defence statement, but also from the fact that the presence at the conference of Mr Nakasone implied an extension of the Atlantic Alliance to include Japan. The French protested energetically against any such interpretation. But the shift in position after Williamsburg also produced a new line from the French Communist Party. They interpreted the joint communiqué as a hardening of Western resolve, since not only was this the first time France had signed a statement to the effect that 'the security of our countries is indivisible', but also the reference to the negotiations deciding the level of missile deployments was seen as acceptance of the fact that some Western missiles would be deployed. Therefore, on 31 May 1983 the political bureau of the PCF, in an important statement critical of the French position at Williamsburg, argued that since the various governments had taken this line on Geneva, the INF talks should be opened up to all European countries. From all sides the criticism of Mitterrand began to pour in. The Gaullists and the Soviet Union joined forces in denouncing his return to 'Atlanticism'.

In the summer of 1983 the diplomatic battle over the Euromissiles saw France at the centre of the controversy in various ways. First, the Soviet proposal that France's arsenal should be put on the table at Geneva became a major sticking-point in INF negotiations. Second, the decision of the French government to break a seventeen-year isolation and act as host to the NATO Council meeting, which was held in Paris in June, gave rise to predictable criticism from Gaullists and communists, not to mention the Kremlin.[9] Third, in his speech to the NATO meeting, Mitterrand came out openly in favour of the 'walk in the woods compromise' in Geneva, which had recently found favour with the SPD, and expressed the hope that Geneva would fix the INF 'balance' at 'the lowest level possible'. This may well have been in part an attempt to stave off a mounting challenge to the French position from a combination of the PCF, the peace movement and the Soviet Union.

On 19 June 1983, the PCF-inspired *Appel des Cent* held a highly successful 'peace picnic' in the forest of Vincennes, which many commentators interpreted as the moment of take-off for the French peace movement. Although the slogans for this demonstration remained as vague as ever, the position of the PCF itself had shifted quite markedly since the Williamsburg declaration. With increasing regularity the PCF was beginning to agitate for France to accept the Andropov proposals that the French nuclear arsenal should together with the British be 'balanced' against the SS-20s. These proposals were made quite explicit after a surprise visit by Georges Marchais, the French Communist Party leader, to Moscow on 12 July. Despite a public relations exercise which consisted of conjuring up a false 'quarrel' between Marchais and Andropov it rapidly transpired that what was afoot was an agreement between the PCF and the CPSU on taking the French weapons 'into consideration' at Geneva. Despite

PCF reassurances to the contrary this probably reinforced the grievances that caused the communists to leave the government in France.

Giscard d'Estaing had been subtly restructuring France's entire defence panoply, including her nuclear arsenal, with a view to rapprochement with the NATO doctrine of 'flexible response'. Now there were indications that Mitterrand wished to reverse this trend. Under the socialist administration there was an unequivocal public return to the doctrine, first theorized under the Gaullists by General Lucien Poirier, of the 'test' or 'ultimatum' shot. Under this theory, the tactical missile is to be used, under the political authority of the President, only in the event of an enemy advance that seemed to be threatening France's 'vital interests'. The very act of firing it is intended as an unambiguous statement that the enemy must stop its advance or else the strategic weapon will be fired almost immediately. The Giscardian notion of tactical missiles as part of a war-fighting or battlefield panoply within the strategic context of 'flexible response' was presented as anathema. In this respect, therefore, there appears to have been a very clear break with the direction Giscard seemed to be taking France under his presidency.[10]

Despite hefty defence cuts by the socialist government in 1982 top priority was given to the strategic arsenal, with substantial resources being channelled into research and development for the mobile SX strategic missile. A completely new strategic context began to emerge. On the very day when Defence Minister Hernu made clear his intentions to afford absolute priority to strategic nuclear weapons (30 September 1982), General Bernard Rogers, Supreme Allied Commander in Europe, delivered a speech in Brussels to launch what was rapidly interpreted in France as a new war-fighting scenario for NATO, in line with the new American strategy of the 'Air-Land Battle'[11] which had been formulated a month previously in the United States, without any consultation with NATO. If France and her NATO allies appear united on deployment of Pershing 2 and cruise as an element of nuclear diplomacy, the new American proposals for the defence of Europe seemed liable to create very serious disruptions in Franco-NATO relations. There were two somewhat separate wings to what has increasingly come to be known as the 'Rogers doctrine'. The first was the desire to increase conventional defence capability in Europe so as to be able to 'raise the nuclear threshold' and possibly make a declaration of 'no early use' (of nuclear weapons). The second, which is much more closely associated with the notion of 'Air-Land Battle', was the prospect of abandoning thirty years of defensive posture on the part of NATO and preparing consciously to adopt an offensive strategy which would, in the early stages of conflict, carry the war into socialist bloc territory using, if necessary, a combination of conventional, chemical and nuclear weapons. While General Rogers gave regular publicity, throughout 1983, to the question of raising the nuclear threshold and increasing conventional defences, the more aggressive war-fighting aspects of the Air-Land Battle scenario have remained confined to the specialist military journals. By 1984, the terminology had already evolved, with 'Air-Land Battle' replaced by 'Deep Strike' and 'Follow On Forces Attack' (FOFA).

The strategic doctrine implicit in either aspect of the new American approach to the defence of Europe conflicted on a number of major points with the professed strategic thinking of the socialist administration in France. This conflict may appear to be masked on the surface by the resemblances between French and NATO military modernization plans at the conventional level. These plans were introduced in France with the important *loi de programmation militaire* which was finally passed by the National Assembly in May 1983. During a much publicized visit to the military camp at Canjuers on 15 October 1982, Mitterrand tried to allay the fears of many army officers by insisting that the land army would continue to play a major role in French defence policy.[12] But he made it clear that that role was to be one of 'global deterrence' in which conventional defence, like the tactical nuclear missiles, is considered to be one element in an overall defence policy whose key is the strategic nuclear arsenal.[13] The basic argument is that all three elements are considered to be part of the 'global deterrent'. The 'deterrent' operates against any threat to France's 'vital interests' (which, in order to increase the level of uncertainty, are never defined). Since it is vital to know whether an enemy, by engaging in a certain form of military action, is seriously intending to threaten those 'vital interests' (as opposed to merely manoeuvring in the hope of gaining some minor advantage), it is necessary, according to French military strategy, to force that enemy to make his intentions crystal clear. If the conventional defence forces are sufficiently well organized, trained and equipped then only a major attack from an enemy could hope to defeat them. A major attack would immediately be interpreted as a threat to the nation's vital interests, and would therefore introduce at once the prospect of recourse to the strategic nuclear arsenal. The tactical nuclear missile might come in at an intermediate state in this process, but the main point is that every aspect of French defence policy is geared to preventing war from breaking out rather than to actually fighting it. If it were to break out despite these precautions, then the doctrine is clear: escalation to the level of strategic nuclear fire would be almost immediate. Such is the theory behind the French notion of 'global deterrence'. It is a very different theory from that of 'flexible response'. Hence, the Mitterrand administration was genuinely shocked by Soviet suggestions that the French nuclear arsenal should be included in the Geneva talks. Mitterrand, Hernu and Cheysson argued that France's nuclear strategy (global deterrence) was quite distinct from that of NATO (flexible response). Therefore, the French argument goes, because the strategic doctrine governing these different systems is so distinct, the systems themselves cannot be lumped together for arms control purposes.

In fact, it became more and more obvious that Mitterrand and Hernu were about to carry out the very policy that, when openly proposed by Giscard in 1976, brought down around his ears the combined wrath of the Gaullists, the socialists and the communists. They were preparing for the first time ever to deploy French divisions on the front line in any future 'forward battle' in Europe. The only difference is that, whereas Giscard felt that, politically, he could weather the storm created by such a proposal, and therefore did not hesitate to make the proposal openly, the socialists know that, politically, they could not survive open admission of such plans, and therefore dress them up as something else (global deterrence). All this is very confusing, and it is hardly surprising that the opinion polls indicate almost universal ignorance about the strategic theories underlying France's weapons systems.

That ignorance and confusin were hardly dispelled by the publication of the Socialists' military white paper, the *loi de programmation militaire 1984–1988*. The most significant feature of the bill was the projected rapid deployment force (FAR). The FAR was to be under one unified command. There are remarkable similarities between this type of modernization and the rapid deployment preparations being made by NATO in the context of the new Deep Strike and FOFA approaches to the defence of Europe. The emphasis is on speed and the ability to carry the war rapidly into enemy territory. In presenting the new force Charles Hernu specifically indicated that discussions would take place with the NATO allies as to how and under what circumstances it might be deployed in conjunction with other allied forces. And under questioning from the parliamentary defence commission on 21 June 1983, he admitted that deployment could only take place with the agreement of the NATO Supreme Commander, since the FAR would be dependent on NATO for air and logistical support. These developments began to look extremely suspicious in various quarters. The PCF issued a strong criticism of any plans to use the FAR in Europe and similar worries were expressed by the dean of post-Gaullist defence strategy, General Poirier.[14]

But both Hernu and the now-retired Supreme Commander of the French armed forces, General Lacaze, have publicly insisted that the FAR will not be used automatically in the event of hostilities in Europe, still less will it be used to cover a section of the West's defences along the 'Iron Curtain'. Moreover, they have repeatedly stressed that FAR is a war-prevention force rather than a war-fighting force. It will be under the political authority of the President of the Republic, and his decision to deploy would symbolize the determination of the state to go to the ultimate extreme if hostilities do not cease immediately. Thus the three legs of the French strategic 'deterrent' are structurally linked in a cohesive unit.

Conclusions

The French approach to détente in Europe, an approach that goes back to the Second World War and is rooted in a much longer tradition of French foreign policy, has at its core the notion of the political autonomy and independence of France. Only a non-aggressive, self-limiting national independence, spread by French example to the other nation-states of Europe (including the Soviet Union), can bring about the loosening of Eastern and Western blocs that is necessary for durable understanding and cooperation; and only by seeing détente in this light can Europe avoid the vagaries of superpower hegemony, in which 'cold war' and 'thaw' (not genuine détente) succeed each other in cycles that are determined by the rituals of bipolar logic but do not alter that logic and its underlying conflictual nature. This approach requires French leaders to perform a continuing balancing act between longer-term aspirations for a Europe-wide settlement, with détente built into its foundations, and the practical need for Atlantic solidarity in a bipolar world. The condition of that balancing act has come to be embodied in French defence policy, with its fundamental consensus on the maintenance of an independent nuclear deterrent along with its running debates on the form and function of that deterrent.

In the 1960s the debate between the Atlanticists and the Gaullists was won essentially by the latter. The Gaullists drew on the heritage from the Fourth Republic and earlier, on their control over the state apparatus in a crucial phase of political, economic and military change and consolidation, and on de Gaulle's own capacity to win symbolic battles while not really challenging the ways in which the Atlantic Alliance worked in practice. In the 1970s the Giscardians, drawn from political groupings traditionally more favourable to Atlanticism, but dependent upon Gaullist support in coalition politics, made moves towards the greater coordination of French forces, strategy and tactics with the United States and NATO. However, they were constrained not only by the Gaullist consensus but also by Giscard d'Estaing's own desire to appear as a strong and independent presidential figure in the world. In the 1980s the socialist government also made moves towards Atlanticism but most of the time it avoided crossing the Gaullist 'bottom line', which was guarded by important factions in the Socialist Party. A genuine belief in the centrality of European détente has drawn even the more pro-Atlanticist French leaders towards the Gaullist approach.

Most crucially, perhaps, two fundamental changes have taken place since the establishment of the Gaullist consensus. In the first place, a phase of détente, both at the superpower level (e.g., in the

Strategic Arms Limitation Talks) and at the European level (in inner-German relations, the Helsinki process, and increasing contact between Eastern and Western Europe on a number of levels), occurred after the mid-1960s. Though stillborn in such areas as human rights in the East and genuine arms reduction, it was successful in ways that might not have been predicted ten years ago. Increasing trade and economic contacts, cultural diffusion, regular intergovernmental consultations, the recognition of international frontiers, all create cross-cutting ties between the more differentiated nation-states of both 'blocs'. Despite Soviet hegemony in the East, the economic reforms of Hungary, the nationalism of Romania, and the impact of Solidarity in Poland have made the Warsaw Pact nations a much more heterogeneous grouping, each with a panoply of quasi-autonomous links with the West and the Third World. The reactions of the new, economically reformist Soviet leadership to this situation will be critical on several dimensions. And despite Reaganism and the 'new patriotism' in the United States, West European nations — and indeed the European Community in some ways — have carved out wider and more differentiated roles for themselves and have a broader complex of linkages with each other, with the East and the Third World, too. In this context, the 'refreezing' of the cold war after 1979 can be seen to be 'one step back' after the 'two steps forward' of the 1960s and 1970s. French independence was a leading catalyst of the détente process, and French leaders will want it to remain so as some signs of the possibility of a new phase of that process seem to appear in the mid-1980s. Such a French role has become not only a 'given' in the practice of foreign and defence policy, but also a condition of domestic institutional and political legitimacy.

Secondly, however, in contrast to these hopeful signs, France's capacity to play such an independent and effective role in pursuing détente has become more complex and problematic. In the context of French politics, the old divisions between Atlanticists and Gaullists are still there, cutting across the lines of parties and coalitions. For all its consensual predominance, Gaullism will never be so easy as under de Gaulle. In the context of the economy, French foreign and defence policy have been rendered more problematic by the recession of the later 1970s and 1980s, a clear contrast to the strong growth of much of the 1960s and early 1970s. Not only has this recession led to a squeeze on defence spending and put pressure on priorities; it has also necessitated trade-offs between economic policy and foreign policy. It was often said in 1982 that Mitterrand's stand on the importance of deployment of Euromissiles was at least in part a (futile) quid pro quo for a more benevolent American attitude towards the new socialist government's economic reforms and Keynesian reflation of the period. And in the military context, perhaps most important of all, the development of weaponry has involved the need to 'keep up' by producing a wider and more complex range of nuclear weapons of all sizes; whilst development of nuclear strategy has meant the need for a tactical nuclear warfighting capability and the question of a European response to the American Strategic Defence Initiative. They have made both the costs and the benefits of nuclear independence more difficult to calculate. It is upon just such a calculation that the capacity of French governments to achieve the political independence necessary to pursue their vision of détente rests. On that capacity may in turn rest the capacity of Europe to define and pursue a kind of détente not merely handed down by the superpowers, when they are in a generous mood, but capable of changing the conflictual logic of the bipolar international system itself.

Notes

1. Cf. P.G. Cerny, *The Politics of Grandeur: Ideological Aspects of de Gaulle's Foreign Policy* (Cambridge: Cambridge University Press, 1980); Michael M. Harrison, *The Reluctant Ally: France and Atlantic Security* (Baltimore, Md.: The Johns Hopkins University Press, 1981); Edward A. Kolodziej, *French International Policy under de Gaulle and Pompidou* (Ithaca, N.Y.: Cornell University Press, 1974); W.W. Kulski, *De Gaulle and the World* (Syracuse, N.Y.: Syracuse University Press, 1966).
2. Alfred Grosser, *La IVe République et sa politique extérieure* (Paris: Armand Colin, 1964), introduction.
3. See Claude Bourdet, 'The Rebirth of a Peace Movement' and Christian Mellon, 'Peace Organizations in France Today' in J. Howorth and P. Chilton, eds, *Defence and Dissent in Contemporary France* (London: Croom Helm, 1984), Chapters 7 and 8. See also J. Howorth, *France: the Politics of Peace* (London: Merlin, 1984).

4. On French strategic theory, cf. Cerny, *The Politics of Grandeur*, op. cit., Chapters 7–9; Howorth and Chilton, op. cit.; Harrison, op. cit.; Wilfrid L. Kohl, *French Nuclear Diplomacy* (Princeton, N.J.: Princeton University Press, 1971); and the various works of General André Beaufre, General Pierre Gallois, General Charles Ailleret, General Michel Fourquet, etc., cited in the above.
5. See John Halliday, *The Making of the Second Cold War* (London: New Left Books, 1983), and also Stanley Hoffmann, *La nouvelle guerre froide* (Paris: Berger-Levrault, 1983).
6. Raymond Aron, *Peace and War: A Theory of International Relations* (London: Wiedenfeld & Nicolson, 1966), p. 490.
7. For a consideration of the systemic implications of this clash, see Alastair Buchan, *The End of the Postwar Era: A New Balance of World Power* (London: Wieldenfeld & Nicolson, 1974).
8. See André Fontaine quoting *Die Welt*, 'Entre la "Suite" et le "Requiem" ', *Le Monde*, 26 January 1983.
9. Details in *Le Monde*, 10 June 1983.
10. For an analysis of the theory of the tactical 'ultimatum' shot and of Giscard's attempts to alter that theory, see General Lucien Poirier, *Essais de stratégie théorique* (Paris Fondation pour les Études de Défense Nationale, 1982), pp. 287–311.
11. On Air-Land Battle, see 'Une nouvelle stratégie atlantique?', *Le Monde*, 5 October 1982; Konrad Age and Martha Wenger, 'La nouvelle doctrine "Air-Land Battle" ', *Le Monde Diplomatique*, February 1983; A.M. Thomas, 'L'Air Land Battle et l'engagement américain en Europe', *Défense Nationale*, April 1983.
12. *Le Monde*, 17–18 October 1982.
13. On 'global deterrence' see Hernu's and Lacaze's speeches to the IHEDN, in *Défense Nationale*, December 1982 and June 1983.
14. Lucien Poirier, 'La greffe', *Défense Nationale*, April 1983. Poirier admitted that he hoped the explanations given by Hernu were the correct ones, but added that the FAR remained very much an unknown quantity. In an interview with the author on 6 August 1983, Admiral Sanguinetti expressed the view that the FAR was intended to be used as part of NATO's panoply.

9 Britain, détente and the Conference on Security and Cooperation in Europe

Philip Williams

British policy towards the Conference on Security and Cooperation in Europe (CSCE) has not been the subject of much scholarly attention. Although one or two scholars in Britain have focused on the implementation of the Helsinki agreement, or have been involved in the monitoring of Soviet and East European conduct on human rights, they have paid little attention to the evolution of British policy as such. If this omission appears rather surprising, it is, in fact, indicative of the relatively low priority given to CSCE in British foreign policy throughout the 1970s. Indeed, British involvement in the CSCE negotiations can most appropriately be characterized as limited or modest in its approach, certainly when compared with the involvement of the Federal Republic of Germany or the neutal and non-aligned states of Europe.

These limits were apparent in all facets of British policy. In the first place, Britain had very limited interests at stake. The Helsinki process was not something that jeopardized vital economic or security interests, while it was clear that any benefits that might accrue to Britain would also be limited. This factor facilitated a degree of detachment about the process that was not shared by at least some of its allies or by the members of the Eastern bloc. The second kind of limitation concerned British expectations about what the process might achieve. This limitation reflected what might be described as a realistic if not sceptical approach to East-West détente as it evolved during the 1970s. To understand British policy towards CSCE, therefore, it is necessary to place it in the broader context of British attitudes and policies on détente. In view of these first two limits, it is hardly surprising that there was limited domestic interest in, or attention to, the Helsinki process. It was not a matter of wide parliamentary or public debate. CSCE was not in fact totally ignored. Although it was sporadic and fragmentary, there was at least some parliamentary oversight. The consequence was that Britain, as well as having limited interests and expectations, also had very limited aims in CSCE. The counterpart of limited aims, however, was that, for Britain, indirect objectives sometimes took on more importance than the ostensible purpose of the negotiations.

The rest of this chapter will elucidate these four kinds of limits in a way that enables the reader to make possible contrasts between British policy and that of the Federal Republic of Germany. Attention is given, not only to the broad attitudes that shaped British policy, but also to the policy-making process through which these attitudes were elaborated. The chapter concludes with an appraisal of British policy which suggests that the British approach, although limited, was far from being negative.

Limited interests: Britain and CSCE

British policy towards the Conference on Security and Cooperation in Europe can be understood in terms of the distinction between direct and indirect interests. British interests were essentially indirect. What was at stake for Britain was the environment in which it would have to operate. If the CSCE process was successful, then East–West relations in Europe would become more congenial and less acrimonious. While such an outcome was to be welcomed, it was not something that was vital for British security. Agreement at the Helsinki Conference would not change the fundamentally antagonistic relationship between East and West in Europe or make it possible to ignore the demands of military preparedness. The converse wa also true: even if CSCE had failed to reach a successful conclusion and provide for more extensive cooperation, it would not have been a disaster for British security policy. In a sense this viewpoint was equally true for Britain's NATO allies. In areas other than military security, however, some of the allies, especially the Federal Republic of Germany, had far more at stake.

Although Britain had an obvious interest in the human rights aspect of the Helsinki Agreement, as enshrined in both Basket One and Basket Three, the free movement of people and information was not vital to it in the same way it was to the Federal Republic. There were specific cases of family reunification that Britain was willing to press hard on — and the number of these increased immediately after the signing of the Final Act in 1975. Furthermore, the issue of Jewish emigration and Soviet treatment of dissidents did at times cause considerable consternation in Britain. At no stage, however, did human rights become as salient an issue as they were in the United States.

Britain's position on cooperation in economics, science, technology, and the environment was very similar. Although Britain played a key role in pushing for Basket Two, it was not a matter of vital interest. The United Kingdom's trade with Eastern Europe was a small proportion of its total trade. From 1963 to 1976 Britain's import and export trade with Eastern Europe fluctuated between 2.7 and 3.2 per cent.[1] While increased export trade in particular was always welcome, the East European market was not of decisive importance for Britain. Nor did Helsinki have any immediate or dramatic impact on the volume of trade. Trade with Eastern Europe constituted 2.86 per cent of Britain's total trade in 1975 and 2.9 per cent in 1976.[2] Apart from the fact that British firms improved their spares and after-sales service in the aftermath of the Final Act, Helsinki seems to have had little economic effect.

In short, in terms of both human rights and economic cooperation, the British stake in ensuring that other signatories lived up to the obligations of the Helsinki Final Act was limited. The other side of this coin, of course, concerned the obligations that Helsinki placed on Britain. Michael Clarke has suggested that 'it is curious that so little attention is ever given to Britain's own compliance with the document'.[3] This lack of attention is readily understandable, however, since Britain starts from a high threshold of compliance, especially in relation to human rights. Even so there have been a few minor isssues that have arisen in relation to British compliance. Perhaps the most serious have been the complaints from the Eastern bloc about the time taken to issue travel visas to applicants from the bloc, as well as about failures to grant them. Although it was suggested that one way of dealing with this issue was for Britain to notify East European governments about the reasons behind its decisions in those cases where applicants were turned down, the Home Office rejected this as inappropriate. This response is not entirely surprising. After all, one of the few protections that democratic societies have available is a degree of discretion about whom they admit to the country.

One of the other issues that was brought up in 1977 by the Defence and External Affairs Subcommittee of the House of Commons Expenditure Committee, in its examination of the progress that was being made towards implementation of the Final Act, was the small amount of funding that the British government was making available in order to promote cultural, economic and scientific exchanges with the Soviet bloc countries. In the period from 1976 to 1979, £100,000 was allocated annually for follow-up expenditure. This allocation was seen essentially as a pump-priming exercise, however, and in the first year only £44,000 was spent. The Treasury refused to allow the remainder to be carried forward.[4] By 1983–4 the follow-up expenditure figure had risen to £190,000, with almost £130,000 of that being channelled through the British Council.[5] Although the amount itself is paltry, it has to be seen against a background in which Britain was already spending £2 million per year on such promotions. At most, therefore, CSCE has had no more than a marginal impact on cultural exchanges.

The point about almost all these issues is that they are related to 'low policy' rather than 'high policy'. For the most part, CSCE did not involve matters that impinged in direct and major ways on British interests. Neither the benefits nor the dangers were particularly pronounced. This fact made it easier for British policy-makers to take a fairly detached approach to the process. Yet the modest expectations that Britain had about the Helsinki Conference have to be seen within the framework of the British approach to détente. And it is this approach that must now be examined.

Limited expectations: Britain and European détente

The development of East–West relations from cold war to détente in the 1960s and 1970s was not something in which Britain played a major role. This low profile in détente is somewhat surprising and puzzling because Britain in the 1950s had been a leading proponent of the argument that it was necessary to search for a less hostile relationship with the Soviet Union.[6] Some time in the early 1960s this clear sense of direction was lost. As a result, British policy was pragmatic and reactive in a period when other states were taking major initiatives designed to establish a *modus vivendi* in Europe.

President de Gaulle of France, of course, with his policy of 'bridge-building', was clearly in the forefront of these efforts in the mid-1960s. De Gaulle may have been, for a short period, an asset to the Soviet Union because of his disruptive impact on NATO. However, his grandiose aspirations for the creation of a Europe 'from the Atlantic to the Urals' posed a direct challenge to Soviet predominance in Eastern Europe. Although détente in Europe began largely through the efforts of Paris, it was not until Bonn made a clear commitment to normalizing relations with its Eastern European neighbours that it started to move rapidly. The Federal Republic's *Ostpolitik* was the key to détente in Europe. It was important not only because it coincided with the Soviet desire to get West German acceptance of the status quo in Europe but also because it helped to galvanize the Nixon administration into formulating its own détente policy. Henry Kissinger, President Nixon's National Security Adviser, was initially very concerned about *Ostpolitik* and became engaged in the détente process in Europe in large part to ensure that the process was disciplined in ways that ensured that it was not inimical to Western interests. This concern was not of course the only motive that impelled the United States into a search for superpower accommodation. American détente policy sought also to encourage Soviet restraint in a period of American military retrenchment. In addition, it represented a serious attempt to transform the superpower relationship from one in which there was intermittent cooperation simply to manage East–West crises to one where there was more extensive cooperation designed to prevent or avoid such confrontations.

In the present context the most important thing about the détente process of the late 1960s and early 1970s is that Britain was 'marginalized'. Certainly Britain did nothing to hold back détente, but by the same token it did little to facilitate or encourage the process. Britain is probably best regarded as one of the recipients of the détente of the 1970s rather than one of its creators. Yet this position was not without some advantages. Détente in Britain was never oversold to the same extent as it was in the United States. It was acknowledged that the 'era of negotiations' had begun, but it was also recognized that this process did not herald a fundamental shift in the nature of the East–West relationship.

The British position on détente was perhaps expressed most clearly in 1976 by Roy Hattersley during a House of Commons debate.[7] As he made clear, détente was not viewed by the British Labour government or Foreign Office as the resolution of fundamental differences. Rather was it seen as simply a reconciliation of contending approaches in an attempt to create an international order within which different political and ideological systems could live together in a stabilized peace with increased commercial and cultural relationships. Détente did not mean an end to East–West differences, but was an attempt to make the world safer in spite of them. Furthermore, Hattersley argued, it was necessary to proceed with caution. Détente was not a substitute for the more traditional approaches to Western European security based upon defence and deterrence. On the contrary, it was necessary to negotiate with the Soviet Union from a position approaching equal military strength. Although it was not essential for NATO to achieve equality with the Warsaw Pact in every category of weapon, it was important to demonstrate that Western Europe continued to take its own security very seriously and would not be lulled into complacency.

Part of this caution stemmed from the fact that détente was seen as a process and, therefore, as something that could be stopped or even reversed. Certainly its continued progress could not be taken for granted. While British policy-makers were anxious that détente should proceed, they had no illusions about the difficulties and setbacks that could occur. To some extent this caution stemmed from a somewhat sceptical attitude towards the Soviet Union in the higher levels of the Foreign Office where détente was seen as a Soviet tactic rather than as a fundamental change in Soviet objectives or ambitions.

If the dominant British perceptions of détente emphasized its limited character, the CSCE process was regarded as an important but limited part of détente. British policy-makers did not expect the

Conference — any more than détente itself — to bring about a dramatic improvement in East–West relations. Indeed, in relation to the Helsinki Final Act the main British concern was to make clear that it was not a legal document and that it did not give *de jure* status to the Soviet position in Eastern Europe. Although the emphasis on the fact that the Helsinki Declaration was not a treaty was a key element in the Western approach as a whole, it accorded perfectly with the low-key approach that had been adopted by Britain throughout the negotiations.

The other themes that were raised in relation to Helsinki by British spokesmen were similar. It was emphasised that the Final Act was a 'framework' and, as with most frameworks, what was crucial was the extent and manner of its implementation. The Declaration was seen as the beginning rather than the end of the process. It was hoped that the political undertakings in the Final Act would provide the basis for the development of a more constructive relationship between East and West. If it was a step in the right direction, it was, however, only a small step — much more remained to be done. Hattersley claimed, for example, that Helsinki was not the achievement of détente, merely a step towards it.

Even so, the Final Act was not to be dismissed as meaningless. It was significant as a set of undertakings or yardsticks against which the future behaviour of the Soviet Union and other Eastern bloc members could be judged or assessed. Terms like 'charter', 'code of conduct', and 'code of behaviour' were frequently used to describe the Final Act.[8] Its normative or prescriptive character was deemed crucial, and there was a recognition that the Soviet Union had provided a device that the West might be able to use as a 'lever' on Soviet policies.

Yet there were no great expectations about the effect of this lever, especially on human rights. Prime Minister Harold Wilson's statement at the final meeting emphasized that détente should be 'reflected in the daily lives of our peoples', but the rhetoric could not hide the recognition that the nature of the Soviet system militated against such an eventuality.[9] British policy-makers were also reluctant to press too publicly for change. Correspondingly, there was a certain amount of dissatisfaction with the highly visible public posturing on human rights that came to the fore in the Carter administration. This dissatisfaction emerged in testimony before the Defence and External Affairs Subcommittee of the House of Commons Public Expenditure Committee in 1977.[10] British officials recognized that the human rights issue could provoke confrontation rather than promote cooperation and had a clear preference for a soft approach based on quiet diplomacy in individual cases. This preference was in turn a reflection of the traditional British approach to foreign policy which was essentially pragmatic and which paid little attention to the internal affairs of other states.

These modest expectations about improvements of human rights in Eastern Europe were accompanied by equally modest assessments of the likely impact of the Helsinki Final Act on other areas of cooperation. In terms of trade and access to the East European and Soviet markets, there were no great hopes or expectations for anything other than a long-term incremental improvement. Trade was not expected to grow at a fast or surprising rate simply because of the economic clauses of the Final Act.

A similar agnosticism was expressed towards the confidence-building measures (CBMs) that were part of Basket One. Although the CBMs, which provided for twenty-one days' advance warning of manœuvres involving more than 25,000 men, were regarded as a useful supplement to national intelligence estimates, they could never provide more than a marginal accretion of security. Indeed, British policy-makers were well aware of one of the main dangers of CBMs — the more reliance that is placed on them, the more they can be exploited by the adversary as part of a comprehensive deception strategy. This caution was combined with the belief that the key issues of military security in Europe were being discussed in other fora, especially the Strategic Arms Limitation Talks and the negotiations on Mutual and Balanced Force Reductions in Europe. Without parallel and almost spectacular progress in both these other sets of negotiations there would be no fundamental improvement in the security position in Europe. At the same time, there was some hope that CSCE would have a spill-over effect and that the Final Act would help to give some impetus to the other negotiations. These hopes should not be exaggerated, however. The British government did not expect a major breakthrough in the MBFR talks. Indeed, the negotiations were seen in London, as elsewhere, as having less to do with mutual force reductions than with forestalling the unilateral reductions in American troop levels that were being demanded by the Democratic Majority leader Mike Mansfield and his supporters in the American Senate. In short, although Britain was a willing participant in the negotiations about European security, it had limited expectations and few illusions about the likely consequences.

This low-key approach both contributed to and was facilitated by the lack of public attention to the CSCE process in Britain. And it is this dimension that must now be examined.

Limited domestic interest

In Britain, unlike the United States, the executive not only proposes in matters of foreign policy; it also disposes. On certain issues, such as the Argentinian invasion of the Falklands, parliamentary intervention can have an important effect. The CSCE process did not have this kind of political salience. There were some comments from Conservative MPs warning of the danger that the Helsinki Final Act might act as a tranquillizer and lead to the relaxation of British defence efforts. These criticisms were fairly easily met, however, since the government itself was not optimistic about the prospects, and had no intention of substituting an uncertain détente for defence and deterrence. In other words, there was a large measure of consensus and bipartisan agreement on this issue.

However, such agreement simply reinforced the structural features of the British political system which militate against controversy on foreign-policy matters. The parliamentary system and party discipline make it almost impossible for individuals to establish an institutional base from which to conduct effective campaigns against government policy, in the way that Senator Henry Jackson and his aide Richard Perle were able to do in the United States. It is difficult in Britain to mobilize support for crusading legislation like the Jackson–Vanik Amendment of 1974, which linked the granting of Most Favoured Nations status to the Soviet Union to Soviet liberalization of its stance on Jewish emigration.

Another difference between Britain and the United States was in the degree of oversight of the Helsinki process. In the United States a Commission on Security and Cooperation in Europe, consisting of members of both the executive and the legislature, was established to monitor observance of the Final Act in the Soviet bloc. In Britain there was no counterpart to this Commission. Furthermore, parliamentary scrutiny of the Final Act and its subsequent implementation was itself rather circumscribed. In March and April of 1977, the Defence and External Affairs Subcommittee of the House of Commons Expenditure Committee heard testimony on five separate occasions. On the first two occasions all seven members of the subcommittee attended; at the next two meetings the subcommittee was a member short; while at the last session there were only five members in attendance. Evidence was heard from one outside expert — Andrew Shonfield, the then Director of the Royal Institute of International Affairs. Nine officials from the Foreign and Commonwealth Office (FCO) came before the subcommittee as did Lord Goronwy-Roberts, the Minister of State at the Foreign Office. In addition, three members of the Department of Trade, one official from the Home Office and one from the Ministry of Defence also appeared before the subcommittee to deal with specific aspects of the Final Act. Although the proceedings were extremely informative, and the subcommittee members raised pertinent and often very detailed issues, it was clear that the proceedings did not generate a great deal of interest beyond the members.

It is hardly surprising, therefore, that the House of Commons has not engaged in any form of sustained scrutiny of the implementation of the Final Act. There have, of course, been occasional debates in Parliament on the violations of human rights in the Eastern bloc as well as some parliamentary questions on the subject. There have also been one or two expressions of strong sentiment on the subject. In May 1977, for example, 143 members of the House of Commons signed a letter to *The Times* expressing their concern over Soviet policy on Jewish emigration. This kind of episode has, however, been the exception rather than the rule. For the most part, policy towards CSCE has been a matter for the Foreign Office — and there has not been a great deal of outside pressure or publicity.

The key role seems to have been played by the small CSCE unit that was established specifically to deal with Helsinki and its aftermath. Although the members of the unit were able to operate relatively free from public or parliamentary pressures, their task was not an easy one in that they had to coordinate the positions of the various departments involved. The CSCE covered such a wide range of activities that it impinged on the responsibilities of the Ministry of Defence, the Department of Trade and the Home Office. By and large, however, the coordination process seems to have been accomplished with considerable effectiveness.

The FCO seems also to have taken the lead in encouraging the establishment of a group outside government to assess compliance with the Final Act. There appears to have been a feeling in some circles that Britain needed a counterpart to the groups that had sprung up in Eastern Europe to monitor the performance of their governments in fulfilling the obligations they had accepted in the CSCE. Although there was apparently some suggestion that Chatham House would provide an appropriate forum for the group, in the end it was decided that the monitoring could more appropriately be undertaken through the David Davies Memorial Institute for International Studies. Consequently, the Helsinki Review Group was established with Lord Thompson as the first chairman.[11] The group members were very much part of the 'Establishment' and, consequently, worked closely and easily on an unofficial basis with the FCO. This relationship was in turn of considerable advantage to officials who could claim that they were under public pressure to ensure that human rights were observed more rigorously in the Soviet bloc. Although there were no illusions about what CSCE could achieve, the FCO thought that it did represent something worthwhile and that, if possible, it should be followed through. The Helsinki Review Group was an important part of the attempt to ensure that the Final Act was not simply a 'code of behaviour' or set of undertakings with no practical import. The Group itself, with Geoffrey Edwards as its rapporteur, produced three balanced and highly informative reports: *From Helsinki to Belgrade; Belgrade and After;* and *Helsinki–Belgrade–Madrid*. In addition, Edwards produced a review of the Madrid follow-up conference in the May 1984 issue of *International Relations*, the David Davies Memorial Institute journal. In many respects the creation of what might appropriately be described as a tame pressure group provided the best of all worlds for the FCO. On the one hand, British representatives at the meetings in Belgrade and Madrid could point to the activities of the Review Group as an example of public interest and public pressure in Britain. On the other hand, the Foreign Office was able to maintain maximum discretion in its approach to the question of Eastern bloc compliance, and did not have to take positions for domestic consumption — as did their counterparts from Washington on occasion. In other words, British policy-makers enjoyed considerable latitude both in choosing and in pursuing their objectives — objectives which were themselves fairly limited.

Limited objectives and initiatives

Britain did not play a major role in the negotiations leading up to the Conference on Security and Cooperation in Europe. This minor role was partly because the early 1970s — when détente diplomacy was coming to the fore — was a period in which Britain was preoccupied with entry into the European Economic Community. Almost all other aspects of foreign policy were of secondary importance in comparison. On the other hand, Britain was not oblivious to the negotiations that preceded the convening of the Helsinki Conference. But these negotiations were dealt with not so much by individual states as by the North Atlantic Council in Brussels, which acted as both coordinator and clearing house. The idea of a pan-European security conference was essentially a Soviet initiative which can be traced back to the mid-1950s. It became more serious in the late 1960s and early 1970s as NATO and the Warsaw Pact engaged in what is sometimes described as a 'dialogue of communiqués'. During this period, meetings of both alliances ended with communiqués spelling out the willingness of the members to negotiate with the rival bloc and the principles on which such negotiations could be based. Although the members of NATO were later to see CSCE as something that could be used against the Soviet Union, they were initially very reluctant to go ahead, partly because of concerns that the Conference was simply a Soviet device to divide the United States from Western Europe. In order to prevent this, NATO established certain preconditions, including the full participation of the United States and Canada in the deliberations. The successful completion of the Quadripartite Agreement on Berlin was also linked to the convening of a European security conference. It is significant too that CSCE only went ahead after the normalization process between the Federal Republic of Germany and its East European neighbours. In fact, the Helsinki process can be understood in part, at least, as a multilateral version of Chancellor Brandt's *Ostpolitik* and Mr Brezhnev's *Westpolitik*. It was also intended as a parallel measure to negotiations on force reductions, which NATO members, for all sorts of reasons, were anxious to get started. Throughout this phase of negotiations about negotiations, the British role was essentially that of good NATO ally. Whilst British policy-makers participated fully and frankly in the discussions and helped to hammer out the common position, they do not seem to have played a major part — which is hardly surprising, in view of the limited interests that they perceived to be at stake for Britain.

During the CSCE negotiations themselves, British participants occasionally took major initiatives. Much of the impetus for Basket Two on economic cooperation came from Britain, while in May 1975 British negotiators intervened decisively to resolve outstanding issues in the texts on domestic contacts and exchanges of information. Britain not only helped to lubricate the process at one or two crucial junctures, it was also prepared to stand firm when this was deemed necessary. One example of this was the question of the language to be used to refer to post-war European frontiers. Britain, together with the other NATO allies, was prepared to accept only the term 'inviolability of frontiers', which has a specific meaning in international law and prohibits attempts to change frontiers by force while acknowledging the legitimacy of peaceful change. In deference to the specific concerns of the Federal Republic of Germany, the Allies refused to accept more far-reaching language such as 'immutability' or 'untouchability' of frontiers which would have ruled out any form of change. The need to maintain alliance cohesion was never far from the surface, and there were times when promoting Western solidarity became almost an end in itself.

During the course of the 1970s, however, there was a subtle

change in British priorities. The desire to be a good European became paramount as the coordination among the European Nine took on more immediacy and importance than coordination in NATO. Although on many issues there were no serious divergences between the European and the American positions, there was not complete unanimity. This problem was especially apparent in the Carter years when the Europeans became unhappy at the crusading vigour with which the United States pushed the issue of human rights violations in the Soviet Union. The differences were apparent both prior to, and during, the Belgrade follow-up meeting — at which the American representative was regarded as something of an 'unguided missile' — with the Europeans advocating a more balanced and low-key approach. By this stage the incidental benefits of cooperation with the European allies had taken on considerable importance for Britain — and this itself was symptomatic of the limited objectives which Britain was pursuing *vis-à-vis* the Soviet bloc. In a sense, the means became more important than the ends. Yet this observation does not imply criticism of British policy. Indeed, any assessment of this policy must acknowledge that the modest approach that was adopted by Britain was not without its advantages. These advantages must now be identified.

Assessment and Conclusion

To emphasize the limits in British policy towards the CSCE is not to condemn that policy. On the contrary, an approach that was both modest and pragmatic had much to recommend it. In the first place, it led to a degree of consistency in British policy that was not always apparent in that of its allies, especially the United States. To some extent this consistency was simply the result of the detached position of Britain. Not only did the issues discussed in CSCE have far less urgency for Britain than they did for the Federal Republic of Germany; they lacked also the emotional overtones that they had in the United States, where the traditional moralistic approach to foreign policy was infused with ethnic indignation. American policy towards the Soviet position in Eastern Europe can only be understood by reference to the large Eastern European émigré community that exists in the United States and that often appears to have a significant influence in Washington.

Though a high degree of detachment was a necessary condition for a balanced approach, it was certainly not a sufficient condition. Yet when combined with the circumspect attitudes of British policy-makers to détente in general, and CSCE in particular, such detachment both facilitated and encouraged the emergence of a balanced and judicious policy. Never as euphoric about détente as the United States, the British government did not end up so disillusioned; not expecting great changes as a result of CSCE it was mildly encouraged rather than disappointed with the results.

Equally important was the fact that a policy of restraint was in many respects the one most appropriate to the circumstances. British policy-makers were perhaps more aware than many of their counterparts elsewhere of the tension in the Helsinki Final Act between the level of inter-state relations (where there was an emphasis on the status quo and the reduction of tensions) and the demands for changes in relations between the individual and the state, demands that could actually aggravate East-West relations if pushed too far. It was about these two levels that Pierre Hassner wrote when he argued that the cold war in Europe had been replaced by a 'hot peace'.[12] During the cold war, both East and West used the rhetoric of the offence but were, in fact, much more concerned with internal bloc consolidation. In the 'hot peace' of the 1970s there was formal acceptance of the status quo, but each side was attempting to change it to its advantage through more subtle means. British policy-makers recognized the dangers in this process. They were aware that too much emphasis on change in Eastern Europe might not only be counterproductive in terms of its purposes, but could spill over and obstruct or undermine the moves towards accommodation that were being made at the formal state level. Although British officials were prepared to press the Soviet Union to uphold the commitments it made in the Final Act, they were sensitive to the dangers of pushing too hard and too publicly. The CSE process had turned into a weapon that could be used by the West; but it was, and is, one which had to be used with care and discrimination.

In other words, British policy-makers were attuned to one of the main dilemmas in East-West relations — how to promote change in Eastern Europe without thereby precipitating instability or provoking the Soviet Union into more repressive measures or direct intervention in its attempt to maintain control of its bloc. It is necessary to steer a middle course between the Sonnenfeldt doctrine which, at least in one possible interpretation, seemed to hold out little prospect of the Eastern Europeans detaching themselves to any significant degree from Moscow, and the statement by Reagan's Secretary of State, George Shultz, at the opening of the Stockholm negotiations on disarmament and confidence building in Europe which denied any legitimacy whatsoever to the Soviet position in Eastern Europe. The record of British policy towards CSCE suggests that this task of handling dilemmas in East–West relations is one to which British policy-makers are well suited. Limits can sometimes be advantageous!

Notes

1. See 'Memorandum by the Department of Trade' in *Fifth Report from the Expenditure Committee, Session 1976–77, on Progress Towards Implementation of the Final Act of the Conference on Security and Cooperation in Europe*, HC 392 (London: HMSO, 1977), p. 53. Hereafter cited as *Report on Progress*.
2. Ibid.
3. Mike Clarke, 'Implementation of Britain's CSCE Policy 1975–84' in M. Clarke and S. Smith, eds, *Foreign Policy Implementation* (London: Allen & Unwin, 1985), p. 149.
4. See *Report on Progress*, p. xxxiv.
5. Clarke, op. cit., p. 151.
6. I am grateful to Brian White of North Staffordshire Polytechnic for this point.
7. See 'Extracts from a debate on East–West relations in the House of Commons on 24 February 1976' in *Miscellaneous No. 17. Selected Documents Relating to Problems of Security and Cooperation in Europe, 1954–77*, Cmnd. 9066 (London: HMSO, 1977), pp. 304–12. Hereafter cited as *Selected Documents*.
8. These terms are used frequently by key British policy-makers. The speeches are contained in *Selected Documents*.
9. For the Wilson speech, see *Selected Documents*, pp. 216–22.
10. See *Report on Progress*, p. 73 for an example.
11. I am grateful to Keith Kyle of Chatham House for his helpful comments on the formation of the Helsinki Review Group.
12. See P. Hassnet, 'Europe: Old Conflicts, New Rules', *Orbis*, vol. 17, no. 3, Autumn, 1973, pp. 895–911.

10 Britain and European Political Cooperation in the CSCE

Michael Clarke

For the Western Europeans, the success of European Political Cooperation (EPC) in the process surrounding the Conference on Security and Cooperation in Europe (CSCE) has been one of the gratifying by-products of a diplomatic negotiation that has otherwise been a very long haul. In a broad perspective it could be argued that EPC was a natural derivative of the CSCE. After all, the CSCE was concerned with a wide range of issues that were of natural interest to the European Economic Community. The Community of the Nine made up a quarter of the thirty-five-nation conference and in any case had major contacts with many of the other participants; and they also cooperated in other diplomatic fora such as the United Nations Economic Commission for Europe and Unesco, in matters that overlapped with CSCE issues. Perhaps it was not surprising that EPC developed strongly. Yet it was not automatic that it should do so. The EEC has proved disappointing in many policy areas where similar advantages would seem to have applied. More to the point, both EPC and the CSCE were processes that began at exactly the same time, between 1970 and 1972, and which at the outset were open-ended and speculative. Certainly British politicians did not entertain particularly high hopes for either diplomatic exercise at the beginning.

The development and the success of EPC grew out of two mutually reinforcing trends. On the one hand, the progress of CSCE, as of détente, was disappointing: this provided a context in which a powerful diplomatic group could influence negotiations. On the other hand, the procedures and coordination of the fledgling EPC proved to be highly appropriate to just this kind of diplomatic long haul. The less success there was for détente, the more there proved to be for EPC. In the case of Britain's reactions to these issues, the relationship between failure in the one sphere and success in the other became reinforced over time until they had some of the attributes of a self-fulfilling prophecy.

The poor performance of the CSCE

One of the major reasons for the general success of EPC has been the poor performance of the CSCE process itself in affecting East–West relations, at least in the way the Final Act seems to envisage. This situation was produced by a number of general factors.

To begin with, the Final Act of 1975 is very much a 'Western document'.[1] All of its authors stress, of course, how carefully balanced it is; they point to the compromises behind all of the final wording and how the Soviet Union has made much of its achievement of the declaration of ten principles in Basket One. In the event, however, the Soviet Union paid a high price for its declaration of principles. The West was determined that the Final Act should be a political document, not a legal one, in order to avoid giving the Soviet Union *de jure* recognition of the ten principles, which the Soviets would have liked to make into a legal cornerstone around which the rest of the document would be cast.[2] The result could have been made to look like a post-war peace treaty for Europe. Not only did the Soviets fail to elevate the status of the principles to something akin to legalism; they also had to agree to the inclusion of several issues, especially in Basket Three, which they would rather not have had included.

The Final Act may be a diplomatically balanced document. In a political sense, however, it is a document in which the ten principles at the beginning are in reality paid for by the Soviet Union with the rest of the CSCE agreement. The Western powers have effectively set the agenda of the CSCE process. As the process has continued through successive review meetings. working groups, and now the Stockholm Conference on Disarmament and Confidence-Building Measures in Europe, so this agenda-setting has become more obvious. Whether or not the West feels it is getting anywhere with the CSCE process, it has found that it has the Soviet Union and many of the Eastern bloc states very much on the defensive all the time. Further reviews of the Final Act, in Belgrade and Madrid, have been occasions to offer interpretations, and in some cases, reinterpretations of the document. The Western states have been firmly in control of this gradual evolution of the process.[3]

Secondly, the CSCE was initiated as part of a grand détente package deal of the late 1960s and early 1970s. It was an important component in keeping up the momentum of *Ostpolitik*, and the Western powers balanced their reservations about attending a European security conference against their keener interest in the establishment of the Mutual and Balanced Force Reduction (MBFR) talks in Vienna. For the Soviet Union, the attraction in the late 1960s of a European security conference was that it would dilute any adverse impact on Eastern Europe of the *Ostpolitik* that was developing at the time; it would serve, in lieu of a peace treaty, to legitimize the Soviet position in Eastern Europe and, most especially, to legitimize the German Democratic Republic, and it would serve as a major forum into which the Eastern governments could channel any embarrassing issues arising from détente, in such a way that nothing tangible need emerge.[4]

As part of a diplomatic package, therefore, the CSCE was a process whose time seemed to have come in the early 1970s. But by 1975, when the Helsinki Final Act was finally signed, the package had already dissolved. The momentum of détente had clearly slowed by that time, and détente — of this vintage, anyway — was at an end by 1979. The various talks that were proceeding at this time (particularly the MBFR and SALT talks) had become essentially self-contained. And for the Soviet Union many of its original diplomatic aims had already been overtaken by events. The GDR had achieved formal diplomatic recognition, the success of *Ostpolitik* had presented the Soviets with greater territorial legitimacy in Eastern Europe, particularly in respect to Poland, and the political cohesion of the Eastern bloc had not been challenged from outside. Moreover, the CSCE took on an unexpected momentum of its own and challenged the political cohesion of the Eastern bloc from the *inside*. It stimulated monitoring groups in Eastern bloc countries; it became identified very potently with human rights and thus quickly became a stick with which the Western powers could beat the Soviet Union over its internal politics and the behaviour of its client governments in Eastern Europe.

Thirdly, in response to this dissolution of the original diplomatic package upon which the CSCE was founded, the subsequent process of review meetings and working groups became a barometer of the declining fortunes of détente and the onset of a new cold war. The Belgrade review meeting of 1977–8 was unable to reach agreement on anything substantive, except that there would be another review: and when there was, the Madrid meeting of 1980–3 opened to the accompaniment of the invasion of Afghanistan and the Polish crisis and closed on the mutual indignation surrounding the shooting down of the Korean airliner.[5] Clearly, the CSCE would have no independent impact on East–West relations or European security in general. It had become a symbol of whatever state the cold war was in.

In these circumstances, the CSCE became trapped in its own internal workings. It was not a major impetus to détente but a reflection of it; it was having no discernible independent impact on the conduct of East-West relations. In the well-chosen words of Professor Helga Haftendorn, we had arrived at the point where, 'the maintenance of the CSCE process consumes more détente than it produces'.[6] Effectively, therefore, the diplomatic process of the Final Act, the review meetings and the working groups became the only major output of the CSCE. In this situation the EPC could develop very successfully, for the European Community states could operate as a caucus in the negotiations. In a conference of thirty-five participants a caucus of nine or ten has obvious advantages. Moreover, since the practical impact of anything agreed in Helsinki, and then reviewed in Belgrade, Madrid or Stockholm, was likely to be small, it was much easier for the Community to submerge natural differences of interest in agreed positions. And since the whole process after 1975 rapidly took on a more stark East-West confrontation aspect, with the East getting the worst of the exchange, there was increasingly more to unite the Community members than to divide them. In short, the type of progress that the CSCE made — the evolution of self-contained conference diplomacy — was highly conducive to the type of progress that EPC *could* make. It turned out to be an excellent vehicle for Community cooperation.

The impressive performance of EPC machinery

A favourable context does not in itself guarantee success. Another major reason for the success of EPC in this case was that, as it happened, Community policy-makers coordinated their positions extremely well. Indeed, in the early history of the CSCE process, the development of EPC was so impressive that it took on a leadership role, tacitly directing the course of negotiations.

The early history of EPC on this issue is one of intensive and overlapping negotiation between Community policy-makers. As early as November 1970 the Foreign Ministers' meeting that approved the Luxembourg Report, which gave expression to European Political Cooperation, identified the CSCE as an area in which political cooperation should, and could be developed.[7] The Political Committee was directed to establish a working group, which it did in March 1971, and this was complemented in May 1971 by an *ad hoc* CSCE working group which enlarged the existing group by including appropriate representatives from the EEC Commission. At the highest level, the President of the Commission would express a view whenever CSCE was being discussed in a summit; below that level the Political Director of Directorate-General I (External Relations) would express the Commission's view to the Political Committee. And below that, at the level of the working groups, the personnel overlapped as they evolved a network of well-understood procedures. The original members of the Political Committee's working group were generally the Eastern European or NATO specialists who would anyway meet twice a year within NATO.[8] The CSCE working group and the *ad hoc* working group coexisted with overlapping membership, and they would normally meet every two months. As the Final Act was actually negotiated, they moved into virtually continuous sessions. The elaborate nature of these arrangements evolved as a response to the different areas of competence that each organization embodied. The vertical division expressed the political rank, from Presidents and Prime Ministers, to Foreign Ministers, to Political Directors, to working group members. At each level there was an expression of the common interests of EPC, as well as a voice for the appropriate representative of the EEC Commission. The horizontal order expressed the functional division of labour; between those issues that involved the security concerns of all the Western states, which were dealt with through NATO, or occasionally on a bilateral basis; those issues that concerned more specifically the European Community states in matters they chose to regard as the substance of EPC; and those issues, for example under Basket Two, that were obviously concerned with the EEC as such, having implications for the workings of the Treaties of Rome.

If such vertical and horizontal divisions seem overelaborate on paper, in practice they worked in a highly coherent way. This outcome was due to the overlapping of personnel and, increasingly, of the issues involved. In 1972–3, during the first twelve months of diplomatic work for the CSCE, the NATO forum seemed the most relevant, since at this stage the negotiations concerned the wider issues of the Soviet Union's insistence on a set of 'security principles' and the diplomatic price that it was prepared to pay for it. When the negotiations moved into a second phase during 1973–5 in Geneva, however, the 'NATO issues' were less prominent, the United States — though a participant — was little more than an observer, and Secretary of State Henry Kissinger seems to have been only mildly interested in the whole affair.[9] It was here that the close coordination of EPC began to make itself felt. The Community emerged as the most coherent single caucus in a conference that, at the time, consisted of a Soviet and East European bloc, a disinterested USA, a contructive but separate Canada, a group of 'neutral and non-aligned' (NNA) states and, within the latter, one or two mavericks, such as Malta, who had very particular concerns to pursue. The Eastern bloc may have been more solid, but the EEC was much more successful as a caucus. It produced positions and extensive drafts, carrying the NNA states with its wording, and in effect it began the process whereby the Final Act and its subsequent interpretations were to become an exercise in the West setting a diplomatic agenda for the East. The preparatory work for the Helsinki Final Act in 1975 had made the EEC member states, therefore, a highly effective caucus, and the composition of the document, particularly in Baskets Two and Three, reflected this fact.[10]

By the time the process of reviewing the CSCE began in 1977, this new diplomatic situation had become even more pronounced. EPC was now functioning extremely well. It had become a process that needed minimal central direction. The policy was coordinated very much from the bottom up. From August 1975 until mid-1976 the preparatory machinery of EPC had concentrated on producing a very extensive commentary on the Final Act, Basket by Basket, line by line. The result was a substantial piece of work that was produced as European Community (not Commission) documents in 1976.[11] More than anything, these documents express the strength of EPC on this issue. They are an agreed interpretation of the Final Act among the Nine and all the institutions of the Community; they mark out the possibilities and limits for the future of the CSCE. There could hardly be a clearer example of the role that the Community states were playing in setting the agenda of the CSCE at this time. The process of coordination and policy-making needed very little political direction from above.

CSCE issues were never prominent in the Foreign Ministers' meetings after 1975. In the public record there is only one Foreign Ministers' meeting, in February 1977, at which any substantive discussion of CSCE took place.[12] For the vast majority of the time policy was evolved within a much lower-level triangle: between fairly small departments in national foreign ministries, the extensive coordination machinery of EPC which had now been functioning in high and low gears for five years, and — a newer element — the national delegations at the review conferences, who were collectively building up a good deal of expertise and experience and were becoming the new *cognoscenti* of the CSCE labyrinth.

By 1977, however, the circumstances had altered. The Soviet Union and the Eastern Europeans were very much on the defensive as the 'Helsinki declaration' had become so identified with human rights issues, and the United States belatedly, began to take a great interest in the CSCE process for exactly the same reasons. The very closeness of the EEC delegations at the Belgrade review meeting began to exacerbate a transatlantic difference within the West. In a practical sense, the EEC delegations would meet, usually three times a week during conference sessions, first thing in the morning. Whilst 'the Nine' were involved in such deliberations, the 'other Six', that is the other members of NATO who were not in the EEC, were unable to coordinate their detailed positions for the imminent working groups until the EEC meetings ended. Frequently, there was just insufficient time to establish a NATO position on many matters of detail, and the European Community position would emerge by default. This tendency was reinforced by the work of DG I at the European Commission, which on certain matters would act as a single coordinator to parcel out new proposals that members of the EEC group were putting forward. In a more political sense, there was a difference in the priorities of the American delegation as opposed to those of the Europeans.[13] The United States was prepared for a confrontation with the Soviet Union over Basket Three issues. It was seeking a clear propaganda victory over the Soviet Union in the matter of human rights, and there was a wealth of Congressional fact-finding and American public emotion behind that desire.[14] The leader of the American delegation, Arthur Goldberg — 'the unguided missile' according to some European press correspondents — felt that he lacked EEC support in many of his sorties. This more overtly confrontational style had not been anticipated by the EEC delegations and was not regarded by them as tactically wise either for the fate of the meeting or for the Eastern European dissidents — as yet unnamed — who were at issue in these exchanges.

The Belgrade meeting dragged on past Christmas until March 1978. In the event, much of the detailed work that the EEC group had done on new proposals and tighter interpretations became irrelevant. As time progressed the meeting revolved increasingly around the attempt simply to agree on a concluding document. There was a brief French desertion from the European ranks as its delegation offered a surprise compromise text of a concluding document. In the end it was only through the work of the NNA states that even the minimal document of Belgrade was agreed upon. It recorded that they had met, exchanged views, and would meet again. The CSCE process had been kept going; the Soviet Union and its allies would be on trial again in Madrid in 1980. Beyond that, almost nothing was possible. Within that restrictive framework, EPC had proved itself triumphant in preparing, organizing and giving weight to the most effective caucus within the thirty-five nation conference. If that was good for the EEC, it had proved to be less good for NATO and cannot be said to have contributed much to security and cooperation in Europe.

Between 1973 and 1978 the process of EPC had been one of the more noticeable products of the CSCE. In so far as it had been possible to lead CSCE somewhere, the EEC states had led it. The Eastern bloc had been reluctant to do anything with the CSCE after 1975; the United States had been quixotic. Moreover, the process of EPC had drawn on the natural magnetism of the EEC states to touch on other European countries. In the early stages, before Community enlargement took place in 1973, Norway (then a prospective member of the EEC) had been included in all preparatory discussions for the CSCE. The Community's economic and political links with the Middle East and North African countries gave it an important interest in the Mediterranean issues that emerged in the Final Act. The Nine had effectively written the Mediterranean Declaration that appeared in the Final Act and were insistent on limiting the demands of Malta that wider Mediterranean issues should be included. This position was successfully maintained throughout the Belgrade meeting and then at a special working group on Mediterranean security in Valetta in February 1979. In a more particular way, Italy acted as a link between the EEC and the Mediterranean states, while Denmark took on a similar role, acting as a liaison with the Scandinavian group. There was also an interesting, unofficial 'German-language group' which consisted of the Federal Republic, the German Democratic Republic, Austria, Switzerland and Liechtenstein; it was concerned to ensure that translations of the texts agreed with a German version.[15] All of these links contributed to the general success of EPC in playing such a leading role in the conferences.

By the time of the Madrid review meeting in 1980, circumstances had shifted once again. The Community states found themselves highly coordinated, but playing a less vital role than at Belgrade. After Belgrade there had been a general recognition on both sides of the Atlantic that coordination within the NATO group would have to improve. There would have to be more timely coordination between the European 'Nine' and the other six NATO states. And the United States appointed as leader of their delegation Ambassador Max Kampelman, who was more experienced in European diplomacy, and who certainly had a long acquaintance with CSCE history. The Western group as a whole was more consensual at

Madrid and less dependent on the running being made either by the United States on human rights or by the EEC on most other issues. Moreover, the whole conference was much more orientated to security issues. The detailed work of the EEC delegations on specific new proposals was easily overshadowed at Madrid by public wrangling between the superpowers over major cold war issues.[16] The agreed text of agreement over Basket Two issues was settled before the end of 1982. It awaited agreement on matters in Basket One, which would have to be settled before a concluding document could be drafted. Ironically, it was in just this area that Madrid eventually made some unexpected progress, in extending the definition of confidence-building measures and agreeing to the Stockholm conference on confidence-building and disarmament. So NATO, and issues most closely linked to NATO, increasingly dominated the proceedings at Madrid. The NNA states still had a useful role to play at Madrid but, like the EEC states, less opportunity to develop it. It had also become clear by 1980 that the machine of EPC was now only one diplomatic machine among several. The CSCE process itself had achieved some institutionalization. The superpowers sent to the conference large and powerful delegations, and the various cross-cutting diplomatic groupings had had five years and the experience of Belgrade to become accustomed to the process. By 1983 the relative advantages that the EPC diplomatic machine had enjoyed between 1973 and 1978 had become diluted by the learning process of others.

The development of British policy

It is possible to understand the development of EPC in these negotiations by reference to the two general trends outlined above: as the CSCE process became less substantive, and more dependent on the mood of East–West relations, it was easier for a caucus like the EEC to reach a genuinely integrated negotiating stance; and, as it happened, the EPC coordinating machinery, particularly at the lower level, produced a very effective caucus. Its effectiveness may have brought diminishing diplomatic returns in the 1980s as the superpowers returned to the front line, as it were. Yet, as the

Community members went into the Stockholm meeting in January 1984, and began preparing for the next review meeting in Vienna in November 1986, there could be no doubt about the effective working of EPC.

In the case of Britain's own policy towards the CSCE over these years, the same trends are accurately mirrored at the national level. However, in this national mirror something else is reflected too; the priorities of British policy went through an evolution as the CSCE process continued, until the success of EPC became the first priority, indeed an end in itself, some way ahead of any goal that the CSCE was capable of offering. Moreover, though it is customary to look at the meagre results of the CSCE with hindsight, and ask what else British policy could pursue, this development was not inevitable. It arose through the way in which the policy was handled.

At first British policy-makers did not automatically interpret the CSCE as a natural vehicle for EPC. The CSCE may have been identified as one of the original concerns of EPC when the process was established, but in 1972 it was not obvious that the EEC would be the most appropriate forum through which Britain should pursue its policy. In any case, the original conception of EPC in 1972, certainly in Britain, was that it was unlikely to be too demanding a process. High-level contacts would be regular but not frequent, and lower-level contacts would be made as and when necessary. NATO seemed a more obvious forum for issues of 'security', and the Council of Europe and established bilateral contacts would seem to provide safe channels for the negotiations of related matters.[17] It was not until 1974–5 that it became clear that the Soviet Union was beginning to lose the argument; 'security' was going to be defined rather widely in the Final Act and linked to 'cooperation', which was also widely defined. Without a clearer American lead, NATO was not so obvious a forum for preparations among the Western Allies. But this situation only became clear towards 1975 as the real nature of the Helsinki package, and American reactions, emerged.

There was also a fair amount of scepticism among British policy-makers during the early stages about what the whole process might achieve. There was a genuine suspicion in both political and diplomatic circles that the West might be entering into this part of the grand détente package deal too cheaply; that it was being manipulated by a crafty Soviet Union into an unjust peace treaty and a communist propaganda jamboree. Britain never felt the same degree of opportunity over the CSCE as the Federal Republic. As Professor Haftendorn has pointed out, the CSCE — being not just a conference but a programme of bilateral and multilateral diplomatic negotiations — was seen as capable of contributing to a framework for future West German *Ostpolitik*.[18] There was, at the time, some concern in the Federal Republic that existing bilateral *Ostpolitik* could otherwise become unstructured and unpredictable. Certainly there was no equivalent in British policy-making circles to the personal commitment of Hans Dietrich Genscher, foreign minister since 1974, to the success of the CSCE process. In short, it appears that British policy aims were not particularly clear in the early stages. Expectations of success in East–West terms were low. There was a determination that the CSCE process, whatever became of it, should not be preprogrammed to arrive at a given result — which would simply accord the Soviet Union the diplomatic victory that it had originally been seeking. It had to be evolutionary. We would simply have to see where the negotiations for Helsinki and the Final Act took us.

In the light of these open-ended expectations it was with pleasure and a certain degree of surprise that British policy-makers reported in 1976 how successful EPC had proved to be. The process of EPC had emerged far more incisively than originally envisaged, and diplomatic officials had embraced the new work with enthusiasm. Because there was so little expectation of an early East–West success, policy-makers latched onto EPC as something tangible that *had* emerged from their work. And it is clear that this outcome had arisen not as a political initiative as such, but as part of the standard procedures of the British diplomatic community. It was acknowledged at the formal level by the Foreign Office Minister responsible for the CSCE; he stressed that the lack of progress in Belgrade had not detracted from the unity of Britain and its allies.[19] It was more forcefully expressed by Foreign Office personnel in evidence to the House of Commons. They pointed out that EPC had become the basis of 'the fundamental work and the most systematic' of its preparations for the CSCE.[20] In private, one Foreign Office official who had been intimately involved at Helsinki and Belgrade commented in 1978 that the 'context of the Nine was absolutely basic to the positions we took'.[21] In the two years between the Final Act and the Belgrade review meeting, therefore, Britain was pursuing a policy that effectively put EPC as a higher priority than NATO, higher than relations with the United States over these matters, and certainly higher than its pursuit of détente as such.

This general bias in favour of EPC was progressively reinforced by other aspects of the process. Firstly, we should be aware of the kind of issues that the CSCE presented to British policy-makers. It was a diplomatic initiative that was supposed to lead to many other organizational contacts between states in Europe; not vice versa. Essentially the diplomacy came before the activity. This situation is not normally the case in diplomacy. In economic relations, for example, the task of diplomacy is more normally to rationalize, facilitate and promote the existing relationships between states and state organizations. The need for diplomacy arises normally from the existence of certain types of connectedness. This relationship was not obviously the case with the CSCE; the Final Act was supposed to make things happen that would not otherwise have done so.[22] As far as British policy-making was concerned, therefore, the CSCE began in the Foreign Office where EPC was much favoured and where the liaison activities of EPC were quickly assimilated.

Secondly, as the negotiations continued, the issues stayed firmly within the Foreign Office. In theory, many other Whitehall departments could have been involved, since the CSCE concerned such a range of military, economic, cultural, personal and educational activities. In practice, however, since expectations of CSCE's impact were low, and since it was seen as a component of détente, it remained a foreign-policy matter and primarily a Foreign Office concern. There was a necessary degree of involvement by the Ministry of Defence in Basket One issues, and some involvement by the Department of Trade and the Home Office, where particular issues arose. Beyond that, however, the CSCE process was overwhelmingly the concern of one Foreign Office Minister of State at any one time, a small 'CSCE Unit' within the Foreign Office, and the particular members of Britain's conference delegations and those officials working within the day-to-day machinery of EPU.

While such centralization of policy-making within the Foreign

Office was not inevitable, it was also not surprising. Its effect was to keep all the various issues involved in the CSCE in the realms of diplomacy. This situation again strengthened the desire to make EPC work. As Andrew Carter has pointed out, CSCE was a unique and successful example of multilateral conference preparations, at a depth never previously achieved.[23] Home departments within Whitehall cannot, of course, avoid the implications of the EPC structure, but the Foreign Office is the ministry most closely involved and naturally committed to the success of EEC collaboration. The CSCE also had no particular backers in Britain. There was no organization or individual whose fate was bound up with the negotiations. The Foreign Office represented the most 'interested party' in Britain (outside some very isolated private organizations) and, as we have seen, officials had much higher hopes for EPC than détente.

Thirdly, as the negotiating process continued through Belgrade to Madrid and Stockholm, the policy machine within Britain became, if anything, more narrow. All the trends and attitudes that we have identified were reinforced by the negotiating success that the Western delegations enjoyed. As the CSCE became a more self-contained diplomatic exercise, there seemed even less need to involve relatively disinterested home departments or outside organizations. Most home departments, as well as the Foreign Office itself, felt that there was singularly little that they had to do in order to live up to the expectations of the Final Act.[24] It is a measure of how thoroughly the Western delegations had effectively drafted the Final Act that most ministries discovered that they were already implementing it; and quite adequately in their own judgements. At a higher level, the British government confirmed this view officially in 1978.[25] There was essentially nothing to do but leave the Foreign Office to carry through the negotiating of the review meetings. There was some evidence of high-level political direction to the British delegation in Madrid to take a tougher line than hitherto on human rights questions, and the Stockholm Conference inevitably involves the Ministry of Defence more than before. Essentially, however, as the process moved further on from the immediate considerations of the Final Act, the active policy-making circle has become smaller rather than larger, routine rather than initiatory, and subordinate to higher priorities within the Foreign Office and in its close liaison with the Cabinet Office. Between these two powerful offices, the priorities of European affairs and the promotion of EPC stand at their highest within the British government: though even the Cabinet Office seems to have accorded the Foreign Office the leading role over EPC itself.

So effective had this Community negotiating machine become that the Eastern Europeans were permanently on the defensive after 1977. They were reduced to simple obstruction and blocking tactics; so much so that some British observers warned that the CSCE, as a détente process, would be effectively stultified by this sort of Western success.[26] There would simply not be enough in it for the Eastern bloc, and particularly the Soviets, to encourage them to negotiate seriously in the future.

In reviewing the years from 1972 to 1985, it becomes clear that Britain's CSCE policy began somewhat tentatively and ambiguously. By force of circumstances, it adopted EPC as its framework and then, after 1975, evolved almost exclusively within that framework with a remarkable degree of consistency. After all, between these years the policy has spanned no less than five governments, four prime ministers, and six foreign secretaries. Political involvement from the top has, however, been minimal and more a matter of emphasis than anything else. Work at the bottom has been detailed, expert and diplomatically effective. And the international context has been such that the negotiations for the CSCE *are*, to all intents and purpose, the output. It says much about the nature of both the CSCE and EPC, and of the relationship between them, that the former has lacked any real vitality while the latter has gained a great deal from the whole process.

Notes

1. *Conference on Security and Cooperation in Europe. Final Act*, Cmnd. 6198 (London: HMSO, 1975).
2. *Coopération Politique Européenne*, GT (76), 4 rev. (Luxembourg: European Community, 1976) pp. 7–9.
3. On the progress of the CSCE see Geoffrey Edwards, 'Belgrade and Human Rights', *Government and Opposition*, vol. 13, no. 3, Summer 1978, pp. 307–22;

G.P. Loescher, 'Human Rights and the Helsinki–Belgrade Process', *Yearbook of World Affairs*, 1981, pp. 62–78; M. Howard, 'Helsinki Reconsidered: East–West Relations Two Years After the Final Act', *Round Table*, vol.67, no. 267, July 1977, pp. 241–5; H.G. Skilling, 'CSCE in Madrid', *Problems of Communism*, July–August 1981, pp. 1–16.

4. See K.J. Holsti, 'Bargaining Theory and Diplomatic Reality: the CSCE Negotiations', *Review of International Studies* vol. 8, no. 3, July 1982, pp. 159–70.
5. For the texts of the Belgrade and Madrid meetings, see *The Meeting Held at Belgrade from 4 October 1977 to 9 March 1978 to Follow up the Conference on Security and Cooperation in Europe*, Cmnd. 7126 (London: HMSO, 1978); and *Concluding Document of the Meeting Held at Madrid from 11 November 1980 to 9 September 1983 to Follow up the Conference on Security and Cooperation in Europe*, Cmnd. 9066 (London: HMSO, 1983).
6. Remark made by Professor Helga Haftendorn at the Conference on CSCE and European Détente, University of Bradford, November 1984.
7. Götz von Groll, 'The Nine at the Conference on Security and Cooperation in Europe' in David Allen, R. Rummel and W. Wessels, eds, *European Political Cooperation: Towards a Foreign Policy for Western Europe* (London: Butterworth, 1982), p. 60.
8. Ibid., pp. 63–4.
9. For a good review of official positions during the negotiations for the Final Act, see *Miscellaneous No. 17. Selected Documents Relating to Problems of Security and Cooperation in Europe 1954–1977*, Cmnd. 6932 (London: HMSO, 1977).
10. Philippe Lemaitre, 'Solidarity Begins at Home', *The Times*, 1 November 1977.
11. See *Coopération Politique Européenne*, vols 1–4.
12. *The Times*, 1 February 1977; *The Guardian*, 16 April 1977.
13. See the annual *Activities Reports* of the independent Congressional Commission on Security and Cooperation in Europe (established in 1976), Washington DC. On the US position in Belgrade see Department of State, *The Belgrade Followup Meeting to the Conference on Security and Cooperation in Europe October 4, 1977 – March 9, 1978*, Special Report no. 43, June 1978, Bureau of Public Affairs, Washington DC, pp. 34–5.
14. See, for example, the speech of Professor Joyce Hughes, a member of the American delegation to Belgrade, *United States Information Service Press Release*, 12 October 1977; and the reaction to it, *New York Times*, 12 October 1977, p. Al.
15. Groll, op. cit., p. 67.
16. J. Sizoo and R. Th. Jurrjens, *CSCE Decision-making: The Madrid Experience* (Netherlands: Kluwer Academic Publishers Group, 1984) Chapters 3 and 6.
17. B. Burrows and G. Edwards, *The Defence of Western Europe* (London: Butterworth, 1982) p. 135.

18. Professor Haftendorn in her remarks to the above conference at the University of Bradford.
19. Statements by Lord Goronwy-Roberts, Minister of State, *The Times*, 10 March 1978, p. 10.
20. House of Commons Expenditure Committee, *Fifth Report from the Expenditure Committee, Session 1976–77, on Progress Towards Implementation of the Final Act of the Conference on Security and Cooperation in Europe*, HC 392 (London: HMSO, 1977) p. 14.
21. Personal interview.
22. See Michael Clarke, 'The Implementation of Britain's CSCE Policy, 1975–84' in Steve Smith and M. Clarke, eds, *Foreign Policy Implementation* (London: George Allen and Unwin, 1985) pp. 142–65.
23. Andrew Carter in his remarks to the above conference at the University of Bradford.
24. House of Commons Expenditure Committee, op. cit., pp. xii, 53, 81.
25. *Fifth Report from the Expenditure Committee, Session 1976–77, on Progress Towards the Implementation of the Final Act of the Conference on Security and Cooperation in Europe. Observations by Government*, Cmnd. 7112 (London: HMSO, 1978).
26. House of Commons Expenditure Committee, op. cit., p. 35; Helsinki Review Group, *Belgrade and After* (London: David Davies Memorial Institute, 1978) p. 22.

11 Conclusions: a three-dimensional view of East–West relations

Kenneth Dyson

The earlier chapters of this book emphasized the historical dimensions and the character and origins of contrasting national conceptions of détente. It is now time to turn to the practical and theoretical implications of the experience of the détente and post-détente phases for the effective management of East–West relations in Europe. The stress that was placed on the complexity, paradox and ambiguity of détente in the introduction and Chapter 1 gave an indication of the nature of the conclusions. Simple views about East–West relations tend to produce inadequate responses to complex problems; sloganeering about 'peace' and 'strength' threatens paralysis of thought and policy; whilst indiscriminate use of the notion of threat and the 'merchandising of fear' can be counter-productive. All too easily the main consideration becomes the use of a particular approach rather than identification of the approach that is appropriate to tackling a specific situation. The central problem in East–West relations is partial or negative effectiveness. Great sophistication is required because policy must master an extensive set of concepts. In other words, East–West relations is a matter for 'policy professionals' who combine extensive experience with historical insight and some theoretical discipline. Sophistication means taking account of the total situation so that the possibility of miscalculation in a complex environment is minimized; it means recognizing that no single approach is always effective; and it means starting squarely with prudence as the organizing value and main issue in East–West relations.

This chapter stresses the need for a three-dimensional view that embraces the roles of ideology, strategy and détente; that analyses the several elements of the European situation as a basis for diagnosing that situation and determining the appropriate combination of the three dimensions in policy; that recognizes that flexibility of approach is essential in order to match style to the changing diagnosis; and that sees the importance of the capability of being able to change a situation so that Europeans can live in greater safety. Greater professional skills of this kind are badly needed in East–West relations. As far as European political leaders were concerned they were woefully lacking in the Kremlin leadership under the aged and ailing Brezhnev, Andropov and Chernenko; whilst both the Carter and Reagan administrations in Washington were slow to come to grips with the peculiar complexities of East–West relations in Europe. What Americans and Russians saw as their resilience of approach under stress appeared to Europeans as rigidity. From the American and Soviet perspectives, their European allies were prone to drift dangerously out of a misplaced desire to 'keep the peace' and lower the pressure on themselves. By contrast, Europeans argued that their flexibility of approach was better matched to the particular situation in Europe. The appropriate approaches were perceived differently because Europeans diagnosed the European situation differently, sensing that Europe really was peculiar.

Prudence is contributing to a safer world by identifying, containing and managing the multiple risks and crises to which international relations are prone. It can seldom be obtained by achieving a single aim, no matter how broadly it is conceived. For instance, strategic security may be obtained at the risk of jeopardizing political relationships or by sacrificing political solidarity. In other words, prudence is multi-dimensional; seeing prudential behaviour in simple black-and-white terms may help in the short rather than long term. Prudence cannot, of course, stand alone as a value in East–West relations. Policy-makers will continue to seek a more 'liberal' world order, based on a concern for human rights and freedom of choice, and greater 'justice' in the relationship between states and their own citizens as well as between each other. Just as properly they will pursue greater security and material improvements for their citizens. There will, accordingly, be continuous, inescapable and controversial trade-offs between values to be made. The prices that have to be paid will be controversial (e.g., security rather than the justice in Eastern Europe); their distribution will also be controversial (e.g., the fact that Americans pay much more for defence than Western Europeans). Yet in an uncertain and exceedingly dangerous region of the world like Europe prudence has a particular appeal. It involves a measured attitude towards values, basing policy on what a reasonable mind estimates is likely to happen. In the minefield of East–West relations prudence involves also a recognition of the inescapable role of accident and back luck. It means constructing through CSCE and inner-German relations political relationships that can endure the wheel of *fortuna*. To repeat once again the words of Talleyrand: 'above all, not too much zeal'.

East–West relations as a learning process

As we saw in the first two chapters, East–West relations have undergone a slow and complex learning process, beginning during the period of wartime alliance and incorporating phases of four-power cooperation, cold war, détente and 'post-détente confrontation. Indeed the learning process was influenced by earlier experiences and memories, in particular of the origins of the German and Soviet states in 1871 and 1917 respectively and their subsequent development as encircled and nervous states into the aggressive politics of Nazism and Stalinism. The imprint of Nazism and Stalinism on East–West relations is a continuing theme. Also, on occasion the learning process was collapsed into a short dramatic period, like that between 1946 and 1948 when the cold war emerged and tore up the structures of four-power collaboration. Later learning did not involve root-and-branch change. 'Post-détente' confrontation left the main structures of European détente intact, though functioning badly. The phase of détente was the product of years of bilateral preparations and 'dialogue by communiqué', as we saw in the chapter on CSCE. It was in fact superimposed on the ideological struggle and strategic suspicions that characterized the cold war. It did not replace or break free from these characteristics of the cold war. Throughout the post-war period East–West relations in Europe have had the underlying continuity provided by this two-dimensional view.

For this reason Pierre Hassner's decription of the early 1970s as a period when cold war in Europe was being replaced by a 'hot peace' seemed most apt.[1] According to Hassner, the cold war was a period when both sides employed aggressive ideological rhetoric as part of their preoccupation with the consolidation of their spheres of influence in Europe. With détente emphasis shifted to the rhetoric of the status quo. Motivated by the desire to gain recognition of the post-war settlement, the Soviet Union sought (unsuccessfully) to incorporate the language of the 'immutability' or 'untouchability' of frontiers into the Helsinki Final Act. At the same time each side sought by subtle means to undermine the position of the other, the West by seeking observance of human rights as a condition for détente and the Soviet Union by its 'peace offensive' under the umbrella of proposals for 'military détente'. So long as the status quo in Europe was ideologically unacceptable or strategically threatening, an adverserial relationship was bound to continue. Learning the limits of détente was a painful process for many in West and East who during the heyday of détente had lost sight of the larger picture.

Towards a situational management of East–West relations

The lesson drawn from the cold war phase, in the wake of the Berlin, Cuban and Sino-Soviet crises, was that an East–West relationship based on the two dimensions of ideological struggle and strategic competition was insufficient to satisfy mutual interests. There was a mutual interest in a revised political framework that could contain and manage crises and that could prevent the diversion of ever more resources into the arms race. The lesson drawn from the phase of détente, in the wake of the Afghanistan, Polish and INF crises, was that effective management of East–West relations required more than the search for improved political communications. The coincidence of American military retrenchment with a Soviet arms build-up in the late 1970s indicated that, at the least, mutual interests had to be pursued in parallel. In response, the Reagan administration sought to remind its European allies that negotiations were fruitless, indeed dangerous, unless conducted from a position of ideological and strategic strength.[2] With the political ascendency of the New

Right détente became a taboo word in Washington. President Reagan's public reference to the Soviet Union as 'the evil empire' symbolized the re-emergence of behaviour that had been characeristic of the cold war. According to Richard Perle, the trap of détente was the assumption that the Soviet Union could be trusted to abide by agreements.

In the 'post-détente' phase of superpower confrontation the Atlantic Alliance went through a very unsettled and troubled period. The Reagan administration's emphasis on the tough ideological and strategic dimensions of East–West relations drew sharp criticism from newly active European peace movement as well as from the traditional European Left. In 1983 Lord Carrington, British Foreign Secretary from 1979 to 1982 and Secretary General of NATO since 1984, delivered a famous speech in which he referred critically to 'facing Russians down in a silent war of nerves, broken only by bursts of megaphone diplomacy . . . crude one-dimensional moralism'. This criticism mirrored many others from trusted and proven friends of the Atlantic Alliance in Europe. The phrase 'dialogue of the deaf' became common currency in European expressions of concern about the deteriorating superpower relationship. What were the implications of this conflict between European and Atlanticist frameworks of action?[3] In one sense there was nothing new. Alternating periods of improvement and decline had been a regular feature of relations within the Atlantic Alliance. On the other hand, European integration might be deepening the structural roots of the antagonism, with for instance growing conflicts over trade and monetary policies. In June 1984 the American Senate voted for the first time ever on an amendment that could have led to American troop cuts in Europe. It was defeated only after strong lobbying from the President. In the American case a growing orientation to Asian and Pacific issues seemed to provide another structural root of the antagonism. Asia was replacing Europe as the principal trading area of the United States. In addition, in the aftermath of the Vietnam War American moralism shifted from internationalism, embodied earlier by President Kennedy, towards neo-isolationism. Despite these intimations of change the pressures of Alliance solidarity remained strong. The general impression of divergence of interests and disagreement about how best to manage East–West relations masked a disjointed yet gradual and slow learning process within the Alliance. The main contribution of Western Europe was to urge policy away from cold-war behaviour; whereas the United States stressed that East–West dialogue could only be fruitful if the right conditions were created. By 1984 the possibility of a new and more sophisticated phase of 'constructive confrontation' was indicated in the views expressed by the American Secretary of State George Shultz, the revised East–West policies of the British Conservative government and the nuances that the Kohl government had given to West German *Ostpolitik*.[4] The American administration began a dialogue with the Soviet Union on separate regional issues, including Afghanistan, the Middle East and the Far East. Though there was a convergence of perspectives, the problem of divided counsels in Washington continued to threaten the learning process of the Atlantic Alliance.[5] George Shultz and his right-hand man in the State Department, Richard Burt, were ranged against Caspar Weinberger and his right-hand man in the Pentagon, Richard Perle. Western Europeans continued to be irritated by the confusion of signals from Washington. At the same time the Western Europeans were in the grip of inertia, unable to respond in an effective and convincing manner to new challenges. Reduction of American troops in Europe is a serious possibility that Western Europeans must address in a practical manner.[6]

What conclusions can be drawn about the type of political strategy required for an effective management of East–West relations? The initial problem is the use of effectiveness as the central issue, for it suggests precise standards and objectives that cannot be established in such complex, multi-faceted and fast-changing relations. More appropriately, East–West relations require prudential management. Two simple conclusions can be drawn: that reliance on a one- or two-dimensional strategy heightens risks; and that it is necessary to achieve an 'appropriate' balance amongst the ideological, strategic and political factors in East–West relations. East–West relations is a highly professional activity precisely because it is not always easy to take account of these factors simultaneously. Political strategy needs to be long-term, flexible and cautious; and, in order to be a strategy, it must be coordinated. Policy-making must avoid being simply reactive to individual threats and outrages. It needs to identify potential for peaceful change and exploit shifting political opportunities in a pragmatic and prudent manner. Such opportunities are likely to continue to appear in Eastern Europe. They must be exploited by reference to the common European heritage that transcends East and West and to what Sir Geoffrey Howe in his speech 'Europe, East and West' at the Hague on 17 June 1985 called 'the special responsibility of Europeans for the peace and well-being of Europe'. Development of human contacts and confidence building become central objectives within the essential framework of Alliance solidarity and broad strategic balance. Flexibility of approach means accepting that ideological, strategic and political factors interact dynamically in East–West relations. Policy-making must cope with the ambiguities and paradoxes of East–West relations outlined in Chapter 1. Caution involves more than just attending to Alliance solidarity and strategic issues. The many-sidedness of international morality suggests the need for a measure of restraint from interference in the Soviet sphere of influence. It means de-emphasizing threats of coercive measures like trade or credit sanctions in favour of the force of good example, most notably by the further development of European integration as living practical embodiment of the human benefits of *détente, entente, coopération*.

The enduring problem is what constitutes an 'appropriate' balance in East–West relations. Theory cannot provide a simple solution to this problem. It can only tell policy-makers what they need to know in order to be better able to live with the difficulties that are posed by these relations. Judgements about the appropriate balance will vary with time and place and need to be refined by careful analysis and debate. Policy-makers require skills of situational judgement. Skill at reading a situation means being able to map the various elements of the situation: ideology, strategy, Alliance solidarity, domestic politics, and Eastern bloc politics. Each element makes demands on the approach to East–West relations. They must in turn be actively managed. As was emphasized in the introduction and Chapter 1, ideology and strategy are the tough elements. Though they influence each other, they remain independent. Singly and together they are hurdles in any process of East–West relations. The ideological climate can be sensed from election results, appointments, promotions, speeches and protocol. Suggestions of greater openness, for instance with the rise of Gorbachev in the Soviet Union, can shift expectations about East–West relations. In practice, however, ideological struggle is never absent. Each side seeks to exploit the nervousness of the other by psychological warfare. The degree of official attention and recognition given to the activities of bodies like the Soviet Peace Committee or the Committee on the Present Danger in the United States are indicators of the level of ideological aggression. Strategy is a powerful influence, not least because of its technological component. The strategic climate can be sensed from the extent to which a particular country or bloc at a particular time justifies its own security in terms that increase the insecurity of others. This problem has bedevilled European security in the late 1970s and 1980s, as can be seen in Chapters 1 and 2. Technological change has been a further factor complicating strategic judgement, notably multiple independently targeted warheads from the 1960s and the strategic defence issue from the 1980s. Alliance solidarity requires intensive interaction so that partners take proper account of each other's interests and expectations. Here again demands may change with election results. Developments in political relations within the Soviet bloc require close and very sensitive monitoring. Importance must be attached not just to real and imminent crises but to more subtle shifts of expectations, of the kind that have taken place in Hungary and more recently in the GDR. The chapters by Andrew Carter and Eberhard Schulz give particular attention to this element. Finally, as emphasized by Phil Cerny and Jolyon Howorth, Michael Sturmer and Phil Williams in their respective chapters on France, the Federal Republic and Britain, the domestic politics of parties and lobbies places contrasting demands on policy-makers in different national contexts. Policy-makers must understand and work with their political system and culture.

At times policy-makers must adapt rather passively to the demands of the situation in which they find themselves. Yet, in the interest of prudence, they need to develop skills of situational management. They must seek to change the demands from one or more elements of the total situation: for instance, by a shift of ideological content, modification of strategy, new programme of official visits or new appointments of promotions. Situational management requires behavioural skills. Relationships are crucial. Hence much depends on the strength and quality of contacts to the situational element that needs to be changed. Typically situational management is a matter of altering unrealistic expectations, for instance about the efficacy of ideological struggle as an approach. In advocating change in East–West relations skills of timing and presentation are essential. Once a particular situational element has been singled out for change it is necessary to decrease resistance to change, for instance by one or more new faces in positions of authority or by offering the prospect of greater access to influence through a more informal relationship. It is also important to indicate that there is important and interesting work to be done in East–West relations and to offer some material gain from change. By these latter means acceptance of change can be increased. These techniques were all apparent in the transition to détente. New figures emerged, like Egon Bahr, the closest adviser of Chancellor Brandt and negotiator of the treaty between the Federal Republic and the Soviet Union of 1970. The replacement of Walter Ulbricht by Erich Honecker in the GDR in 1971 indicated the resolve for change in the Soviet bloc. Bahr's formula of 'change through *rapprochement*' (*Wandel durch Annäherung*) referred to détente as a means of making living conditions in different social systems more equal. At the provisional signing of the Basic Treaty between the Federal Republic and the GDR in November 1972 he emphasized that this was the beginning of a road 'which would lead beyond organized coexistence (*nebeneinander*) to good-neighbourly relations (*miteinander*) . . . we have set great value on the practical measures affecting all important aspects of everyday life'. In the closing speeches at the Helsinki Conference in 1975 the British Prime Minister, Harold Wilson, spoke also of the need for CSCE to find expression in the daily lives of Europeans. CSCE's failure to live up to such expectations explains the disillusionment with it. By contrast, as Eberhard Schulz indicates in this book, the fruits of détente are much more visible and widely distributed in the Federal Republic.

The dimension of détente

One of the greatest dangers in East–West relations is a loss of faith in dialogue. On occasion guile and intransigence seem to be the only defining characteristics; subversion rules. Such loss of faith represents a flight from the inherent ambiguity of East–West relations, the subject of Chapter 1. One side's subtlety is another's guile; one side's conviction is another's intransigence. A continuity of confrontational politics is to be expected in ideology and strategy. The central political requirement is sufficient mutual respect, as 'honourable men', for a constructive dimension to be developed. There is a shared interest in avoiding the frustrations, fears and misunderstandings that are engendered by lack of communications; in the common European heritage; and in what Sir Geoffrey Howe has called 'the special responsibility of Europeans for the peace and well-being of Europe'. The perils of the nuclear age are particularly acute in Europe where short-range tactical nuclear weapons, as well as INF, are strategic in impact; where conventional and nuclear forces are mixed in a confusing fashion; and where crisis could come suddenly and from an unexpected quarter and, consequently, overburden the competence of decision-makers. Not least, a joint sense of responsibility needs to be developed through economic relations. They help to build bridges and to create a common interest in containing crises. Accordingly, détente must remain an essential part of the 'appropriate' balance in East–West relations. Its purpose is to create a framework of political and economic relationships out of which new structures of cooperation can be built. These structures of cooperation will in turn help to redefine the terms of ideological and strategic interaction. Inner-German relations illustrates the potential as well as problems of this process. CSCE may yet focus more of its immediate attention on Basket Two rather than Basket Three; whilst discussions on Basket One may begin to concentrate more clearly on new structures for crisis management in Europe.

What, then, are the prospects for détente in Europe? One answer might be that they would be better if a new word were used. After all, George Shultz was not prepared to use the word détente at the tenth anniversary celebrations of the Final Act in 1985. The modest and more conventional term 'dialogue' has been common currency amongst the advocates of 'constructive' confrontation, like Shultz and Howe. The chapters on inner-German relations and CSCE in this book indicate a continuing recognition of the need for serious and sustained political dialogue in Europe, at bilateral and multilateral levels. Indeed, in the mid-1980s Britain became a more significant in bilateral relations with Eastern Europe. Margaret Thatcher's official visit to Hungary in January 1984 was the 'curtain-opener' for a new policy that involved visits by the Foreign Secretary to a series of East European countries.

In order to assess the prospects for fruitful negotiation one must exercise situational judgement. It is essential to remember that negotiations do not occur in a vacuum; that platitudes about the need for negotiations fail to take account of the political consequences of their failure; and that progress in negotiations depends on certain conditions. Four conditions are essential:

1. evidence to both Moscow and Washington that ideological rhetoric and guile are impotent;
2. the continuing unity and resilience of the Atlantic Alliance in the face of Soviet threat and attempts to exploit public opinion in Western Europe (from this point of view the NATO 'dual-track' decision of 1979 was a mistake; by seeking negotiations before deployment of INF it gave an opportunity to the Soviet Union to divide the Alliance);
3. the absence of Soviet fears of imminent and sudden erosion of socialist solidarity in Eastern Europe (thus the Czech crisis of 1968 disrupted the preparation of Soviet détente policies and led to the Brezhnev doctrine);
4. a Western strategy that encourages moderates in the Eastern bloc to justify negotiations as indispensable to achieving at least some Soviet objectives (like stabilization of Eastern Europe through maintaining prosperity there or its own greater economic efficiency).

One of the skills of détente diplomacy is knowing when to negotiate. Indeed a paradox of détente is that it may involve the prudential decision at a particular time not to negotiate. Another skill of détente diplomacy is the ability to identify the particular subjects that are ripe for negotiation. Arms control negotiations are not always to be recommended. Indeed the experience of the MBFR negotiations and the INF negotiations in Geneva suggests that too much has been expected from this dimension of East–West relations. The more successful negotiations in inner-German relations have focused on a combination of political and economic concessions. By creating a broader web of mutual interests in this way it may be possible to reduce tensions and thereby create a political climate for arms control negotiations. The exercise of both these skills requires intensive, careful 'back-door' diplomacy over years. Successful summits are the outcome of a slow-moving process of this type. They contribute little in themselves. The nature of the time scales in East–West relations is revealed most clearly in the chapters on CSCE and West German détente policies.

This emphasis on East–West relations as a professional activity suggests the importance of insulation from domestic politics. Though an eminently political process, requiring democratic accountability, East–West relations is an activity *sui generis*. Appropriate domestic political structures provide an additional, fifth condition for effective negotiations. The techniques of détente diplomacy tend to wither in the open political market-place, where promises of 'quick fixes' vie with apocalyptic imagery as politicians seek to impress domestic political audiences. In East–West relations the test of the 'professional' politician is that he or she appreciates the conditions for effective negotiations and focuses on how to create and use such conditions. The chief qualities of such a politician are a measure of restraint, precision, and bipartisanship. Restraint comes from a sense of responsibility to numerous international audiences rather than a single domestic audience. Precision stems from a recognition that the agenda must be delimited if negotiations are to make progress and that it must relate to the general conditions of East–West relations. Bipartisanship is linked to the need to diminish the leverage available to the other side, not least to procrastinate in the expectation of more favourable political opportunities. Domestic political structures must encourage the development of these professional qualities. 'Back-door' diplomacy can then be effectively harnessed to negotiations about high-level political objectives for East–West relations over the medium term. Also, some guarantee can be offered that these objectives can be sustained in domestic politics.

The relationship between political strategy and domestic structure is a central problem of East–West relations. Within the context of geopolitical interests, strategy has tended to follow domestic structure. A major factor in the divergence of approach to East–West relations within the Atlantic Alliance has been the difference between the open and very pluralistic structures of American government and the more closed and unified structures of Western European governments; between a politicized and competitive administration and strong public service traditions. The effects of this difference of domestic structure have been compounded by contrasts of geopolitical interests as American interests have become more bound up with the Pacific basin. In addition to geopolitical doubts, Western Europe faces the question of whether the United States can develop domestic structures that are appropriate to a professional management of East–West relations. If the answer is negative, Western Europe must strengthen its collective role and voice within the Atlantic Alliance with the aim of counterbalancing the weaknesses in American strategy towards Europe. In other words, professional management of East–West relations in Europe requires structural reforms: strengthening the European pillar of NATO by reform of the Western European Union; building a stronger role for European Political Cooperation in East–West relations beyond CSCE negotiations; encouraging a stronger role for the EEC in security discussions and in economic diplomacy *vis-à-vis* Eastern Europe; and providing opportunities for the neutral and non-aligned states to act as 'bridge-builders' and in 'crisis-management' structures. The problem of structural reforms in Western Europe is not just political inertia. The need to minimize adverse impacts of such reforms on the four conditions for effective negotiations in East–West relations provides a constraint. At the same time Western Europe has a golden political opportunity to make an impression on East–West relations by force of good example. Whether that opportunity is realized will depend on the philosophy of East–West relations that finds expression in these structural reforms. A period of reform will require the highest standards of professionalism from Western European politicians.

Towards a philosophy of East–West relations

The problem in East–West relations is not the absence of proposals for improvement; it is the lack of an adequate organizing framework for them. Proposals for improvement roll all too readily off the tongues of politicians and from the pens of publicists. By contrast, academics have been unprepared or unwilling to tread the path of earlier philosophers like the Abbé de St Pierre and Immanuel Kant. Both sought to elaborate the principles on which a European 'peace order' could be constructed. Post-war discussions about East–West relations have tended either to occur in an ethical vacuum of 'realist' political strategies of effective deterrence and nuclear war-fighting or to acquire a tone of moral superiority and exclusiveness from liberal ideology or Marxism-Leninism. Neither tendency recognizes and responds to the complexities, ambiguities and paradoxes of East–West relations; neither encourages a flexible strategy of 'situational' management. What, however, is to guide 'situational' management in East–West relations and to sustain professional conduct?

It is necessary to return to the statement with which this book began — that we live in an age of mounting potential for mass destruction, by conventional as well as nuclear weapons. It is also essential to note that even radical arms control and disarmament measures would be likely to leave a concentration of weaponry capable of eliminating modern Europe. They would have marginal, if any, significance. Against the background of these detestable and detested realities of modern warfare, East–West relations can less afford illusion and zeal than in any past period of European diplomacy. Moral zeal must give way to the elementary human principle of 'live and let live'.[7] Millions of living Western Europeans and Americans are infinitely preferable to millions of dead Eastern Europeans and Russians. On this basis excessive reliance on nuclear weapons threatens strategy with paralysis and problems of credibility. They are not to be envisaged as effective instruments of war. A war involving nuclear weapons would be uncontrollable and disastrous to one's own side; a peace based on the cataclysmic destructiveness of nuclear weapons encourages a democratic public to retreat to pacifism and unilateral disarmament. Accordingly, the central political objectives in East–West negotiations must be to restructure ideological argument and strategic deployments in accordance with the principle of 'live and let live'. Strategy must emphasize strong defensive deployments and conventional forces, accompanying a pledge of 'no early use' of nuclear weapons with withdrawal of tactical nuclear weapons from the front line. It must manage technological change — like strategic defence — with the aim of so complicating the strategy of each side that rational incentives for war are diminished and incentives for radical arms control measures increased. Strategy must also stress the importance of establishing facilities that can be used to confer in time of crises: perhaps a European monitoring station manned by the neutral and non-aligned states under the auspices of CSCE. A combination of practical proposals of this kind with limited measures of 'good will' would be a signal for inter-alliance negotiations: though its success would depend on a careful reading of the conditions for negotiations. Restructuring ideological argument would be at least as difficult. Coexistence at the ideological level is not part of the Soviet concept of 'peaceful' coexistence. Yet lack of rules of the ideological game unsettles negotiating conditions in the interconnected games of strategy and détente. Paradoxically, and perhaps foolishly, in the Helsinki Final Act the Soviet Union accepted the rules of an ideological game that favoured the West. Self-restraint in this area would also be a signal for negotiations, again depending on careful reading of conditions.

The complexity and scale of risks in East–West relations means that policy makers must give central place to the value of prudence.[8] Prudence means safeguarding one's ideology, with its views on liberty and justice; it means providing an adequate response to strategic threats; and it means cultivating the political relationships on which East–West affairs depend. In essence, prudence entails keeping alive a three-dimensional view of East–West relations and attaining a measured balance in its conduct. A 'measured' balance requires forebearance, adhering to certain rules; otherwise confidence can never be built. Neither side can guarantee responsible conduct by the other. Yet each has an obligation to chart a responsible course of its own. At the same time, by stressing the use of intelligent foresight to avert future harm, and of reasonable argument, prudence injects a sense of worldliness into judgement. Ultimately moral considerations in East–West relations cannot be drawn into a single unified account from which appropriate behaviour can be deduced. In this sense the skills of policy-makers are not primarily philosophical. They must be good at 'situational' management, and their philosophy must be able to encompass the complexity of their subject matter.

Europe and détente: a final thought

Western European policy-makers are faced in the mid 1980s with important and exciting opportunities for building new institutions and developing common policies. The role of détente in rehabilitating Europe is far from exhausted for, as we have seen, it has a particular practical relevance and historical resonance to Europeans. Europe is, of course, not an island that can be insulated from international affairs. East–West relations in Europe is subject to *de facto* linkage with developments and events elsewhere, like the Gulf or South-East Asia. At the same time, détente has become part of the search for identity of Europeans, a word as well as a process with a recognizable European pedigree. Europeans have sensed the dangers in tearing apart the complex tapestry of détente in Europe; more positively, some of them are beginning to recognize the opportunities for European political development that are offered by continuing to weave the tapestry of détente. CSCE has at least provided Europeans with the chance to move beyond an 'off-stage' role as dramatic critics of the theatricalities of superpower relations. It has given them the possibility of becoming promising new actors on the stage of East–West relations, of creating a model of civilized regional political behaviour. By this means Europe can once again become a source of political inspiration in a world that can no longer afford the traditional forms of power conflict associated with the modern state, Europe's past legacy to the world.

How this new career for European states develops will depend not just on the CSCE itself, which is not equipped to perform as an engine of détente. The challenge must be taken up in West European subgroupings like the EEC, the WEU and the neutral and non-aligned group, and not least in Eastern Europe; and it will require political professionalism as well as propitious circumstances. Western Europe must concentrate its minds in particular on the possibility of American troop reductions in Europe and on Soviet anxieties about its own and Eastern European inefficiency. Closer Western European integration in security and diplomacy can be justified to the United States in terms of 'burden-sharing' within the Alliance. It can also enjoy Soviet support as a means of helping Western Europe to exert a stronger moderating influence in Washington. At the same time the Soviet objective of uncoupling Western Europe from the American deterrent must be met by the argument of consequences: if uncoupling is a serious prospect, the Federal Republic of Germany will be likely to emerge as a partner in a new Western European nuclear force. The process of Western European integration would then act as a test to see whether Soviet fear of a more 'free-wheeling' Federal Republic, uncontained by the American presence, was greater than its fear of American extended deterrence. Whatever the outcome of this test of Soviet motivation, Soviet recognition of Western European security concerns will remain difficult to achieve.

Notes

1. Pierre Hassner, 'Europe: Old Conflicts, New Fears', *Orbis*, vol. 17, no. 3 Autumn 1973, pp. 895–911.
2. J.R. Schlesinger et al., *Defending America: Towards a New Role in the Post-Détente World* (New York; Basic Books, 1977); W.S. Thompson, ed., *National Security in the 1980s: From Weakness to Strength* (New Brunswick: Transaction Books, 1980); and *Realism, Strength, Negotiation: Key Foreign Policy Statements of the Reagan Administration* (Washington, DC: Department of State, 1984).
3. Laurence Freedman, ed., *Troubled Alliance* (London: Heinemann, 1983); L.B. Burrows and G. Edwards, *The Defence of Western Europe* (Borough Green: Butterworth, 1982); and Michael Smith, *Western Europe and the United States: The Uncertain Alliance* (London: Allen & Unwin, 1984).
4. George Shultz, 'New Realities and New Ways of Thinking', *Foreign Affairs*, 1985; Sir Geoffrey Howe, 'Europe, East and West', speech at the Hague, 17 June 1985; on *Ostpolitik* see Sturmer's chapter in this volume.
5. The nature of the divided counsels in Washington is discussed in Strobe Talbott, *Deadly Gambits: The Reagan Administration and the Stalemate in Nuclear Arms Control* (London: Picador, 1984). On the influence of the Committee on the Present Danger, which when founded in 1976 included Reagan, on the

Reagan administration, see Jerry Sanders, *Peddlers of Crisis* (London: Pluto Press, 1983).
6. Phil Williams, *US Troops in Europe* (London: Royal Institute of International Affairs, 1984). On the opportunities for, and problems of European defence cooperation, see Trevor Taylor, *European Defence Cooperation* (London: Royal Institute of International Affairs, 1984).
7. Freeman Dyson, *Weapons and Hope* (New York: Harper and Row, 1984).
8. This point was made more generally in Maurice Cranston, *Politics and Ethics* (London: LSE, Inaugural Lecture, 1972); and in W.B. Gallie, 'Wanted: A Philosophy of International Relations', *Political Studies*, vol. 27, September 1973, pp. 484–92.

Index

Abgrenzung 118-9, 159
Abrasimov, Peter 162
Adenauer, Chancellor Konrad 3, 135, 138, 147, 156
Afghanistan 46, 48, 56, 65, 71-2, 84, 102, 108, 152, 159, 190, 202, 209, 240, 257
Africa 72, 210
'Air-Land Battle' 213-14, 216
Alexander I 172
Algeria 2, 60, 200
Allied Control Council 19, 27-8, 31, 115
Andropov, Yuri 56, 57, 161, 163, 164, 165, 210, 212, 255
Angola 64
Arab-Israeli War 1973 93, 94
Arms control 8-9, 11, 37, 40 *passim*, 68-70, 81, 130, 131
Atlantic Charter 24, 36
Attlee, Clement 19
Austria 2, 18, 27, 32, 47, 75, 90, 92, 94, 95, 182, 191, 245,

Backfire bombers 43
Bahr, Egon 60, 262
Balkans 25-6
Baruch, Bernard 31
Basic Treaty between the two German states 88, 89, 106, 134-5, 137, 140, 159, 262
Belgium 88, 91
Belgrade CSCE meeting 63, 99-102, 105, 127, 189, 190, 234, 240, 243-4, 248, 249
Berlin 6, 16, 19, 21, 25, 27, 38, 60, 62, 89, 100, 106, 114-20, 132, 136, 139, 143, 150-1, 157

Berlin crisis 1948 ix, 31, 34, 36, 106, 142, 146, 156
Berlin crisis 1958 ix, 34, 36, 117, 142, 149, 257
Bevin, Ernest 19
Bezymensky, Lev 166
Bidault, Georges 144
Bismarck, Otto von 3, 128, 166
Bizonal Economic Council 29
Bodin, Jean 1
Bohemia 17
Brandt, Chancellor Willy 22, 60, 88, 92, 94, 135, 150, 157, 179, 211, 233, 262
Brezinski, Zbigniew 14, 15
Brezhnev doctrine 33, 58, 77, 87, 96, 97, 185, 188, 194, 264
Brezhnev, Leonid 44, 46, 57, 158, 161, 175, 176, 178, 179, 180, 185, 190, 199, 233, 255
Britain 2, 3, 19, 20, 21, 43, 49, 91, 107, 148, 155, 199, 202, 221-53 *passim*, 259, 264
Brown, Harold 66
Bucharest Declaration 40, 87, 176, 181
Budapest Appeal 40, 87, 178
Budapest Memorandum 88, 90
Bulgaria 18, 20, 25, 26, 33, 52, 70, 73, 76, 109, 162, 163, 168
Burt, Richard 259
Bush, George 49, 208
Byelorussia 17
Byrnes, James 19

Carrington, Lord 38, 258
Carter, Andrew 250
Carter, President Jimmy 3, 14, 56, 64,

Carter, President Jimmy (*continued*) 77, 100, 108, 159, 234, 255
Casablanca meeting 16
Catherine II 172
Ceauşescu, Nicolae 70, 73, 77
Charter 77 65, 101
Chernenko, Konstantin 56, 57, 162, 165, 170, 255
Cheysson, Claude 209, 215
China 35, 43, 58, 61, 71, 88, 145, 179, 207
Christian Democratic Union (CDU), West German 48, 60, 92
Christian Social Union (CSU), West German 48, 92
Churchill, Winston 16, 17, 20, 24, 25, 28, 30, 34, 53, 134, 199
Clay, Lucius 29
Cold War 9, 31, 137, 256–7
Collective security system in Europe, Soviet proposals for 39, 86–8, 172–97 *passim*
Cominform 33
Committee on the Present Danger, US 261, 270
Communist Party of the Soviet Union 10–11
Communist Party, French 200, 201, 211, 212
Concert of Europe 49, 188
Conference on Security and Cooperation in Europe (CSCE) 2, 47, 63, 83–112 *passim*, 119–20, 130–2, 152, 186 *passim*, 203, 221–53 *passim*, 263, 266, 269–70
Confidence-Building Measures (CBMs) 9, 39, 41–2, 97–8, 103–4, 187, 191, 192, 228
Congressional Commission on Security and Cooperation in Europe, US 100, 230
Containment 10, 19, 34, 146–9
Council for Mutual Economic Assistance (CMEA) 71, 74, 76, 80, 95, 104, 109, 139, 140, 171

Council of Foreign Ministers 19, 31
COCOM 78, 82, 108
cruise ix, 43, 57, 66, 159, 209
Cuban missile crisis (1962) 34, 38, 43, 57–8, 149, 152, 201, 202, 207, 257
Curzon Line 53
Cyprus 94, 96
Czechoslovakia ix, 7, 18, 19, 33, 46, 57, 62, 71, 73, 76, 77, 89, 90, 101, 120, 123, 157, 165, 168, 182, 185, 264

David Davies Memorial Institute 231
de Gaulle, Charles ix, 22, 24, 28, 60, 88, 144, 175, 186, 198 *passim*, 225
Denmark 88, 91, 94, 245
détente, definition of ix, 4–11, 22, 23 36 *passim*, 45 *passim*, 63 *passim*, 83, 198–9, 202–3, 207–8, 216–9, 224–9, 263–6
deterrence doctrine 8, 19, 41, 42 *passim*, 201, 214–16, 267
Deutschlandpolitik 47, 113–71 *passim*
Diepgen, Eberhard 114
Dominican Republic 57
Dregger, Alfred 168–9
Dresden 17

East Prussia 17, 20
Eden, Sir Anthony 54
Eisenhower, Dwight 20, 25, 57, 205
entente, definition of ix
Erhard, Ludwig 29, 137, 150
Estonia 20
Eurocommunism x, 101
European Advisory Commission 27–8
European Coal and Steel Community 30, 148
European Defence Community 30, 39, 148, 201
European Economic Community 30, 47, 76, 85, 91, 92, 98, 104, 132, 182, 200, 234, 237–53 *passim*, 266, 269
European Political Cooperation 47, 92–3, 94, 198, 237–53 *passim*, 266

Fabius, Laurent 170
Finland, 2, 47, 83, 84, 91-2, 94, 95, 104
Fischer, Oskar 160
flexible response doctrine 43, 193, 206, 213-5
force de frappe, French 6, 60, 148, 203-5, 208
France xi, 2, 3, 6, 7, 15, 17, 27, 28, 30, 43, 48, 50, 60, 61, 78, 87, 88, 90-1, 93, 103, 128, 148, 150, 155, 176, 191, 198-20 *passim* 225, 244
Franco-German collaboration 15, 51
Franco-Prussian War 1, 15
Franco-Soviet relations 28, 60, 87, 199
French Empire 200, 201

'gas-for-pipelines' deal 78, 108, 209, 210
Gaullism 198-208, 217
General Agreement on Tariffs and Trade (GATT) 33
Genscher, Hans Dietrich 248
Gera 141, 159-60, 168
German Democratic Republic (GDR) x, xi, 6, 7, 29, 32, 34, 35, 47, 48, 60, 62, 70, 71, 73, 76, 90, 98, 110, 113-71 *passim*, 174, 178, 183-4, 185, 239, 245, 261, 262
German-Polish Treaty 1970 88, 106
German-Soviet Trade Treaty 1978 108, 109
German-Soviet Treaty 1970 88, 90, 106, 134, 158, 169, 186, 262
Germany, Federal Republic of ix, 6, 7, 29, 31-2, 34, 39, 48, 60, 62, 85, 87, 88, 91, 92, 93, 94, 97, 107, 113-71 *passim*, 176, 179, 184, 185-6, 202, 210, 211, 222, 225, 234, 245, 262
Germany, occupied 26 *passim*, 115, 155-6
Giscard d'Estaing, Valéry 199, 202, 204, 213, 215, 217
Glienicke bridge (Berlin) 114-16

Goldberg, Arthur 100, 244
Gorbachev, Mikhail 56, 57, 67-8, 70, 79, 80, 85, 104, 171, 261
Goronwy-Roberts, Lord 230
Greece 20, 25, 34, 101
Green Party, West German 48, 137, 153
Grenada 72
Gromyko, Andrei 44, 155, 159, 176

Haftendorn, Helga 240, 248
Hager, Kurt 166, 169
Hallstein doctrine 32
Harmel Report 40, 60, 88-9, 106, 152
Hassner, Pierre 235, 256-7
Hattersley, Roy 226, 227
Helsinki Final Act ix, 4, 38, 42, 63, 65, 83-112 *passim*, 116-7, 120, 125, 126-7, 152, 154, 155, 167, 187-8, 238, 257 *see also* CSCE
Hernu, Charles 213, 215, 216
Hiroshima 17, 18, 46
Hitler, Adolf 3, 22, 25, 124, 129, 144, 145, 148 *see also* Third Reich
Hoffmann, Heinz 161
holocaust 16
Holy Alliance 128, 172
Honecker, Erich 3, 6, 48, 70, 90, 122, 123, 139, 141, 142, 158, 161, 162-79, 262
Hopkins, Harry 54
Horizont 167
'hot line' 38, 41, 149
Howe, Sir Geoffrey 170, 260, 263, 264
Hull, Cordell 54
human rights ix, 3, 5, 36-7, 39, 63, 64, 65, 83, 96, 99, 100-2, 105, 107, 109-10, 126, 129, 189-90, 191, 222-3, 227-8, 234, 239
Hungary x, 8, 18, 20, 25, 26, 33, 34, 48, 65, 68, 71, 73, 74-5, 76, 77, 90, 98, 109, 120, 125, 149, 163-4, 218, 261, 264

Ideology 7-8, 36 *passim*, 260-1 *see also* Marxism-Leninism
Indo-China 2, 202 *see also* Vietnam War
Inner-German relations x, 2-3, 5, 6, 87, 92, 113-71, 172-97 *passim*, 265
Intermediate-range nuclear forces (INF) 42, 43-5, 48, 70, 71, 72, 78, 84, 85, 152, 159, 162-5, 167, 169, 208-12, 257, 263, 264, 265
International Monetary Fund (IMF) 33, 109
Italy 20, 26, 88, 93, 170, 245

Jackson-Vanick Amendment (1974) 64, 108, 229
Japan 18, 20, 31, 61, 71, 78, 211
Jaruzelski, General 73, 75, 161
Jewish emigration (from the Soviet Union) 64, 110, 223, 229, 230

Kampelman, Max 245
Kant, Immanuel 267
Katyn massacre 17, 26
Kennan, George 19, 36
Kennedy, President John F. 59, 206, 258
Khrushchev, Nikita 57, 58, 117, 149, 157, 174, 175
Kissinger, Henry 35, 44, 46, 61-2, 64, 77, 93, 100, 106, 135, 136, 151, 203, 225, 242
Kochemasov, Vyacheslav 114, 162
Kohl, Chancellor Helmut 6, 48, 113, 127, 135, 163, 164, 166, 168, 169, 259
Korean airliner incident 67, 102, 240
Korean War 147, 148

Latvia 20
Le Monde 6
Lellouche, Pierre 14-15
Leningrad 17, 21
Linkage, doctrine of 11, 46, 61-2, 64

Lithuania 20
London protocols 1944 27-8, 115, 117
London Programme 31
Luxembourg Report 241

Mackinder, Halford 24, 50, 145
Madrid CSCE meeting 63, 102-3, 105, 127, 130, 190-1, 240, 244, 245-6
Malta 98, 190, 242
Mansfield, Mike 229
Marchais, Georges 212
Marshall Plan 18, 20, 29, 31, 33, 34, 146
Marxism-Leninism 7-8, 10-11, 18, 23, 74, 120, 158, 267
Marx, Karl 10
Mediterranean region 98, 190, 245
Metternich, Prince 61
Mitterrand, President François 25, 48, 49, 51-2, 198, 202, 208 *passim*
Molotov, Vyacheslav 19, 174
Morgenthau, Henry 27
Mozambique 64
Munich Agreement 1938 6, 19, 22, 92
Mutual Balanced Force Reduction (MBFR) talks 42, 63, 84, 85, 89-90, 91, 97, 100, 104, 106, 228, 239, 265

Nagasaki, 17, 18, 46
Napoleon Bonaparte 49
National Socialism, German 6, 8, 23, 124, 256 *see also* Third Reich and Hitler
Nazi-Soviet Pact (1939) 22-3
NATO ix, x, 8, 22, 32, 34, 40, 43, 44, 60, 66, 69-70, 72, 78, 88-9, 94, 113, 127, 152, 156, 159, 160, 167, 176, 177, 179, 181, 182, 183, 186, 191, 192, 201, 205-8, 208-9, 212, 213, 214, 215, 216, 217, 226, 232, 233, 241, 242, 243-4, 246, 247, 264
Nemmersdorf massacre 17

Index

Netherlands 88, 93
Neues Deutschland 167, 168
neutral and non-aligned states (NNAs) 2, 47, 85, 86, 91–2, 93, 94–5, 96, 97, 99, 102, 103, 104, 105–6, 107, 181, 242, 246, 266, 268, 269
New York Times 6
Nicaragua 79, 202
Nixon, President Richard 35, 58, 61, 62, 77, 88, 89, 93, 94, 135, 203, 225
Nixon–Brezhnev Summit 89, 91
Norway 91, 94, 98
Novoe Vremya 165
Nuclear Non-Proliferation Treaty 38, 57, 179
Nuclear Test Ban Treaty 38, 57
nuclear weapons 46–7, 51, 208–19, 267–8
nuclear-free zones 41, 97, 174–5, 192
Nunn amendment 78

Oder–Neisse line 16, 21, 26, 174, 177, 179
Ogarkov, Marshal Nikolai 44, 165, 166, 169
oil crisis 1973 94
Olympic boycotts 71, 77, 102
Orlov, Yuri 86, 100
Ostpolitik, West German x, 49, 62, 91, 92, 113–71 *passim*, 179, 185, 225, 239, 248, 259
Ottawa meeting on human rights 103, 191

Palme Commission (1983) 40
Papandreou, Andreas 166
peace movement 3, 45, 50–1, 78, 127, 163
peaceful coexistence, concept of 37, 46, 61
Perle, Richard 229, 258, 259
Pershing 2 ix, 43, 44, 57, 66, 159, 209
Peter, Janos 183

Pieck, Wilhelm 28
Pleven Plan 30, 148
Poirier, General Lucien 213, 216, 220
Poland ix, x, 7, 8, 16–17, 18, 19, 20, 22, 25, 26, 29, 33, 34, 35, 48, 53, 56, 62, 65, 66, 67, 68, 73, 75, 76, 77, 80, 84, 86, 90, 102, 106, 109, 110, 119, 120, 125, 128, 139, 149, 152, 157, 158, 159, 161, 168, 175–6, 179, 185, 190, 192, 218, 239, 240, 257
Pompidou, President Georges 94, 203, 204
Ponomarev, Boris 189
Popieluszko, Father Jerzy 75
Potsdam Conference (1945) 17, 18, 19, 21, 24, 25, 26, 28, 84, 143, 145, 155, 169
Prague Declaration 40, 88, 96, 179–80
'Prague Spring' 8, 57–8, 59, 68, 87, 178
Pravda 46, 48, 166, 167

Quadripartite Agreement on Berlin 1971 ix, 62, 106, 115, 117–18, 122, 142, 150–1, 158, 179, 185, 186

Rapacki, Adam 87, 174–5, 179
Rapallo Treaty 1922 147
Rapid Deployment Force (FAR), French 216
Reagan, President Ronald 3, 45, 56, 67, 68–9, 72, 77, 79, 85, 100, 104, 209, 210, 211, 255, 257, 258
Reparations, against Germany 26, 27, 29–30
Rogers, General Bernard 213–14
Romania x, 18, 20, 25, 26, 33, 48, 52, 62, 65, 70, 73, 76, 77, 87, 90, 94, 95, 96, 97, 98, 109, 168, 177, 179, 181, 184–5, 187, 191, 218
Roosevelt, President Frederick Delano 16, 19, 20, 24, 25, 50, 145, 173

278 Index

Royal Institute of International Affairs 230, 231
Rude Pravo 165
Rusk, Dean 24

Sakharov, Andrei 86, 100
Sanctions, against Soviet Union ix, 78, 105, 209
Schmidt, Chancellor Helmut 6, 25, 43, 51, 91, 92, 106, 127, 135, 152, 161, 167, 209
Schulz, Eberhard 110, 262
Schultz, George 24, 49, 83, 85, 236, 259, 268, 264
Schuman Plan 30, 148
Security 8, 39, 40 passim, 50-1 see also strategy
Shcharansky, Anatoly 86, 100
Shonfield, Andrew 230
Silesia 17, 21
Sino-Soviet relations 35, 58, 179, 257
Social Democratic Party, West German (SPD) 48, 60, 127, 153, 211, 212
Socialist Unity Party, East German (SED) 28, 122, 139, 158
Sokolowski 44
Solidarity, Polish 66, 67, 80, 120, 218
Solzhenitsyn, Alexander 99
Soviet Union (USSR) x, 1, 5, 6, 7, 8, 10-11, 17, 18, 19, 21, 22-3, 24, 26, 29, 32, 33, 34-5, 39, 41-2, 43-5, 47, 56-82 passim, 83, 86 passim, 96, 101, 103-4, 105, 109, 114-20, 126, 130, 139, 140-1, 144, 145-6, 147, 149, 155-97 passim, 209, 225, 226, 227, 232, 238, 239, 243, 255, 257, 258, 264, 270
Speidel, General Hans 147
SS-20s 43, 57, 66, 106, 127, 152
St Pierre, Abbé de 267
Stalingrad 21
Stalin, Joseph 20, 21, 25, 27, 29, 33, 34, 36, 57, 58, 145, 148, 155, 156, 173, 174, 256
Stockholm Conference on Confidence and Security-Building Measures and Disarmament in Europe 40, 85, 103-4, 130, 191-2, 236
Strang, William 27
Strategic Arms Limitation Talks (SALT) 38, 44, 63, 66, 84, 89, 106, 218, 228, 239
Strategic Defence Initiative (SDI) ix, 45, 68-70, 72, 219, 261
Strategic Nuclear Force (FNS) French 204-5, 208
strategy 8, 39, 40 passim, 68-70, 261, 268 see also security
Strauss, Franz Josef 92, 162, 211
Suez 2
Sweden 2, 47, 92, 94, 95, 104
Switzerland 2, 47, 93, 94, 95, 96, 187, 245
Szuros, Matyas 164

Talleyrand, Charles-Maurice de 256
Tarsadalmi Szemle 164
Technology transfer 59, 78, 123, 152 see also COCOM
Tehran meeting 17, 24, 25, 26
Thatcher, Margaret 211, 264
The Times ix
Third Reich (1933-45) 10, 15, 16-17, 20, 22-3, 125
Thirty Years War 1, 15
Thompson, Lord 231
Tito, Marshal 34
Truman doctrine 34, 147 see also containment
Truman, President Harry 19

Ulbricht, Walter 28, 90, 122, 158, 184, 185, 262
United Nations 24, 33, 62, 100, 120, 159, 169, 237
United States x, 1, 2, 3-4, 5, 8, 10, 15, 18, 19, 21, 24, 33-4, 42, 43, 56-82 passim, 88, 91, 100-1, 108, 129, 130,

146–9, 151–2, 153, 158, 159, 173–4, 175, 176, 177, 179, 180–1, 186, 200, 201, 203, 205–8, 210, 229–30, 234, 242, 243, 244, 255, 266, 270

Versailles Peace Settlement (1919) 16, 19, 107, 129
Vienna Congress (1815) 16, 107, 128, 132, 143
Vietnam War 2, 57, 59, 64, 151, 175, 176, 258

Warsaw Pact 32, 39, 40, 69, 79, 81, 82, 86, 87, 88, 89, 94, 95, 97, 113, 157, 165, 176, 178, 181, 182, 184
Watergate scandal 64, 94, 151
Weber, Max 154
Weinberger, Caspar 259
Weizsäcker, Richard von 108
Western European Union (WEU) 22, 78, 266, 269
Westphalia, Peace of (1648) 1, 16, 128, 132, 143
Williamsburg summit (1983) 71, 211–12
Wilson, Harold 227, 262
World Bank 33
World War, First 1, 16, 50
World War, Second 1, 6, 16 *passim*, 24 *passim*, 35, 84

Xiaoping, Deng 71

Yalta Conference 17, 20, 24–5, 26, 27, 28, 29, 47, 49, 53, 115, 173
Yugoslavia 2, 25, 34, 47, 90, 96, 97, 98, 177, 184

Zamyatin 180, 183
Zhivkov, Todor 70